Fixing Haiti

**The Centre for International Governance Innovation**

**Centre pour l'innovation dans la gouvernance internationale**

The Centre for International Governance Innovation (CIGI) is an independent, non-partisan think tank that addresses international governance challenges. Led by a group of experienced practitioners and distinguished academics, CIGI aims to anticipate emerging trends in international governance and to strengthen multilateral responses to the world's most pressing problems. CIGI advances policy ideas and debate by conducting studies, forming networks and convening scholars, practitioners and policymakers. By operating an active program of publications, events, conferences and workshops, CIGI builds capacity to effect change in international public policy. CIGI was founded in 2001 by Research In Motion (RIM) co-CEO and philanthropist Jim Balsillie, who serves as CIGI's chair. CIGI is advised by an International Advisory Board.

www.cigionline.org

# Fixing Haiti: MINUSTAH and beyond

Edited by Jorge Heine and Andrew S. Thompson

**United Nations
University Press**

TOKYO · NEW YORK · PARIS

United Nations University Press
United Nations University, 53-70, Jingumae 5-chome,
Shibuya-ku, Tokyo 150-8925, Japan
Tel: +81-3-5467-1212   Fax: +81-3-3406-7345
E-mail: sales@unu.edu   general enquiries: press@unu.edu
http://www.unu.edu

United Nations University Office at the United Nations, New York
2 United Nations Plaza, Room DC2-2062, New York, NY 10017, USA
Tel: +1-212-963-6387   Fax: +1-212-371-9454
E-mail: unuony@unu.edu

United Nations University Press is the publishing division of the United Nations University.

Cover design by Mea Rhee

Cover art by Stivenson Magloire, *Sans titre*, acrylic on cloth © 1990.

Printed in the United States of America

ISBN 978-92-808-1197-1

Library of Congress Cataloging-in-Publication Data

Fixing Haiti : MINUSTAH and beyond / edited by Jorge Heine and Andrew S. Thompson.
    p.  cm.
  Includes bibliographical references and index.
  ISBN 978-9280811971 (pbk.)
   1. Haiti—Politics and government—21st century. 2. Failed states—Haiti.
3. United Nations Stabilization Mission in Haiti. 4. United Nations—
Peacekeeping forces—Haiti. 5. Peacebuilding—Haiti—International
cooperation. 6. Economic assistance—Haiti. 7. Technical assistance—Haiti.
I. Heine, Jorge. II. Thompson, Andrew S. (Andrew Stuart), 1975–
F1928.2.F5   2011
972.9407'3—dc23                                                    2011021069

To the memory of Gerard Le Chevallier and all those who died in Haiti
on 12 January 2010

# Endorsements

"Library shelves sag under the weight of books on Haiti. Many are truly exceptional studies probing and dissecting the causes of Haiti's repeated failures at sustaining development and good governance: French colonialism, European racism, US failures to plumb its 'culture of poverty', ecological devastation – and repeatedly and often mindlessly – the laying of historical blame on what is invariably called 'the Haitian elite'.

All this, of course, is useful preface to understanding contemporary Haiti which is presently at yet another of those terrible political impasses. The well-documented economic complexity and labyrinthine nature of the island's politics have now been magnified by a devastating earthquake, multiple killer hurricanes, and virtually out-of-control urbanization. The presence of the UN military peacekeeping and election monitoring contingents is struggling to keep the peace. Such conditions require fresh analysis, a multifaceted focus by an array of hands-on experts. This is precisely what this book offers in a straight and unvarnished fashion. Nothing presently in print equals it in terms of analytical depth and breadth. Its contents will most probably leave you thinking that solutions are not yet within our reach. This is as it should be if we are to join necessary caution to an equally necessary hope that a better future is indeed possible."

**Anthony P. Maingot,** *Professor Emeritus of Sociology, Florida International University, and past president, Caribbean Studies Association.*

"This superb volume reflects the most sophisticated thinking about the challenges posed by Haiti and the international community's response, including after the devastating earthquake. The first-rate authors have no illusions about the magnitude of the task. Their appraisal of the performance of the UN and key hemispheric players in helping Haiti deal with its profound problems is refreshingly balanced and clear-headed. They chart a way forward that tries to align the capacities of international actors with realities on the ground. For policy officials and decision makers concerned about Haiti's future, this is an indispensable guide."

**Michael Shifter,** *President, Inter-American Dialogue*

# Contents

# Figures and tables

# Contributors

**Eduardo Aldunate** Brigadier General (R) Aldunate was an infantry officer in the Chilean Army. He holds master's degrees in Military History and Military Sciences and was Professor of Military Strategy and History at the Army War College. He has written three books on leadership and civil-military relations. Between September 2005 and September 2006, he served as Deputy Commander of the UN Military Forces in Haiti, MINUSTAH. His book *Backpacks Full of Hope: The UN Mission in Haiti* has been published by Wilfrid Laurier University Press (2010).

**Stephen Baranyi** is Associate Professor at the School of International Development and Global Studies, University of Ottawa, Canada. Over the past 15 years, he has worked as a human rights advocate in the European Union, a policy adviser to government agencies in Canada, a grant manager at the International Development Research Centre, Ottawa, Canada and a principal researcher at the North-South Institute, also in Ottawa. He has published widely on issues at the interface of development and security.

**Marcel Biato** is the Ambassador of Brazil to Bolivia. From 2003 to 2010 he served in Planalto, Brazil's presidential palace, as an assistant to President Lula's chief foreign policy advisor. A career diplomat for thirty years, he has served as a political officer at Brazil's Embassy in London and in the Consulate General in Berlin, as well as a legal advisor to his country's UN mission. In Itamaraty, Brazil's Foreign Ministry, he has covered Latin American and military issues, having been an advisor to the Brazilian principal during the Peru-Ecuador peace negotiations (1995–1998). He holds an M.A. in Political Sociology from the London School of

Economics, and has published extensively on Latin American politics, Brazilian foreign policy, the International Criminal Court and global governance issues more generally.

**Juan Emilio Cheyre** is the founding Director of the Center of International Studies at the Pontifical Catholic University of Chile. He is also the former Commander-in-Chief of the Chilean Army (2002–2006). He holds a PhD in Political Science and Sociology from Complutense University of Madrid and is a former director of the Chilean Army War College. He has published extensively on issues related to military strategy, peacekeeping and international relations more generally.

**Paul Collier** is Professor of Economics at Oxford University and Director of the Centre for the Study of African Economies, as well as Co-Director of the International Growth Centre of the London School of Economics and Oxford University. He was previously (1998–2003) Director of the Research Department at the World Bank. He has been a Visiting Professor at the Kennedy School of Government at Harvard and at the Sorbonne. His books include *The Plundered Planet* (with Lisa Chauvet and Anke Hoeffer) Oxford University Press and Penguin, 2010, *Wars, Guns and Votes: Democracy in Dangerous Places* (Harper Collins/Random House, 2009) and *The Bottom Billion* (Oxford University Press, 2007). He holds honorary doctorates from the University of Auvergne and the

University of Sheffield. In 2008, *Prospect* magazine ranked him among the "World's Top One Hundred Public Intellectuals" and *Foreign Policy* magazine put him among the "Top Global Thinkers of 2009".

**Timothy Donais** is Assistant Professor in the Department of Global Studies at Wilfrid Laurier University in Waterloo, Canada. He taught previously in the Department of Political Science at the University of Windsor, Ontario, Canada. His primary research interests lie in the area of post-conflict peace-building. He is the author of *The Political Economy of Peacebuilding in Post-Dayton Bosnia* (Routledge, 2006), and more recently edited the volume *Local Ownership and Security Sector Reform* (Lit Verlag, 2008).

**Robert Fatton Jr.** is the Julia A. Cooper Professor of Government and Foreign Affairs in the Department of Politics at the University of Virginia, Charlottesville USA. His publications include: *Black Consciousness in South Africa* (State University of New York Press, 1986); *The Making of a Liberal Democracy: Senegal's Passive Revolution, 1975–1985* (Lynne Rienner, 1987); *Predatory Rule: State and Civil Society in Africa* (Lynne Rienner, 1992); *Haiti's Predatory Republic: The Unending Transition to Democracy* (Lynne Rienner, 2002); and *The Roots of Haitian Despotism* (Lynne Rienner, 2007). He is also co-editor with R. K. Ramazani of *The Future of Liberal Democracy: Thomas Jefferson and the Contemporary World* (Palgrave, 2004); and *Religion, State, and*

*Society* (Palgrave Macmillan, 2009). Born and raised in Port-au-Prince, Haiti, Fatton Jr. studied in the mid-1970s in France, later earning an MA and a PhD from the University of Notre Dame.

**Amélie Gauthier** is a former researcher for the Spanish think tank FRIDE. She holds an MA in International Cooperation and Project Management from the Ortega and Gasset Institute in Madrid. Prior to joining FRIDE, she worked as a political analyst for the Canadian Embassy in Madrid (2005–2006). She has also worked for the Hispanic-Canadian International Cooperation programme at the Spanish Confederation of Business Organizations (2000–2001).

**Jorge Heine** holds the Chair in Global Governance at the Balsillie School of International Affairs, is Professor of Political Science at Wilfrid Laurier University and a Distinguished Fellow at the Centre for International Governance Innovation (CIGI) in Waterloo, Ontario. From 2006 to 2009 he served as vice-president of the International Political Science Association (IPSA). He previously served as Chile's ambassador to India, Bangladesh and Sri Lanka (2003–2007) and as ambassador to South Africa (1994–1999). He is the author, co-author or editor of 10 books, including *Which Way Latin America? Hemispheric Politics Meet Globalization* (United Nations University Press, 2009) and, with former Haitian president Leslie Manigat, *Cross Currents and Cleavages: International Relations of the Contemporary Caribbean*

(Holmes & Meier, 1988) and of some 70 articles in journals and symposium volumes. His opinion pieces have been published in the *New York Times*, the *Washington Post* and the *International Herald Tribune*.

**Gerard Le Chevallier (1954–2010)** was Director of Political Affairs and Planning from October 2006 to January 2010 for the United Nations Stabilization Mission in Haiti (MINUSTAH), and before that was MINUSTAH's Chief Electoral Officer. Before joining the United Nations in August 2004, he was a senior associate and the Regional Director for the Latin American and Caribbean region at the Washington, DC-based National Democratic Institute for International Affairs (NDI). He also served as the NDI's field director in Paraguay (1996–1998), Bosnia (1996) and Haiti (1995–1996). During his political career in El Salvador (1979–1994), Le Chevallier became a national leader of the Christian Democratic Party and served as a cabinet minister and MP, and as a founding member of the Central American Parliament. He was one of the key negotiators of the Salvadorean Peace Accords. He graduated from the Hautes Études Commerciales (HEC) in France and has been awarded two honorary doctorate degrees.

**Robert Maguire** is Associate Professor of International Affairs at Trinity University in Washington, DC. and Director of the Trinity Haiti Program. He has been involved with Haiti since the mid-1970s through affiliations with the Inter-American

Foundation, the Department of State and Johns Hopkins, Brown and Georgetown Universities. From 1994 to 2001, Maguire directed the Georgetown University Haiti Program. Since 1990, he has chaired the Haiti Advanced Area Studies at the US State Department's Foreign Service Institute. In 2008–2009 he was a Jennings Randolph Senior Fellow at the United States Institute of Peace (USIP). Currently he is Chair of the USIP Haiti Working Group.

**Mirlande Manigat** is Vice-Rector for Research and International Affairs at the Université Quisqueya in Port-au-Prince, Haiti. Following education in Haiti, she went to Paris, France, where she earned Licence degrees in History at the Sorbonne, and in Political Science at the Institute of Political Science. She is author of nine books and over 50 articles and has held positions at the Centre d'Études des Relations Internationales in Paris, the Institute of International Relations at the University of the West Indies in Trinidad and at the Universidad Simon Bolivar in Caracas, Venezuela. She is currently the Secretary-General of the Rassemblement des Démocrates Nationaux Progréssistes (RNDP), one of Haiti's leading political parties, and has served as a senator in the Haitian Senate.

**Johanna Mendelson Forman** is a senior associate with the Americas Program at the Center for Strategic and International Studies (CSIS), Washington, DC, where she works on renewable energy, the Americas, civil–military relations and post-conflict reconstruction. A former

co-director of the Post-Conflict Reconstruction Project (CSIS), she has written extensively on security-sector reform in conflict states. She has held senior positions at the US Agency for International Development, the Bureau for Humanitarian Response and the Office of Transition Initiatives, as well as at the World Bank's Post-Conflict Unit. She has been a senior fellow with the Association of the United States Army, a guest scholar at the US Institute of Peace and an adviser to the UN Mission in Haiti. She holds adjunct faculty appointments at the American University and at Georgetown University, USA.

**Madalena Moita** has been a specialist in conflict resolution and post-conflict peace-building for the past seven years. She has worked as a consultant on Haiti with institutions such as the European Commission and the International Peace Institute. A researcher with the Spanish think tank FRIDE, she holds an MA in Peace and War Studies from the Universidade Autónomo de Lisboa and is currently finishing her PhD at the Complutense University of Madrid.

**José Raúl Perales** is a senior associate of the Latin American Program at the Woodrow Wilson International Center for Scholars, Washington, DC. He is an expert on Latin American relations, with particular emphasis on trade policy, domestic and international economic institutions, especially in Southern Cone and Caribbean countries and Brazil, and in Central American political economy. He has been a trade policy adviser to the government of Puerto Rico; visiting researcher at institutions in Chile, Argentina, Uruguay and France; and instructor at Michigan State University, USA.

**Patrick Sylvain** is an academic, poet, writer, photographer and social critic. He teaches at Brown University's Center for Latin American and Caribbean Studies. He has been published in numerous anthologies and journals, including: *African American Review, Agni, American Poetry Anthology, American Poetry Review, The Best of Beacon 1999, The Butterfly's Way, Human Architecture, the Journal of Sociology of Self-Knowledge, Massachusetts Review, The Oxford Book of Caribbean Verse* and *Ploughshares.* Sylvain's work was recently featured on a PBS NewsHour broadcast as well as on National Public Radio's *Here and Now*; and in the collection *Poets for Haiti* (Yileen Press, 2010). He is a contributor to CNN.com and to the *Boston Haitian Reporter*.

**Andrew S. Thompson** is an adjunct assistant professor of Political Science at the University of Waterloo, Canada, and the Programme Officer for the Global Governance programmes at the Balsillie School of International Affairs, Waterloo. He is a specialist in the fields of international human rights, civil society movements and fragile states. He has written and co-edited four books, as well as a number of journal articles and book chapters. He has also appeared as an expert witness before the Canadian House of Commons Standing Committee on Foreign Affairs and International Development, and the Canadian Senate Standing Committee on Human Rights. From 2006 to 2009 he was a fellow at the Centre for International Governance Innovation in Waterloo, Canada. Prior to pursuing his doctoral studies, he worked for Amnesty International's Canadian Section in Ottawa, and in 2004 he represented the organization as a member of a human rights lobbying and fact-finding mission to Haiti. He holds a PhD in History from the University of Waterloo.

# Foreword

*Paul Collier*

Haiti has suffered a series of recent misfortunes: hurricanes, an earthquake, cholera and a discredited election. Unsurprisingly, people tend to lose sight of more hopeful developments. Yet, on the day I write this Foreword (11 January 2011), The *Wall Street Journal* is running a story on how Haiti has attracted a major investment from Korea: the world's leading garment firm will establish a factory that will directly employ 20,000 people. By far the most difficult investment to attract is the first: firms reduce their costs by clustering together. Now that one garment firm has invested, others will face lower costs and so are likely to follow. Hence, the initial 20,000 jobs are likely to be multiplied. Further, each job in the garment industry will create indirect employment as workers spend their income locally. And each job can support a family. This is the sort of success that Haiti needs to transform its society from poverty and despair: waged jobs provide dignity, structure and income for ordinary families.

The Korean decision to invest was not a stroke of luck: it was the end result of a coordinated effort by government and international actors. The necessary foundation for such investment is security; this is what MINUSTAH has provided. Investment also requires a market opportunity for its output; this was created by the US Congress, which, following the catastrophe of the earthquake, was persuaded to improve market access for Haitian-produced garments. A priority for the Haitian government post-earthquake has been to relocate the population from Port-au-Prince to places less liable to shocks. The new jobs will be located on a new site in the north-east of the country, but for this to be viable required the provision of a range of infrastructure that is complementary to the private investment. For example, the European Union is financing the necessary new roads. Manufacturing requires electricity, which in turn has required finance from the Inter-American Development Bank and authorizations from the government. These, and similar support from the United States Agency for International Development and the International Finance Corporation, are a model for of the sort of policy coordination that will be needed to transform Haiti from poverty to prosperity.

Obviously, jobs are not enough: Haiti needs radical improvements in basic social services, and a massive programme to rehouse the population. But, as with the story of the clothing factory, international public action can be effective as long as it is smart, coordinated and supported by timely action by the Haitian authorities. As the essays in this volume indicate, these conditions are far from easy. During my work for the secretary-general and the government of Haiti, I was impressed by the dedication of the United Nations' team that was valiantly trying to achieve them. Many members of this team were killed in the earthquake: their fine work deserves to be remembered.

*Oxford, January 2011*

# Acknowledgements

This book would not have been possible without the help, guidance and support of a number of organizations and people. We would like to thank the Centre for International Governance Innovation (CIGI) and the Laurier Centre for Military Strategic and Disarmament Studies for their financial support. We would also like to extend our gratitude to the many colleagues at CIGI, the University of Waterloo and Wilfrid Laurier University, and the Balsillie School of International Affairs who assisted us with the workshop that launched this project, and the book itself. Special thanks go to Yasmine Shamsie for all of her help with the conceptualization of the initial workshop in 2008; Briton Dowhaniuk and the events team at CIGI for their invaluable assistance with the organization and logistics of the conference; Max Brem and his publications team for their wisdom and guidance during the final stages of the production process; and last but not least to Joe Turcotte, an outstanding doctoral student, who has done a masterful job with the formatting and copy-editing of the manuscript. We are indebted to all of our contributors – some of the world's leading voices on Haiti – for their ongoing dedication to this project, which took on a whole new complexity and saliency following the earthquake of 12 January 2010. We would like to thank the United Nations University Press in Tokyo for all of its superb work in producing the book in such a timely manner. Finally, we would like to thank the two anonymous peer reviewers whose collective criticisms have had such a positive influence on the final product.

# Abbreviations

| | |
|---|---|
| ABC | Argentina, Brazil, and Chile |
| ADIH | Association des Industries d'Haïti |
| ALCOPAZ | Latin American Association of Peacekeeping Operations Training Centers |
| AOR | Area of Operation |
| CAECOPAZ | Argentine Joint Peacekeeping Training Centre |
| CARICOM | Caribbean Community |
| CASECs | Administrative Council of the Rural Sections |
| CBC | Congressional Black Caucus |
| CCC | Civilian Conservation Corps |
| CECI | Centre for International Studies and Cooperation |
| CECOPAC | Chilean Joint Peacekeeping Operations Centre |
| CEP | Permanent Electoral Council |
| CHAN | Canada–Haitian Action Network |
| CIDA | Canadian International Development Agency |
| CIRH | Interim Commission for the Reconstruction of Haiti |
| CIVPOL | Civilian Policing Division of the Department of Peacekeeping Operations |
| CNDDR | National Commission for Disarmament, Demobilization and Reintegration |
| CNSA | National Council for Food Security |
| CPA | Canadian Police Arrangement |
| CPI | Consumer Price Index |
| CPP | Concertation des Parlementaires Progressistes |
| CSOs | Civil Society Organizations |
| CSS | South American Defense Council |

| | |
|---|---|
| DDR | Disarmament, Demobilization and Reintegration Programme |
| DEA | Drug Enforcement Administration |
| DPKO | Department of Peacekeeping Operations |
| DSNCRP | National Strategy Document for Growth and Poverty Reduction; Document de Stratégie Nationale pour la Croissance et la Réduction de la Pauvreté |
| EOPE | Army Peacekeeping Operations School (Uruguay) |
| FAD'H | Haitian Armed Forces |
| FDI | Foreign Direct Investment |
| FRAPH | Front pour l'Avancement et le Progrès d'Haïti |
| GDP | Gross Domestic Product |
| GOH | Government of Haiti |
| HELP Act | Haiti Economic Lift Program Act |
| HIPC | Heavily Indebted Poor Countries |
| HNP | Haitian National Police |
| HOPE Act | Haitian Hemispheric Opportunity through Partnership Encouragement Act |
| ICF | Interim Cooperation Framework |
| IDB | Inter-American Development Bank |
| IFIs | International Financial Institutions |
| IHRC | Interim Haiti Recovery Commission |
| IICA | Inter-American Institute for Agriculture |
| IMF | International Monetary Fund |
| I-PRSP | Interim Poverty Reduction Strategy Paper |
| IRI | International Republican Institute for International Affairs |
| JMAC | Joint Mission Analysis Centre |
| LACs | Latin American Countries |
| MCFDF | Ministry for the Rights of Women |
| MFO | Multinational Force and Observers |
| MICAH | International Civilian Support Mission |
| MICIVIH | United Nations/Organization of American States Civilian Mission to Haiti |
| MIF/MIFH | Multinational Interim Force in Haiti |
| MINUSAL | United Nations Mission in El Salvador |
| MINUSTAH | United Nations Stabilization Mission in Haiti |
| MIPONUH | United Nations Civilian Police Mission in Haiti |
| MP | Military personnel |
| MSF | Médecins sans Frontières |
| MSPP | Haitian Ministry of Health |
| NGOs | Non-governmental Organizations |
| NSI | North-South Institute |
| OAS | Organization of American States |
| ODA | Official Development Assistance |
| OECD | Organisation for Economic Co-operation and Development |
| OECD DAC | Development Assistance Committee of the Organisation for Economic Co-operation and Development |

| ONUCA | United Nations Observer Group in Central America |
|-------|--------------------------------------------------|
| ONUSAL | United Nations Observer Mission in El Salvador |
| PAHO | Pan-American Health Organization |
| PD | Paris Declaration |
| PKOs | Peacekeeping Operations |
| PRSP | Poverty Reduction and Strategy Paper |
| RCMP | Royal Canadian Mounted Police |
| RDNP | Rassemblement Des Démocrates Nationaux Progréssistes; Rally of the National and Progressive Democrats |
| ROE | Rules of Engagement |
| SIDS | Small-island developing states |
| SRSG | Special Representative of the Secretary-General |
| SSR | Security Sector Reform |
| START | Stabilization and Reconstruction Taskforce |
| TPS | Temporary Protected Status |
| UNASUR | Union of South American Nations |
| UNDP | United Nations Development Programme |
| UNMIH | United Nations Mission in Haiti |
| UNMOGIP | United Nations Military Observer Group in India and Pakistan |
| UNOC | United Nations Operation in the Congo |
| UNPOL | United Nations Police |
| UNSC | United Nations Security Council |
| UNSMIH | United Nations Support Mission in Haiti |
| UNTMIH | United Nations Transition Mission in Haiti |
| UNTSO | United Nations Truce Supervision Organization |
| WB | World Bank |
| WFP | United Nations World Food Programme |

# Introduction: Haiti's governance challenges and the international community

*Jorge Heine and Andrew S. Thompson*

Haiti clearly is unable to sort itself out, and the effect of leaving it alone would be continued or worsening chaos. Our globalized world cannot afford such a political vacuum, whether in the mountains of Afghanistan or on the very doorstep of the sole remaining superpower.

Kofi Annan, 2004

Haiti may well be the only country in the Americas with a last name. References to the land of the "black Jacobins" are almost always followed by "the poorest country in the Western Hemisphere".[1] To that dubious distinction, on 12 January 2010 the world's first black republic added another, when it was hit by the most devastating natural disaster to occur in the Americas, a 7.0 Richter-scale earthquake. The latter, whose epicenter was in the Caribbean Sea just outside Port-au-Prince – in a shallow area, which made its surface tremors stronger – ripped with deadly force through the Haitian capital and its adjoining areas, reaching as far as the southern city of Jacmel.

Some 230,000 people lost their lives, 300,000 were injured, 1.5 million displaced and 2 million left in need of food assistance. The total value of the damage inflicted that day is estimated at US$11 billion. Some 285,000 homes were destroyed, as were the buildings of the Presidency, the Parliament and the Supreme Court and 15 of the 17 ministries.[2] The grandiose, domed, white stucco presidential palace – long a symbol of the "Big Man", cut-throat, predatory politics that has dominated Haiti from the days of Dessalines and Toussaint L'Ouverture to the more recent ones of the Duvaliers and Jean-Bertrand Aristide – fell on itself, as if in a

*Fixing Haiti: MINUSTAH and beyond, Heine and Thompson (eds),*
*United Nations University Press, 2011, ISBN 978-92-808-1197-1*

poignant reminder that an era had come to an end. A vibrant Caribbean capital with a rich history was transformed into a tent city, where, in improvised field hospitals, doctors and other medical personnel from all over the world did their best to save the lives and limbs of those who managed to get out from under the rubble.[3]

The reasons for such devastation are not difficult to fathom. As far as earthquakes go, 7.0 is way below many others that have hit in the Americas and the rest of the world and caused less mayhem. In the case of Haiti, the lack of proper building codes in an area that had not been hit by a quake of that magnitude in two centuries; the lax enforcement of whatever codes existed in a country where government oversight of rules and regulations is virtually non-existent; and the fact that many *bidonvilles* are built on the barren, vegetation-denuded hills that surround the Haitian capital, all add up to a recipe for disaster once any natural disaster strikes – be they hurricanes, tropical storms or earthquakes.

As if to underscore that nature in its fury spares no one, the 12 January Haiti earthquake also caused the largest one-day tragedy in UN history. A total of 102 UN employees from 30 different countries lost their lives that day, the majority of them at the MINUSTAH headquarters in the former Hotel Christopher in Port-au-Prince (MacFarquhar, 2010). Hédi Annabi, the mission head and Special Representative of the Secretary-General, (who was meeting a Chinese delegation in his office at the time of the quake); his deputy, Luiz Carlos da Costa and seven of the mission's political officers were among the casualties. The latter included Gerard Le Chevallier, an elections expert who played a key role in setting up the 2006 presidential elections and one of the contributors to this book.

Over the past two decades, the United Nations has taken a special interest in Haiti, often hand in hand with the Organization of American States (OAS). The United Nations first became involved in Haiti in 1990, when it helped organize the 16 December 1990 presidential elections won by Jean-Bertrand Aristide at the helm of the Lavalas Party (Fatton Jr., 2002). After the latter's ouster in a military coup (one of the 34 coups Haiti has undergone in its independent history) in September 1991, the United Nations returned to Haiti in 1993 in a civilian mission – Mission Civile Internationale en Haïti (MICIVIH). The expulsion of this mission by the military regime was followed by a 1994 UN Security Council-authorized peacekeeping operation designed to restore democracy and bring President Aristide back to power. After withdrawing its unified civilian and military mission (MICAH) in 2000, the United Nations returned to Haiti in March 2004 for a mopping-up operation designed to restore law and order. Previously, on 29 February of that year, President Aristide had been forced to flee the country in the face of the threat of a rebel militia descending on the capital from the northern city of Gonaives (Dupuy, 2005). In June 2004, MINUSTAH (The United Nations Stabilization Mission in Haiti) was established by the UN Security Council, and finds itself in Haiti to this day, with some 7,000 soldiers and 2,000 policemen, in addition to civilian personnel (Henry L. Stimson Center, 2007). This is the first UN peacekeeping mission to have a majority of Latin American troops; Brazil, with the largest contingent, has taken the lead, also providing the military commander of the peacekeeping forces (see Biato, Chapter 11, this volume).

This long-term, sustained UN commitment to Haiti reflects the concern of the international community in helping Haiti lift itself by its bootstraps. World reaction to the Haitian quake was swift and generous. The United States, Canada and France were among those at the forefront, as were Brazil and Cuba. Presidents Nicolas Sarkozy (in the very first visit to Haiti by a French president), Michelle Bachelet of Chile and Luiz Inacio Lula da Silva of Brazil visited Haiti, as did Prime Minister Stephen Harper of Canada, US Secretary of State Hillary Clinton, US First Lady Michelle Obama, former presidents Bill Clinton and George W. Bush, and UN Secretary-General Ban Ki-moon.

At a time when "donor fatigue" is the byword at many international meetings held to raise funds for post-disaster relief, the 31 March 2010 conference held at UN headquarters in New York was a remarkable success. Although Haitian President René Préval had requested US$4 billion in cooperation for a three-year period (of which 1.3 billion would be used for humanitarian aid in 2010–2011), the total pledged was more than double that amount, at US$10 billion, with the United States (with US$1.15 billion) and the European Union (with US$1.6 billion) leading the way. Even if there is some slippage, as there tends to be, between pledged funds and those actually disbursed and transferred to the recipient country, this would still constitute a significant sum from which to provide a new impetus to Haitian development – not just for the reconstruction of the old Haiti but for the launch of a new one. As former US president Bill Clinton put it at the New York conference, "Haiti could become the first completely wireless country in the Caribbean. Haiti could become the first completely self-sufficient country in energy."

Are such proposals at all feasible, or even realistic?

## Haiti as a fragile state

This is, after all, a country with a per capita income of US$1,180 dollars, one in which 72 per cent of the population lives on US$2 a day, where the adult illiteracy rate is 55 per cent, where life expectancy for women is 58 years and for men 55, and where the AIDS incidence is 6 per cent.

Haiti is a country where even before the 12 January earthquake, power supply was intermittent at best and the infrastructure in utter disrepair, making transport of goods and people both time-consuming and expensive; it is a country where unemployment is estimated to reach 60 per cent, yet where the port of Port-au-Prince has the highest charges in the Caribbean. Does it make sense to talk about a "wireless Haiti" when a regular electricity supply is a scarce commodity?

Until recently, Haiti was largely studied and analysed as a unique social formation – its special history as the first black republic; the first independent nation in Latin America and the Caribbean; the land where the first successful slave rebellion in the Americas took place; and as a French- and Creole-speaking nation surrounded by Spanish- and English-speaking ones (Danner, 2009). These factors have given rise to an extensive and stimulating social science and historical literature, and to some fine scholarship, much of it emphasizing Haiti's rich cultural heritage, its religion, its painters and its music (Heinl and Heinl, 1978; James, 1963).

In the first decade of the twenty-first century, however, and especially after 9/11, the emergence of the concepts of "fragile" and "failed" states, something that has taken place largely within the field of political science (Rotberg, 2003, 2004), has meant that Haiti suddenly became an altogether different unit for analysis. From being studied by a highly specialized category of Caribbeanists, often anthropologists and historians (see Leyburn, 1966 and Métraux, 1972), who feel more comfortable discussing the distant Haitian past than its conflicted present (as the saying goes, "the owl of Minerva flows at dusk"), it has now become a subject for political scientists and economists.

In the wake of 9/11 (an undertaking masterminded in Central Asia, funded from West Asia and with trial runs in East Africa), the notion that in the post-Cold War era the main threat to Western powers no longer came from a defunct Soviet Union or from a fast-growing China but rather from "ungoverned spaces" across the former Third World gained traction. Somalia, Afghanistan, the Democratic Republic of the Congo, Yemen, and yes, Haiti, were identified, variously, as "failed", "failing" or "fragile" states, from where all sorts of threats could and did emerge.

According to one definition, fragile states are those "where the state power is unable and/or unwilling to deliver core functions to the majority of its people: security, protection of property, basic public services and essential infrastructure" (Cammack and Macleod, 2006). Under different circumstances, such conditions (taking place, as Joseph Chamberlain said of Czechoslovakia in the thirties, "in a faraway country of which we know nothing") might have been of little concern to the Big Powers. During the Cold War, such ostensibly "empty spaces" were quickly occupied by proxies enlisted by either of the two superpowers of the extant bipolar system. Yet, in the age of globalization, the latter's "dark side" can quickly raise its ugly head. The territory of fragile states can thus become a base for activities such as international terrorism, drug trafficking, money laundering and the illegal arms trade (Heine and Thakur, 2010).

To identify, classify and rank fragile states thus became one of the fastest-growing areas in comparative and international politics. The development of a wide panoply of indicators to measure degrees and dimensions of fragility, an important prerequisite for "fixing" fragile states – that is, providing them with the proper "good governance" institutions – was an important part of this exercise (Carment, 2003).

Whereas international interventions in Haiti in the 1990s were largely intended to help the country's transition to democracy and to protect human rights, they later evolved into something much more ambitious. Matters such as the building of the Haitian National Police (HNP), the strengthening of the judiciary and of the penitentiary system, among other tasks since 2004 in which the international community through MINUSTAH and other players has been involved, entail a much broader agenda, although progress in these areas has been slow (Mendelson-Forman, 2008).

The relationship between the elected government in such fragile states and the international military and civilian missions ostensibly there to fix them is an uneasy one. The public differences that emerged between Afghan President Hamid Karzai and the Obama administration in April 2010 are an example of these tensions, as were earlier ones between Iraqi Prime Minister Nouri al-Maliki and the Bush administration in 2008.

## The Préval administration

Despite minor questions of emphasis, no such differences have become public in Haiti between the democratically elected government of President René Préval and MINUSTAH and Haiti's leading international partners. The very name of the UN mission indicates that its main objective is the *stabilization* of Haiti, after 20 rocky years of the region's most difficult transition to democracy (Fatton Jr., 2002; Heine, 1988). This has also been very much the goal of Préval – a low-key leader and agronomist by profession, from the small town of Marmelade, who likes quiet deal-making behind closed doors than being out in front haranguing the crowds, as so many other Haitian party leaders prefer to do (Williams, 2007). By refusing to raise expectations and by lowering the political temperature, Préval is the Haitian head of state who has been longest in office since the end of Duvalierism in 1986. In a country where rule has alternated between bloodthirsty dictators in office for decades and weak presidents who last a few months, this in itself is an achievement.

After the interim government of Prime Minister Gérard Latortue (2004–2006), with all the limitations of an unelected government and an ex officio prime minister, from 2006 to 2010 the Préval administration made considerable progress. The security situation improved, with a drop in the number of kidnappings; economic activity picked up – in 2007 economic growth reached 3.8 per cent; and in 2009, with 2.4 per cent growth, Haiti was one of two countries in all the Americas to experience economic growth. In a country famous for its corruption, Préval's personal integrity (no one has ever accused him of anything untoward) has provided the role model Haitians have longed for in their president but seldom got.

This does not mean that Préval, known for his sangfroid when dealing with the daily challenges thrown up by a dysfunctional political system, has not faced difficulties. In February 2008, international food price spikes led to steep increases in local prices (Haiti, as a result of lowering its tariffs in the 1990s, under pressure from the international financial institutions, now imports most of the rice it consumes instead of producing it in the plains of Artibonite, as it did in the past). The ensuing riots led to the fall of the government of Prime Minister Jacques-Édouard Alexis. Later that year, two hurricanes and two tropical storms caused some 800 deaths and over one billion dollars in damages. Given the emergency situation, Parliament, which had been dithering on the confirmation of a new prime minister, approved the appointment to that position of Michèle Pierre Louis, a confidante of President Préval, who had been the long-time head of FOKAL (La Fondation Connaissance et Liberté), a local NGO.

It is a measure of how inured the international donor community had become to Haiti's difficulties that the donor appeal for post-hurricane relief on that occasion found few takers. Yet, Préval's steady hand, which provided continuity and predictability, was starting to pay off. International investors, lured by former US president Bill Clinton, appointed by the United Nations as a special envoy to Haiti, started to look at business opportunities there. By 2009, international chains like Best Western were starting to build hotels in Port-au-Prince. It was precisely at that point that the next earthquake struck.

## A Marshall Plan for Haiti?

Much as nature seemed determined to inflict one setback after another on Haiti – we find it difficult to believe that such different natural disasters as hurricanes, tropical storms and earthquakes would hit a single country, some of them repeatedly, in the short span of 16 months – in early 2010 the international political stars seemed to be aligning with Haiti, rather than against it. In the United States, by far the biggest and most significant player in Haiti, a sympathetic Obama administration responded, indicating its unwavering commitment to the post-quake Haitian relief and reconstruction effort. Secretary of State Hillary Clinton, who has had a long-standing personal interest in Haiti, was equally responsive, and, as mentioned above, many international leaders visited Haiti in the weeks following 12 January.

In contrast to the tepid response to the international hurricane relief fund for Haiti set up in 2008, this time the reaction of the international community was enthusiastic and open-ended. The enormity of the death toll and the damage caused by the earthquake jolted many governments, IOs and NGOs into action. It helped that, for the first time in many decades, there existed in Haiti a democratically elected government, now in power for four years, headed by a leader who was a known quantity and somebody who could be depended upon – however weak his government may have appeared to be after the earthquake, when cabinet meetings had to be held in the down-at-heel quarters of a modest police station, since there was nowhere else to hold them.

Yet another reason for this almost overwhelming international response was the existence of a specific, well-thought-out plan. Over the previous two years a leading development economist, Paul Collier of Oxford University (formerly of the World Bank), had been working with the UN Secretariat and with the Haitian government on a poverty reduction plan for Haiti, a plan that had been caught up in the various political and atmospheric crises that had hit the country in 2008 but that now could serve as a blueprint to lift Haiti from the rubble (Collier, 2009). The hurricanes of 2008 also inspired some additional disaster-relief/cum reconstruction policy proposals that were tabled in the course of 2009. Thus, in the immediate aftermath of the January 2010 earthquake, instead of having to start from scratch, the Haitian government, international organizations and partner countries had a plan in hand.

It was in this context that the proposal for a "Marshall Plan for Haiti" was made (Collier and Warnholz, 2010). There is an element of metaphor here, since the absolute amount involved is much smaller, by several orders of magnitude, than that of the original Marshall Plan applied in the aftermath of the Second World War to stimulate the economies of post-war Western Europe. But the central concept behind the notion is not altogether different. Much as countries like Germany, France and Italy needed a massive infusion of resources to rebuild their cities, regenerate their industries and relaunch aggregate demand, Haiti, where the capital city that housed one-third of its population lies in ruins, needs a concerted international effort to lift itself up again. This is especially true of a country whose situation, even before the earthquake, was critical and lagging far behind the rest of the Americas. According to most indicators, Haiti is largely an "outlier" in Latin America and the Caribbean, a region that grew at an annual average of 5 per cent from 2003 to 2008, and where several countries are now in the middle-income category, though none has made the full jump into the status of developed nation.

The diagnosis on which this proposal was based is straightforward, and relies on what it considers to be Haiti's comparative advantages (Collier 2009; Collier and Warnholz, 2010) as follows:

1. Located in a largely peaceful and relatively prosperous part of the world;
2. Having no deep-seated societal structural problems (i.e., ethnic, ideological or religious divisions; rebel movements; coup-prone armed forces);
3. Endowed with a responsible and dependable political leadership;
4. Possessing a significant, nearby diaspora (which translates into major remittance flows);
5. Having considerable political influence in countries such as Canada and the United States;
6. Having privileged access to the largest market in the world – that of the United States – through HOPE II legislation: duty-free, quota-free until 2018.

It is in this context that the various policy proposals on building up Haiti's infrastructure and economic security – covering jobs, services, food security and the environment – are set forth, exploring alternative paths from those taken in the past.

Under the circumstances, and given arguments of long-standing about the need to channel international cooperation to those who need it the most (rather than, say, countries slightly above the very bottom), and especially so after a natural disaster so devastating that it killed a quarter of a million people and left many more homeless, one would think this would be an unobjectionable proposal. Yet, that has not been the case.

## The response

Although the reaction of the donor community, as witnessed at the 31 March 2010 UN meeting in New York, was overwhelmingly positive to the "Marshall Plan" proposal, the same cannot be said for the academic community. A number of specialists on fragile states, drawing on the literature on the subject and on their own data bases, have criticized the proposal. In more general terms, the very notion of a "Marshall Plan" has been subjected to scathing critiques, as an ineffective approach premised on the notion that "throwing money at problems" is the best way to solve them, thus ignoring a wealth of evidence pointing in a different direction (Naím, 2010). More specifically, the question of whether Haiti would be able to make productive use of such massive resources has also been mooted (Carment and Samy, 2010a, 2010b).

Rather than focusing on the locational and societal advantages of Haiti and its potential, these authors have pointed to the country's dismal record in handling international cooperative efforts in the past and its limited state capacity to do so in the present. The argument against a Marshall Plan for Haiti, such as the one put forward by economists like Paul Collier and Jeffrey Sachs, is based on the particular conditions of Haiti and on a more general argument about fragile states. It goes as follows:

1. Haiti has received a large amount of foreign aid in the course of the past half century (up to US$9 billion according to some estimates), and it is not evident that it has been put to good use.
2. Despite all this aid, Haiti continues to be ranked at the bottom of many development indicators: 149th out of 182 countries in Human Development and 169th out of 180 in the corruption ranking of Transparency International.
3. In some ways Haiti is the ultimate fragile state. Using an "authority, legitimacy, capacity" (ALC) framework, Carment and Samy rank it among the top 10 fragile states during 1983–1994, among the top 20 for much of 1995–2003 and among the top 10 again in 2004–2007.
4. In this context, a key question becomes absorptive capacity (Feeny and McGillivray, 2009). According to some studies, diminishing returns on aid would start when the latter reaches 15 per cent of GDP (it was 13 per cent in Haiti in 2008), and if anything like a Marshall Plan is applied in Haiti, it would vastly exceed that figure.
5. Accordingly, rather than *increase* the amount of aid to Haiti and work closely with the Haitian government (whose lack of capacity has been amply demonstrated), international donors should be more parsimonious and finicky in its dispensation, should try to channel resources to NGOs and, if certain specified goals are not met, just pull out.

This is a very different approach to the Haitian post-earthquake challenges.

## Which way forward?

The first point raised by the critique of the "Marshall Plan" proposal for Haiti relates to the very purpose of international cooperation. At a time when aid has been dropping as a share of the GDP of developed countries (it is at 0.31 per cent of GDP among the 23 OECD members used to measure it, far away from the 0.7 per cent once targeted as a goal), and the income gap between the richest and the poorest countries has been increasing, it seems incongruous to argue against more aid for one of the poorest countries anywhere, that has just been hit by the most deadly calamity in the Western Hemisphere in many decades.

Quite apart from issues such as state capacity, international cooperation primarily serves a humanitarian purpose. The reason that so many US and Canadian citizens donated so generously to the Haiti relief fund immediately after the quake is because there are several million Haitians in acute need of such help. These needs will not go away in a few months. It could be argued that a great danger is that the situation at the height of what many Haitians went through in the early part of 2010 will "normalize" itself in the worst kind of way – by making makeshift tents their semi-permanent or permanent homes. The notion that international cooperation should be withheld, or, at least, made available more sparingly, is at variance with the very rationale for foreign aid and disaster relief in the first place. In this initial phase, whether this aid is channeled through the Haitian government or NGOs is somewhat beside the point; the main point is that it should reach Haiti, and once there, that it is made available to those who need it.

A second point relates to the distinction between reconstruction and long-term development. Once the more immediate relief tasks are taken care of, the next question becomes that of reconstruction proper. Given the destruction of fixed capital that a natural calamity like the 12 January Haiti earthquake causes, merely restoring the situation ex ante is a major project in itself. In so doing, of course, one may want to do things somewhat differently, both to avoid the repetition of a comparably tragic occurrence and to increase productivity and job creation. This is not a task that a state like Haiti is in a condition to take on by itself, and the international community can and should play a role in it. The post-2004 Asian tsunami international efforts in countries like Sri Lanka and the Indonesian province of Aceh are proof positive that such efforts can succeed.

This example, in turn, relates to state capacity. Given Haiti's weaknesses, it could be argued that whereas states like those of Sri Lanka and Indonesia, no matter what other faults they might have, did have whatever was necessary to make the most of international post-disaster relief aid, whereas Haiti does not – and that would mark a crucial difference. Yet, in many ways this is the real challenge of international cooperation vis-à-vis fragile states. A recent study of Haiti (Buss, 2008) concluded that one reason international cooperation had failed in the past is because donors started from the premise that Haiti is a state like any other, whereas it is not. Buss's conclusions are that, concomitantly with substantive aid programmes that help the Haitian people, it is key to implement programmes that enhance the capacity of the Haitian state itself, so that it is able to administer external resources, provide services to its citizens and otherwise discharge normal state functions.

External assistance alone cannot guarantee economic growth in the long term, which is part of the underlying argument of those who oppose any grandiose aid schemes for Haiti. But this does not mean that building up a functioning state apparatus there is impossible. This is the premise on which this book is based. It is about Haiti's governance challenges and the responses of the international community since the insurrection of February 2004. It is an attempt to understand the obstacles that are inhibiting the emergence of a more prosperous and cohesive society, and the ways in which various actors, both domestic and international, are attempting to overcome them. It is also about the ascendency of new actors in the Americas since the end of the Cold War.

Traditionally, the main external actors in Haiti have been the "Big Three" from the north – the United States, France and Canada – countries that, for a whole host of reasons, have a vested national interest in a stable Haiti, and which, for better or worse, took the lead in the United Nations/Organization of American States (OAS)-sanctioned efforts to restore order and democratic rule to the country following the first military coup d'état against Aristide that lasted from 1991 to 1994. Since 2004, a new grouping of states from the south has risen to the forefront of the current UN mission. These are the "ABC countries" – Argentina, Brazil and Chile – that have taken on much of the responsibility for ensuring a measure of stability in Haiti. Hence, a second aim of the book is to evaluate the effectiveness of their efforts roughly six years after the current UN Stabilization Mission in Haiti (MINUSTAH) was established in June 2004. But more than this, it is an attempt to make sense of the changing geopolitical dynamics within the Americas, particularly between the north and south, as seen through the lens of the current international reconstruction effort in Haiti.

## Haiti's governance challenges

As Robert Fatton Jr. (2007) has argued, the historical roots of Haiti's instability can be traced back to the period when Haiti was a French colony. In order to ensure that the plantation economy would be profitable, the French established an authoritarian system of rule. Following independence in 1804, the country's elite maintained this system. Haiti thus has a history of deep class and racial conflict (those in power tend to be mulatto or "blancs"). This conflict has been perpetuated and buttressed by a dictatorial political system of "strong-man rule" in which power lies in the hands of one individual, the president. Under this system, violence has become the favoured means for "resolving and instigating problems" (Fatton Jr., 2006, 2007).

Beginning in 1957, François "Papa Doc" Duvalier and his infamous Tonton Macoutes ruled Haiti with legendary harshness. In 1971, Jean-Claude "Baby Doc" Duvalier took over following the death of his father, and for a time conditions in Haiti improved. However, Baby Doc's presidency was marked by a series of confrontations between the military and civilian authorities, as well as widespread economic stagnation (from 1980 to 1986, Haiti's GDP fell by 15 per cent). Political unrest and economic desperation fuelled anti-Duvalier sentiments. In January 1986, a popular revolt triggered by the shooting of four school children during a demonstration in Gonaives brought the crisis to a boil. Jean-Claude Duvalier and his wife Michele Bennett were forced to flee the country on a jet provided by the US embassy, and to seek asylum in France.

This transition from authoritarianism (or, strictly speaking, the *parenthèse*, as the Haitians refer to the interlude between two strongmen) was marred by deadly violence and political instability (Heine, 1988). The challenge of uprooting (*dechoukaj* is the Haitian expression) the legacy of dictatorship proved daunting. Five different military and civilian governments succeeded one another in the first four years after Baby Doc's departure.[4] The 1990s proved to be equally difficult. Jean-Bertrand Aristide's internationally recognized election victory on 16 December 1990 brought renewed hope that Haiti had emerged from the chaos of the previous half decade to become the hemisphere's newest democracy. But that hope was soon dashed. Aristide's mercurial and unpredictable behaviour undermined his standing. The country's elite soon lost what little patience it had for either representative government or Aristide's economic reforms. On 1 October 1991, General Raoul Cédras and his Front pour l'Avancement et le Progrès d'Haïti (FRAPH) staged a military coup against the newly elected president, forcing him into exile. Cédras and his supporters controlled Haiti for three years, during which time an overall climate of insecurity cast a long shadow over the country. The coup prompted the OAS and the United Nations to intervene, as the situation deteriorated to the point that it constituted a threat to international peace and security. The international community was eventually able to restore Aristide to office through a series of coercive measures that included diplomatic pressure, economic sanctions and military force, but not after much turmoil and hardship.[5]

Governing in the post-coup period proved difficult. A toxic combination of domestic political paralysis and a tepid international commitment to peacebuilding, as evidenced by a gradual scaling back of international aid and resources to the joint UN/OAS mission, prevailed. The situation worsened following Aristide's re-election in 2000. During his second term he relied increasingly on heavy-handed tactics and the use of armed militias (*les chimères*) in order to maintain his authority. By February 2004, he had alienated many of his supporters and effectively lost control of the country. This provided an opening for the insurgents to act.

## A new international response?

The February 2004 insurrection negated many of the gains that had been achieved during the intervention of the 1990s, forcing the international community to "start all over again". Whereas the intervention of the 1990s was principally concerned with restoring democratic governance and stability, the second has had to focus on addressing the systemic human rights and human security problems that have been at the root of Haiti's fragility. The differences between the Security Council resolutions of the 1990s and those of the post-2004 era are reflective of wider changes in the United Nations' approach to peacebuilding in post-conflict environments.

The first difference is a greater emphasis on security, particularly the security of the individual. Security Council Resolution 940 of January 1995, which formally established the UN Mission in Haiti (UNMIH), authorized a force comprising 6,000 troops and almost 800 police officers. Resolution 1048 of 29 February 1996 reduced levels to 1,200 troops and 300 police officers, while Resolution 1063 of 28 June 1996 cut another 600 soldiers from the UN force. With Resolution 1141 of 28 November 1997, which authorized the creation of the UN Civilian Police Mission in Haiti (MIPONUH), the Security Council withdrew the last of the UN's military presence in Haiti, reducing the organization's security presence to a measly 300 police officers.[6] These resolutions were also virtually silent on the state of the human rights situation in Haiti, and none made mention of any problem that could be considered as a threat to human security, an emerging concept at the time. They did make reference to the New York Pact, an addendum to the 1993 Governors Island Agreement, which was the settlement that attempted to establish the terms of the political truce between Aristide and Cédras during the coup of the early 1990s. Among other things, the pact did call for an end to arbitrary arrests and torture, the release of all political prisoners, respect for fundamental freedoms and compensation to the victims of the coup. During this time the joint UN/OAS Civilian Mission to Haiti (MICIVIH) was actively engaged in human rights monitoring and capacity-building programmes under extremely difficult conditions. However, as alluded to above, the Mission's ability to operate was limited by budgetary constraints.

Contrast these priorities with those of the resolutions that followed the February 2004 insurrection. First, the Security Council appears to have learned the lesson that it cannot cut corners when it comes to providing security. Resolution 1542 of 30 April 2004, which established the UN Stabilization Mission in Haiti (MINUSTAH), authorized an initial force consisting of 6,700 troops and 1,622 civilian police officers. Prior to the presidential election of February 2006 these numbers were raised to 7,500 and 1,897, respectively. Six months later, troop levels were lowered to 7,200, but civilian police levels rose to 1,951.[7] Of course, these numbers are still insufficient for the size of the population, and there have been occasions, particularly during the transitional period, in which the blue helmets and police officers in Haiti were accused of violating the standards for peacekeeping and policing established in international law.[8] Nonetheless, the fact that the levels of security personnel have remained relatively consistent since 2004, and have even been augmented since the earthquake, suggests that there is an explicit acknowledgement on the part of the Security Council that long-term stability can only be achieved if individual rights are protected and collective threats to vulnerable populations eliminated.

Unlike the resolutions of the 1990s, the post-February 2004 resolutions place human rights and issues that generally fall under a human security framework at the heart of the UN's presence in Haiti. Security Council Resolution 1542 (2004) is particularly telling. Passed on 30 April 2004, Resolution 1542 authorized the creation of MINUSTAH. Interestingly, MINUSTAH's legitimacy centred on its ability to bring an end to the rights violations that were taking place as a result of the insurrection, and make "a State based on the rule of law and an independent judiciary ... among its highest priorities". Section III, which is dedicated entirely to human rights, authorized MINUSTAH to do the following: support the promotion of human rights; "monitor and report on the human rights situation, in cooperation with the Office of the High Commissioner for Human Rights, including on the situation of returned refugees and displaced persons"; and assist with the investigation of human rights violations, again in cooperation with the Office of the High Commissioner, in order "to put an end to impunity". Resolution 1542 also makes reference to the "human security resolutions" of the early 2000s which gave the Council the authority to include the protection of vulnerable populations in the mandates of UN missions. These include Resolution 1325 (2000) on women, peace and security; Resolutions 1379 (2001), 1460 (2003) and 1539 (2004) on children in armed conflicts; and Resolutions 1265 (1999) and 1296 (2000) on the protection of civilians in armed conflicts. Resolution 1542 also authorized MINUSTAH to work with the Transitional government in creating a nationwide Disarmament, Demobilization and Rehabilitation (DDR) programme, and it even lists sensitizing peacekeepers to the need to control the spread of HIV/AIDS and other communicable diseases as a priority. Since then, subsequent resolutions have also emphasized similar human rights and human security priorities, and in some cases the language used in them is even stronger.[9] Taken together, the result is an extremely robust and ambitious agenda for engagement in Haiti.

To what can this shift in focus between the interventions of the mid-1990s and post-2004 period be attributed? There are probably several explanations, but the most obvious one is that the intervention of the mid-1990s is really a model of how not to intervene in a fragile state. The general consensus is that the United Nations left Haiti prematurely before any meaningful reforms could take hold, and that long-term stability is contingent upon the elimination of collective threats, both physical and economic, to the Haitian population.

Still, since its establishment in June 2004, MINUSTAH's presence in Haiti has at times been problematic, even divisive. Some, although not all, of the problem has stemmed from its weak mandate. Despite the attention to human rights and human security, Resolution 1542 requires that MINUSTAH work alongside the Haitian National Police (HNP) on all issues involving policing. As such, it has never been given the authority to engage in independent policing activities, although it does have power to "vet and certify new and existing HNP personnel for service".[10] Because of this, a number of questions have been raised about its neutrality, as it is seen to be in league with some of the more abusive elements of the HNP. Compounding this legitimacy deficit is that UN forces initially struggled to provide security for all sectors of society. More specifically, peacekeepers were slow to confront the gang violence. The first major initiative to neutralize those located in the slums of Cité Soleil took place only in early 2007.

## Fixing Haiti

In the backdrop of the 2010 earthquake in Haiti and the international response to the crisis, this volume seeks to put the country's current challenges in context. The majority of these chapters were originally presented at a conference held by the Centre for International Governance Innovation (CIGI) in September of 2008 entitled "Haiti's governance challenges and the international community". The chapters have been updated to take into account the devastation that the earthquake has caused. The volume is set out in three parts.

First, "Haiti's Governance Challenges" examines the structural and governance difficulties that afflict the country. Amélie Gauthier and Madalena Moita discuss both how Haiti's fragility and vulnerability is exacerbated by external shocks, and what can be done to insulate the country from future shocks.

Robert Fatton Jr., one of the more eminent political scientists writing on his native Haiti, follows this discussion of the absence of a sense of constitutionalism among Haitians, and the impacts that this has on the state's ability to respond to crises such as the 2008 international food crisis – which as a result of the political crisis and massive street demonstrations triggered by the rise in price of basic food staples brought down the government – and the 2010 earthquake. Moreover, as Mirlande Manigat, a respected constitutional scholar, a former senator and an eminent political leader in her own right (and the candidate who won a plurality of the votes in the 28 November 2010 presidential elections) describes it, Haiti's 1987 constitution complicates the ways in which the country's government must operate. Haiti has ended up with an odd hybrid between presidentialism and parliamentarianism, an unmanageable elections calendar that puts an enormous strain on the nation's budget and a large number of local government assemblies which do much the same. Most observers agree that constitutional reform to streamline this system is needed. Yet such efforts are viewed with suspicion by many Haitians, some of whom consider them nothing but sinister plots designed to aggrandize presidential powers to recreate the Big Man, strong-armed politics of the past, in which leaders would do anything to get to occupy *le Fauteuil* (the presidential chair), and once there, attempt to rule as kings. Similarly, Patrick Sylvain, from Brown University, places the Préval government and international community's responses to the earthquake in the larger context of Haitian history by drawing parallels with the equally destructive earthquake of 1842, which led to the demise of the Jean-Pierre Boyer government and left Haiti in a state of "structural chaos".

If constitutional and political reforms have not made much progress, security sector reform has. The abolition of the Haitian armed forces in 1995 by the government of Jean-Bertrand Aristide has been an unmixed blessing, eliminating the possibility of military coups, of which the country has had 34 in the course of its independent history. This puts a special burden on the shoulders of the national police. In fact, since 2004, the creation of a viable and respected Haitian National Police (HNP) has been one of the main objectives of MINUSTAH and the international community more generally. Although various studies showed that, given Haiti's population, the minimum size of such a force would need to reach

14,000, and the goal was to reach this number by 2011, in early 2010 the HNP had not reached beyond 8,000. The complexities of the vetting process, the length of the training time needed for new police cadets and the steady loss of serving policemen for a variety of reasons (77 of them died in the 12 January earthquake, which also destroyed almost half of all police stations in Port-au-Prince) are adduced as reasons for this delay. However that may be, this is one of the yardsticks along which MINUSTAH's performance is being measured. In the concluding chapter to the section, Timothy Donais analyses this process in some detail, and makes the case that a "community-based" approach to policing is essential if Haitians are ever to achieve a sustainable peace.

In the second section, the volume focuses on the involvement of the United Nations and its MINUSTAH mission. Gerard Le Chevallier, a former legislator from El Salvador, oversaw the electoral system for MINUSTAH during Haiti's 2006 elections, and along with 101 other members of the MINUSTAH mission, died in the January 2010 quake. In his precise, no-holds barred prose, he dissects what the UN mission in Haiti had achieved and what it had failed to do from 2004 to 2008. He was updating an edited version of his chapter when the quake struck. Although his chapter does not address developments since January 2010, his insights remain poignant nonetheless. Haitians have a love-hate relationship with MINUSTAH. On the one hand, quite understandably, they do not like to have a 9,000-strong foreign military and police force in their own country. Haiti does have rather traumatic memories of previous such occasions, such as the US occupation from 1915 to 1934. On the other hand, they are aware of the continuing internal security challenges the country faces, and, if anything, one widespread criticism of MINUSTAH is that it is not forceful enough in clamping down on Haiti's criminal gangs, though some progress has been made (Dziedzic and Perito, 2008). Many Haitians also realize that MINUSTAH cannot simply leave, although they would like to see them laying the ground for making that possible.

General (R), Eduardo Aldunate, of the Chilean Army, who served with Le Chevallier as a member of MINUSTAH, takes on the subject of how best to engage the local population during a stabilization mission. Aldunate's chapter highlights that force alone will not solve the problems that the country is facing, and that it is important to understand the actual needs of the Haitian people and to respond to them proactively. Aldunate, one of Chile's leading military thinkers and a former professor of strategy at Chile's War Academy, served during an especially difficult time as the Deputy Commander of the UN peacekeeping forces. His tenure overlapped with the repeatedly postponed presidential elections (whose success was such an important part of MINUSTAH's mandate), finally held on 7 February 2006, as well as with the tragic death of General Bacellar, his immediate superior, and Commander of the blue helmets.

Johanna Mendelson Forman, a leading specialist on peacekeeping, who has often visited Haiti, focuses on how the engagement of significant numbers of Latin American troops in Haiti's United Nations Peacekeeping Operations (UNPKO) marks the beginning of a new era of regional cooperation in Latin America and the Caribbean. She pays special attention to the shift this also signals in civil–military relations in the region, and the implications this has for a new domestic role for the Latin American armed forces within their own countries, as they leave behind their praetorian past and focus on the sort of professional duties that will mark the twenty-first century.

In this context, the chapter by General Juan Emilio Cheyre is particularly valuable. As a former commander-in-chief of the Chilean Army, Cheyre was responsible for deploying the bulk of the Chilean troops that were dispatched to Haiti in March 2004, and later overseeing, from Santiago, the mission of Chilean Army personnel there through 2006. From this unique vantage point, Cheyre, today one of the region's leading defence strategists, and the founding director of the Centre for International Studies at the Catholic University of Chile, sets MINUSTAH in the broader context of the participation of Latin American units in UN peacekeeping operations around the world, the domestic conditions that have made this possible and the implications this has for the professional growth, modernization and development of Latin American armed forces.

In the final section titled "Hemispheric players", José Raúl Perales explores how engagement with Haiti, and Haiti's position in the Western hemisphere, affects regional cooperation. As Brazil becomes an increasingly vocal player in international affairs, its transition from a regional middle power to an emerging one with global aspirations is becoming evident. Marcel Biato, an adviser to Brazil's president Luiz Inacio Lula da Silva, uses this country's engagement in Haiti as a lens through which Brazil's new regional role can be framed. By taking on a leadership mantle in Haiti, Brazil is showing its commitment to stabilizing the country and discharging its international civic duties.

Stephen Baranyi moves the discussion to the far north by focusing on Canadian policy towards Haiti. Canada has many connections with its regional neighbour to the south, including a large Haitian community (many in Montreal) as well as the visibility and prominence of Michaëlle Jean, Canada's Governor General from 2005 to 2010, and a native Haitian, who gave a tearful appeal for aid for Haiti in the wake of the 2010 earthquake. But Baranyi is critical of Canadian policies, which he suggests have been both generous but also damaging, and have contributed to Haiti's "condition of fragility and dependence".

The section concludes by examining Haiti's relationship with the largest player in the hemisphere, the United States. Robert Maguire compares the George W. Bush administration's policies towards Haiti to those of the Obama administration. He argues that there has been a "new" and more progressive approach to Haiti by the Obama administration, one that emphasizes democracy and human rights promotion, poverty alleviation, and confronting narco-trafficing, but warns that much more needs to be done to include Haitians in the implementation of these aims, not just for Washington's sake, but for Haiti's as well.

## Looking ahead

In light of the January 2010 earthquake, this volume examines the challenges that the country will face moving forward. Haitians' attitudes towards MINUSTAH and international engagement have been mixed. On the one hand, there is a general acknowledgement that chaos could once again erupt if the United Nations and other actors pulled out. On the other hand, there is resentment and even a sense of humiliation among many Haitians who have been forced to accept that, at least for the immediate future, they are not in complete control of their own destiny. This is deeply frustrating. For Haitians, the concern is not that MINUS-TAH leave Haiti; rather, that when it does leave, the conditions are such that it does not have to return.

Still, there remains a widely held view within the international community that Haiti's problems are intractable. Previous attempts at nation-building, particularly those of the 1990s, produced few lasting results, so much so that Haiti has often been described as a "graveyard of aid projects". For their part, donor nations have, in the past, developed "Haiti fatigue", and have withheld development aid, in part because of a lack of hard evidence that their investments had born any fruit. In doing so, a vicious cycle arose: the absence of progress prompted a reduction in aid, which in turn hampered progress and contributed to the disintegration of the country's social fabric. The notion that the situation was hopeless became a self-fulfilling prophecy.

There is a distinct possibility that the current international reconstruction efforts could suffer a similar fate. While most observers agree that the costs of not strengthening Haiti are high, the international community has been down this road before. True security dictates that donors adopt a holistic approach to engagement in Haiti that aims to address the root causes of fragility. And yet there is a substantial divide between the aims laid out by the United Nations Security Council and the international community, and realities on the ground. Even with the support of the hemisphere, there is a danger that history will repeat itself; that if substantive signs of progress are not visible soon, donors may be tempted to withdraw before genuine reform is allowed to take hold. It is the hope of the contributors of this volume that this will not be the case.

## Notes

1. The insight is of Haitian poet Jean-Claude Martineau.
2. For these statistics and an otherwise full report of the Haitian post-quake situation, see International Crisis Group (2010).
3. For a powerful documentary on the quake and its aftermath, see *Haiti: The Quake*, a Frontline production, shown on PBS, April 2010.
4. They were: General Henri Namphy (7 February 1986 to 17 January 1988, 20 June to 18 September 1988), who took control of the country immediately after the revolution; Leslie Manigat (7 February to 20 June 1988), who was elected under disputed circumstances, and eventually displaced by Namphy after serving only five months in office; Lt-General Prosper Avril (18 September 1988 to 11 March 1990), who staged a coup d'état against Namphy and finally Judge Ertha Pascal Trouillot (10 March to 16 December 1990), who was appointed by Avril.
5. Security Council Resolution 875 authorized the body to "consider further necessary measures to ensure full compliance with the provisions of relevant Security Council resolutions", which included economic sanctions. See United Nations Security Council (1993). UN Security Council Resolution 940 was authorized for the creation of a Multinational Force (MNF) under Chapter VII of the United Nations Charter, its mandate "to use all necessary means to facilitate the departure from Haiti of the military leadership ... the prompt return of the legitimately elected President and the restoration of the legitimate authorities of the Government of Haiti, and to establish and maintain a secure and stable environment ..." (United Nations Security Council, 1994, p. 2).

    The sanctions had a devastating effect on the population, and arguably exacerbated the crisis. Another consequence of the coup was a massive exodus of boat people fleeing Haiti. By August, estimates suggested that the number of Haitians intercepted by the US Coast Guard since October 1991 had risen to 38, 000. See Amnesty International (1992).
6. See United Nations Security Council (1994; 1996a; 1996b; 1997a; 1997b).
7. See United Nations Security Council (2004a; 2005b; 2006b).
8. These include documents such as the UN Code of Conduct for Law Enforcement Officials; UN Basic Principles on the Use of Force and Firearms by Law Enforcement Officials; the UN Principles on the Effective Prevention and Investigation of Extra-Legal, Arbitrary and Summary Executions; and the UN Standard Minimum Rules for the Treatment of Prisoners.
9. See United Nations Security Council (2004b; 2005a; 2005b; 2006a; 2006b; 2007).
10. See Paragraph 8, United Nations Security Council (2005b). Paragraph 10 "*Urges* the Transitional Government to conduct thorough and transparent investigations into cases of human rights violations, particularly those allegedly involving HNP officers; *requests* that in order to support this effort MINUSTAH make the Joint Special Investigation Unit operational as soon as possible."

# REFERENCES

Annan, Kofi (2004) "In Haiti for the Long Haul", *Wall Street Journal*, 16 March.

Buss, Terry with Adam Gardner (2008) *Why Foreign Aid to Haiti has Failed and What We Can Do About It*. Washington DC: Brookings Institution Press.

Amnesty International (1992) "Haiti: Human Rights Held to Ransom", AMR 36/41/92, August.

Cammack, D. and D. Macleod et al. (2006) *Donors and the "Fragile States" Agenda: A Survey of Current Thinking and Practice*. London: Overseas Development Institute.

Carment, David (2003) "Assessing State Failure: Implications for Theory and Policy", *Third World Quarterly*, 24(3): 407–427.

Carment, David and Yiagadeesen Samy (2010a) "Haiti Without Tears: Getting Aid right", *Policy Options*, April: 57–63.

Carment, David and Yiagadeesen Samy (2010b) "A Marshall Plan for Haiti? Think Again", *Globe and Mail*, 20 February.

Collier, Paul (2009) "Haiti: From Natural Catastrophe to Economic Security", A Report for the Secretary-General of the United Nations, January (mimeo).

Collier, Paul and Jean Louis Warnholz (2010) "We need a Marshall Plan for Haiti", *Globe and Mail*, 13 January.

Danner, Mark (2009) "Beyond the Mountains" in Mark Danner, *Stripping Bare the Body: Politics, Violence, War*. New York: Nation Books, pp. 1–122.

Dupuy, Alex (2005) "From Jean Bertrand Aristide to Gerard Latortue: The Unending Crisis of Democratization in Haiti", *Journal of Latin American Anthropology*, 10(1): 186–205.

Dziedzic, Michael and Robert M. Perito (2008) "Haiti: Confronting the Gangs of Port-au-Prince", *USIP Special Report*. Washington DC: United States Institute of Peace.

Fatton Jr., Robert (2002) *Haiti's Predatory Republic: The Unending Transition to Democracy*. Boulder: Lynne Rienner.

Fatton Jr., Robert (2006) "The Fall of Aristide and Haiti's Current Predicament" in Yasmine Shamsie and Andrew S. Thompson (eds), *Haiti: Hope for a Fragile State*. Waterloo: Wilfrid Laurier University Press, pp. 15–24.

Fatton Jr., Robert (2007) *The Roots of Haitian Despotism*. Boulder: Lynne Rienner.

Feeny, Simon and Mark McGillivray (2009) "Aid Allocation to Fragile States: Absorptive Capacity Constraints", *Journal of International Development*, 21: 618–632.

Heine, Jorge (1988) "Transition to Nowhere: How Haiti's Transition Might Have Worked", *Caribbean Review*, 16(2): 4–6.

Heine, Jorge and Ramesh Thakur (eds) (2010) *The Dark Side of Globalization*. Tokyo: United Nations University Press.

Heinl, Robert Debs Jr. and Nancy Gordon Heinl (1978) *Written in Blood: A History of the Haitian People 1492–1971*. Boston: Houghton Mifflin.

International Crisis Group (2010) "Haiti: Stabilisation and Reconstruction After the Quake", *Latin America/Caribbean Report*, 32, 31 March.

James, C.L.R. (1963) *The Black Jacobins: Toussaint L'Ouverture and the San Domingo Revolution*. New York: Vintage.

Leyburn, James (1966) *The Haitian People*. New Haven: Yale University Press.

MacFarquhar, Neil (2010) "UN Honors the 101 Who Served and Died in Haiti", *New York Times*, 10 March.

Mendelson Forman, Johanna (2008) "Security Sector Reform in Haiti", *International Peacekeeping*, 13(1): 14–27.

Métraux, Alfred (1972) *Vodoo in Haiti*. New York: Schocken.

Naím, Moisés (2010) "Mixed Metaphors", *Foreign Policy*, March–April: 112–111.

Rotberg, Robert I. (2003) *State Failure and State Weakness in a Time of Terror*. Washington DC: Brookings Institution Press.

Rotberg, Robert I. (ed.) (2004) *When States Fail: Causes and Consequences*. Princeton: Princeton University Press.

Shah, Kamil (2009) "The Failure of State Building and the Promise of State Failure: Reinterpreting the Security-development Nexus in Haiti", *Third World Quarterly*, 30(1): 17–34.

United Nations Security Council (1993) "Resolution 875", 16 October. Available at http://www.securitycouncilreport.org/atf/cf/%7B65BFCF9B-6D27-4E9C-8CD3-CF6E4FF96FF9%7D/Chap%20VII%20SRES%20875.pdf

United Nations Security Council (1994) "Resolution 940", S/RES/940, 31 July. Available at http://daccess-dds-ny.un.org/doc/UNDOC/GEN/N94/312/22/PDF/N9431222.pdf?OpenElement

United Nations Security Council (1996a) "Resolution 1063", S/RES/1063, 28 June. Available at http://daccess-dds-ny.un.org/doc/UNDOC/GEN/N96/162/13/PDF/N9616213.pdf?OpenElement

United Nations Security Council (1996b) "Resolution 1086", S/RES/1086, 5 December. Available at http://daccess-dds-ny.un.org/doc/UNDOC/GEN/N96/351/21/PDF/N9635121.pdf?OpenElement

United Nations Security Council (1997a) "Resolution 1123", S/RES/1123, 30 July. Available at http://daccess-dds-ny.un.org/doc/UNDOC/GEN/N97/206/88/PDF/N9720688.pdf?OpenElement

United Nations Security Council (1997b) "Resolution 1141", S/RES/1141, 28 November. Available at http://daccess-dds-ny.un.org/doc/UNDOC/GEN/N97/340/85/PDF/N9734085.pdf?OpenElement

United Nations Security Council (2004a) "Resolution 1542", S/RES/1542, 30 April. Available at http://daccess-dds-ny.un.org/doc/UNDOC/GEN/N04/332/98/PDF/N0433298.pdf?OpenElement

United Nations Security Council (2004b) "Resolution 1576", S/RES/1576, 29 November. Available at http://daccess-dds-ny.un.org/doc/UNDOC/GEN/N04/626/12/PDF/N0462612.pdf?OpenElement

United Nations Security Council (2005a) "Resolution 1601", S/RES/1601, 31 May. Available at http://daccess-dds-ny.un.org/doc/UNDOC/GEN/N05/367/82/PDF/N0536782.pdf?OpenElement

United Nations Security Council (2005b) "Resolution 1608", S/RES/1608, 22 June. Available at http://daccess-dds-ny.un.org/doc/UNDOC/GEN/N05/395/57/PDF/N0539557.pdf?OpenElement

United Nations Security Council (2006a) "Resolution 1658", S/RES/1658, 14 February. Available at http://daccess-dds-ny.un.org/doc/UNDOC/GEN/N06/242/88/PDF/N0624288.pdf?OpenElement

United Nations Security Council (2006b) "Resolution 1702", S/RES/1702, 15 August. Available at http://daccess-dds-ny.un.org/doc/UNDOC/GEN/N06/468/77/PDF/N0646877.pdf?OpenElement

United Nations Security Council (2007) "Resolution 1743", S/RES/1743, 15 February. Available at http://daccess-dds-ny.un.org/doc/UNDOC/GEN/N07/240/92/PDF/N0724092.pdf?OpenElement

Williams, Carol (2007) "Haiti Tastes Peace Under Preval", *Los Angeles Times,* 25 July.

# Part I

# Haiti's governance challenges

# 1

# External shocks to fragile states: Building resilience in Haiti

*Amélie Gauthier and Madalena Moita*

Whereas the earthquake of 12 January 2010 was an "internal shock" to Haiti, several external shocks had a dramatic impact on the life of Haitians in 2008. That these shocks erupted from exogenous sources is evidence that, in an interdependent global system, all states – but particularly those that are fragile and suffer from weak governance – are vulnerable to phenomena beyond their control: soaring prices of food caused by diverse factors from around the world; climate change and extreme weather, which is prompting stronger and more frequent natural disasters; and the global financial crisis. Around the world these shocks caused major social distress and instigated complex political crises. Together and independently, all three exposed several countries' vulnerabilities as well as the inability of these states to respond to them. Whereas developed states with large and diversified economies were better positioned to adapt, vulnerable and fragile states were nowhere near as resilient, and often suffered important setbacks on the way out of poverty and underdevelopment. Perhaps nowhere was this more evident than in Haiti, a clear case in which both conditions – vulnerability and fragility – aggravate the quality of life of its population. This chapter sets out to do three things: first, to examine the causes of and links between Haiti's vulnerability and fragility; second, to assess the negative effects of the three grave crises of 2008 on the statebuilding process; and third, to explore possible ways donors can help to mitigate vulnerability in order to diminish the impact of future external shocks as the country attempts to recover from the worst internal shock of its modern history.

*Fixing Haiti: MINUSTAH and beyond, Heine and Thompson (eds), United Nations University Press, 2011, ISBN 978-92-808-1197-1*

## Haiti's vulnerability and fragility

Like many other countries in the Caribbean, Haiti is highly vulnerable to external shocks; but it is the only fragile state in the region. When identifying and categorizing fragile states, it is important to define and identify some of the internal and external causes of the fragility, including historical trends that help to explain the weakness of the state. The basic functions of the modern state can be grouped around three areas: security, representation and welfare. According to the Organisation for Economic Co-operation and Development (OECD) Development Assistance Committee's (2007: 2) "principles for good international engagement in fragile states and situations", states are fragile "when state structures lack political will and/or capacity to provide the basic functions needed for poverty reduction, development and to safeguard the security and human rights of their populations".

According to this functional approach, the state is ineffective because it is unable to perform its expected duties. The state has a very thin presence in the country and most basic services are privatized (George, 2004). Fragile states are also weak in a relational perspective: they fail to interact with civil society, and thus fail to recognize and honour the social, political and economic contract between society and the state. Because the state is incapable of fulfilling its responsibilities to its citizenry, individuals are often reluctant to accept or even recognize a common set of rules or to perform their own duties to the rest of society. When individuals do not become "citizens", the social contract is non-existent, and state institutions become tools for advancing the interests of a narrow set of privileged, predatory groups. Such fragile states thus lack both effectiveness and legitimacy. In their absence, a fragile state will often enter into a vicious cycle of structural governance dysfunctionality.

State fragility is often aggravated in times of crisis. The example of Haiti in 2008 is paradigmatic. Social disturbances due to rising food prices caused a political crisis. For five months Haiti waited for a new prime minister. But even when the executive branch of the government has worked properly, Haiti's political elite have been unable to design and implement public policies. Given this reality, the Haitian government has been forced to search for legitimacy elsewhere. Traditionally, elites have found it by establishing a "prebendary" state (Dupuy, 2007: 25) which they maintain through the loyalty of their constituencies. In this context, the majority of the population has no access to any kind of public service, as the state apparatus exists to serve the private interests of the ruling elite. This model was especially evident during the Duvalier dictatorships that ruled Haiti from 1957 to 1986.

Prior to the earthquake, the Haitian state's inability and unwillingness to provide public services was perhaps most evident in the lack of investment in education or job generation, investments which could, in time, be converted into production and ultimately state revenues. Most schools in the country are private, and an estimated 40 per cent of the poorest families' budget is used for education. Without revenues, social expenditure remains dramatically low, and any kind of social safety net is unattainable.

As the poorest country in the Western hemisphere with 76 per cent of its population living on less than US$2 a day (EIU, 2008: 7), Haiti's obstacles to development have been considerable, but the fragility of the social contract works both ways. As mentioned above, if the state does not respond to the demands of its community, individuals do not and will not feel obliged to respect their half of the bargain. Massive migration, corruption and informal and illegal economies are the responses to the absence of a sense of citizenship, only reinforcing the cycle of weak governance. For those who resist migrating, opportunities to improve their living conditions are rare, as social mobility is rigid. Without sound public policies, breaking out of the poverty cycle is not viable. Corruption, crime and the drug trade become alternatives to legal economic activities.

Haiti's economy is one of the most open in Latin America, and the most open of all least developed countries (Borgatti, 2006: 13). In the 1970s, the average tariff was 28 per cent; in 2002, it was 2.9 per cent, following the implementation of structural adjustment plans in the 1990s that promoted liberalization, privatization of state assets and deregulation of the economy. But Haiti has not reaped the benefits of a liberalized economy. In fact, the opposite has been true: from 1990 to 2005 Haiti had negative economic growth, minus 2.0 per cent GDP/per capita growth, and (minus 2.2 per cent from 1970 to 2005) (UNDP, 2007/2008).

The lowering of tariffs also diminished state revenues. To recoup shortfalls, a consumer tax was introduced. This policy had the effect of shifting the tax burden to the population, the vast majority of which lives in conditions of extreme poverty. Thus, economic openness not only exposed Haiti to external economic forces, but it had the added effect of inhibiting the state from being able to protect and thus support the domestic economy.

In an integrated global economy that rewards specialization, Haiti's main competitive advantages have been its abundance of low-wage, unskilled workers and its proximity to the United States, its biggest trading partner. Depending on the source of the information, the United States accounts for 73–85 per cent of Haiti's trade, followed by the Dominican Republic at 9 per cent and Canada at 3 per cent. Prior to the earthquake it had developed an export-directed clothing sector, which represented 67 per cent of the country's exports (all destined for the United States), and served as the main stimulus to economic growth.[1]

Such a high degree of concentration is problematic in times of economic recession and depression. In 2008 the United States approved legislation as part of the Haitian Hemispheric Opportunity through Partnership II Act (HOPE II Act), providing duty-free imports for Haitian apparel, thereby creating further incentives to concentrate, and, consequently, become more dependent on exogenous factors.[2] Following the earthquake, the US senate passed a new bill, the Haiti Economic Lift Program Act (HELP Act), which extends the duty-free agreements for a period of 10 years. In contrast, before the earthquake, Haiti's imports were three times the size of its exports, resulting in a huge commercial deficit that further indebted the country. These imports were not inconsequential, consisting of mostly food and fuel. The prices of food increased 83 per cent from 2005 to 2008, while the price of oil tripled in two years, peaking at US$150 a barrel in June 2008. One effect of Haiti's exposure to these fluctuations in world market prices and supply was that it made government expenditures highly unpredictable.

## Three external shocks

Many countries suffered external shocks in 2008, but the effects of the soaring prices of food and fuel, of natural disasters and of the global financial crisis added considerable stress to Haiti's already fragile development and statebuilding processes. Haiti's vulnerability and its economic weakness, combined with state fragility and external dependence, left it struggling, although other countries facing similar threats showed resilience, preparedness and recovery. In 2008, the Haitian government was ill prepared to face such diverse and intense crises, all of which occurred in the space of 12 months. And as the 2010 earthquake has demonstrated, being unprepared for crises can be disastrous. The external shocks of 2008 should serve as a lesson of what not to do in response to an earthquake.

### Food and fuel crisis

The crisis into the spring of 2008 arising from the worldwide food price inflation had a major impact (CNSA, 2008). Moreover, Haiti's high exposure to world food price fluctuations illustrated the state's ineffectiveness, delegitimization and unaccountability, as well as its enormous distance from the people. As Robert Fatton Jr. explains in his chapter in this volume, it allowed for the political manipulation of the crisis, led to millions of dollars in property and private asset losses, and millions of people going hungry that year. One of the effects of the crisis was a rise in political instability and insecurity. It prompted rioting in most major cities in Haiti, resulting in the deaths of four civilians and a UN officer, more than a hundred injured, hundreds of damaged buildings and losses of US$100 million in an already depressed Haitian economy. The state–society divide thus became especially acute.

This inflation-led crisis also exacerbated political cleavages. It led to the fall of Prime Minister Jacques-Édouard Alexis, and triggered a five-month-long political crisis that ended only after the Haitian Parliament finally agreed on his replacement. Indeed, while the political elite debated, discussed, voted and vetoed candidates for prime minister, and the international community pressed for the installation of a new government, the population suffered the effects of soaring prices. Haiti was, and remains, the only country in the world in which the increase in food prices brought down a government.

As alluded to in the previous section, the effects of the global food crisis in Haiti are linked, both directly and indirectly, to the Washington Consensus model imposed on the country in the 1990s. In Haiti, the agricultural sector employs a large proportion of the country's rural – and especially poor – population. Haiti is a prime example of a country in which global agricultural trade has had a direct and profound impact on the life and even death of local farmers and consumers.

Haiti was once a producer and exporter of rice. However, it suffered a strong decline in its agricultural sector, partly due the imports of highly subsidized American rice with which local producers could not compete, the result being the destruction of an important sector of the local economy. Rice imports from the United States went from 7,300 metric tons to 219,600 between 1985 and 2000 (George, 2004; see also Fatton Jr., this volume). Moreover, during that period, Haiti also entered the International Monetary Fund's (IMF) structural adjustment plan and was forced to reduce its import tariff on rice from 35 per cent to just 3 per cent, very low when compared to the average tariff among Caribbean Community (CARICOM) countries, which is 25 per cent (ibid.). Producers in Haiti simply could not compete with imported foods. However, there was little that Haitian authorities could do about it since, given its relative size, Haiti does not have any negotiating power with international financial institutions such as the IMF and the World Bank.

Today, national production is insufficient to supply enough food for the population, meeting only 43 per cent of the country's needs (52 per cent of the food is imported and 5 per cent is provided by humanitarian assistance). To cover the gap, the state is forced to import a large amount of staple foods, such as cassava, corn, millet and rice. In turn, the external dependency on financing the budget and the unpredictability of aid flows make it difficult to disburse funds rapidly and for the state to respond effectively in times of crisis. In the case of the food crisis of 2008, the government's reaction was slow, its inaction a combination of state incapacity and a general unwillingness to respond (Gauthier, 2008). Weeks went by before it was able to secure an agreement with rice importers to lower the price of imported rice by 15 per cent. This subsidy policy did give some relief to the population; however, it was not a sustainable solution to the shortcomings in supply, scarcity and soaring prices that have been forecast for the years to come (EIU, 2008: 8).

## Natural disasters

Haiti is particularly prone to both small and large natural disasters, such as hurricanes, floods and, of course, earthquakes (UNDP, 2010). The damages that the four tropical storms and hurricanes of the summer of 2008 left behind are telling, but nothing compared to the devastating effects caused by the 2010 earthquake: 793 deaths, 548 people injured, 310 missing; more than 165,000 families – 800,000 people – were affected, especially in the Artibonite, south and south-east regions, as a result of the severe weather that destroyed or damaged houses (around 100,000) and led to tremendous losses to what were already precarious livelihoods (United Nations, 2009). Total losses and damages have been estimated at 15 per cent of GDP or US$900 million. Although hurricanes had had devastating effects in previous years – such as Hurricane Jeanne in 2004, which killed more than 3,000 in Gonaives – the storms of 2008 were particularly destructive. The minister of agriculture in Haiti estimated that 60 per cent of that year's food harvest was destroyed by the hurricanes, representing around a US$180 million loss in revenues (EIU, 2008).

In contrast, Cuba, with a similar geographical location and similar size in population, suffered a minimal death toll, totalling only seven during the same period. According to Jan Egeland, Cuba is the world's best prepared country for facing natural disasters. The government has mobilized communities to participate in evaluating vulnerable areas, planning and recovery. It has also made it a priority to establish special training and funds for civil defence that enables the government to respond immediately after a hurricane has struck. Cuba has also established a well-functioning national communication network that has become integral to warning citizens in times of upcoming hurricanes (Thompson and Gaviria, 2004). At least with respect to this issue, the central government is highly committed to the protection of its citizens.

Some countries manage to bounce back quickly from the storms by using the aid funds they receive for reconstruction, job generation and growth. The minimum state structure required to manage aid funds has been absent in Haiti. The material and human destruction of the hurricanes generated major setbacks: infrastructure in certain parts of the country was completely destroyed, including bridges and roads, making large parts of country incommunicable except by helicopters. The urgency of the crisis prompted the senate to approve the nominee for prime minister at the time, Michèle Pierre-Louis, in order to allow her to coordinate the government's response with the international community.

*Global financial turmoil*

The financial and economic recession of 2008 came as a surprise and an unpredictable shock to much of the world. Still, large and diversified economies such as those in the United States and Europe have had the ability, resources and resilience to respond quickly. Global responses were proposed, rescue packages were developed and strategies to minimize the impacts of losses on the international markets and sustain confidence in institutions were coordinated. Haiti is financially isolated from the centre of the credit meltdown in large part because its banking system is nationally owned and cross-border issues are of little relevance to it. Most banks reported high rates of solvency, at least according the IMF (2008: 18).

The impacts of declining growth, recession and unemployment in the United States and Europe have, however, already been felt beyond their own borders. Less developed countries, isolated from the immediate impact of bank system failure and credit bubbles, have been hit hard by the aftershocks: falling demand for exports, slowing capital flows, reduced remittances, sluggish growth and the threat of development aid drying up (Geldof, 2008; see Te Velde, 2008: 3).

Haiti is no exception. Even prior to the earthquake, its economic outlook was bleak. As indicated above, the country's proximity to the United States has not only made it highly dependent, exposed and vulnerable to decreases in both the demand for exported goods but also in remittances. In fact, the remittances sent by the Haitian diaspora constitute a fundamental part of the country's revenue, supporting up to 70 per cent of households and representing more than twice the earnings from exports (EIU, 2008; CIA, 2007). Close to 73 per cent of Haiti's exports go to the United States; in the first three quarters of 2008, even before the financial crisis, exports to the United States fell by 13 per cent.[3]

Investment in Haiti was already scarce before 2008, although the outlook was definitely brighter prior to the meltdown. The damages caused by the social unrest to real estate and private assets, the government's lack of commitment to protect private investments and the wreckage of already deficient infrastructure have destroyed what few incentives there are to invest in Haiti. In aggregate terms, Foreign Direct Investment (FDI) in developing countries has shrunk from 40 per cent in the 1990s to 20 per cent in the 2000s, leaving many underdeveloped countries competing with each other for a meagre amount of funds (Wade, 2005: 22).

Haiti's economic growth rate of 1.5 per cent in 2008, with a 20 per cent inflation rate, meant that Haiti's economy was effectively shrinking by 2 per cent on a per capita basis (CEPAL, 2008). Moreover, the Haitian population is young, with more than 50 per cent under the age of 25, increasingly urban and eager to find a stable way of living (Pierre, 2008). The World Bank anticipates that the decline in growth in developing countries will lead to more poverty and unemployment, especially among the young. The lack of job opportunities is even more pronounced in times of crises; often the result is that it encourages young people to migrate and/or work in informal and illicit means of subsistence, thus contributing to rising levels of crime.

If the food crisis raised questions about the effects of climate change, the agriculture production model of fragile states or their alimentary dependence, the financial crisis alerted the world to the fragility of the global economic system. The global recession of 2008 has led to calls for a critical reflection on the unsustainability of today's economic model and the inadequacies of global governance mechanisms. The financial crisis could turn out to be an opportunity for change, an opportunity to promote a more transparent and solid financial system in order to avoid future collapses (see Cooper and Subacchi, 2010). It could also be an opportunity to rethink international actors' statebuilding strategies. Regardless of the legacies of the crisis, models of state fragility must incorporate sufficient considerations of sustained long-term economic development, given its importance in fostering a lasting and stable peace (Carment et al., 2004: 16).

## Challenges for donors

The international community has been intervening in Haiti since the departure of Jean-Bertrand Aristide in February 2004. It has provided multilateral and bilateral funding, a medium-sized peacekeeping operation at a cost of some US$500 million a year and financed the Interim Cooperation Framework (ICF) (which later became the Strategic National Document for Growth and Poverty Reduction), which had estimated that Haiti would need nearly US$4 billion from 2008 to 2011 in order to pay for the reconstruction effort stemming from the 2008 natural disasters. In the aftermath of the 2010 earthquake, international donors have held international donor conferences to coordinate the $3.8 billion in reconstruction funds that have been committed (Jimenez, 2010). The United Nations Development Programme (UNDP) as well as 10 other UN agencies have implemented programmes – while the World Bank, the European Union, the Organization of American States (OAS), traditional and new partners in Latin America – are all committed to Haiti's recovery. Still, the reaction to the 2008 natural disasters provides insights into the country's current challenges. What was the reaction to the tragic events of 2008? How did donors react to the crisis and, moreover, to the deterioration of the situation and the negative impacts of these factors? Was Haiti in a "stabilization" process, or is it constantly falling back into crisis mode, unable to reach recovery and development stages?[4]

The overarching priority for the international community in Haiti is statebuilding through the development of technical, strategic and administrative capacities. This means the creation of effective institutions that are able to service the population.[5] However, the model that has been adopted in Haiti in that past has been the standard "one size fits all" model that is applied in multilateral interventions from Afghanistan to the Democratic Republic of Congo; it does not consider the specific characteristics of the country's economic and environmental vulnerability. Building resilience to external shocks through a more diversified economy and through improved environmental conditions and reforestation will help Haiti to recover faster from future crises. As such, policymakers have much to gain by considering economic vulnerability and state fragility in tandem.

All of this has led to the constant shift in the Haitian government's priorities. Following the food crisis and the international conference in Madrid, Spain (July 2008), on food security and rural development, the agricultural sector became, for a time, a priority. But following the hurricanes, the rebuilding of the country's infrastructures became the government's most pressing focus, resulting in an allocation of more than 50 per cent of the 2008–2009 budget to the telecommunications sector, and 2.9 per cent of the budget to improving the environment. At the beginning of September 2008, an initial Flash Appeal was launched, calling on donors to contribute US$108 million in humanitarian assistance. But by the end of the month only 2 per cent of the funds pledged were actually given, and only 48 per cent of a revised post-disaster reconstruction plan was actually financed by the international community.

Sadly, Haiti suffers from donor fatigue syndrome. After six years, and millions of dollars in aid (even more so with the new reconstruction plan estimated at US$5.3 billion in the 18 months following the 2010 earthquake), socioeconomic development had not improved, causing some to question the legitimacy of the international community's intervention. Haiti has not yet received the "peace dividend", (Annabi, 2008), nor is it likely to in the near future. Moreover, the crises exposed a distant government, one that is unable and unwilling to help its citizens. Transforming Haiti from a fragile state to a functioning one is still a work in progress.

Generating economic growth and revenue for the state is essential if states are to resist external shocks. In Haiti, the agricultural sector represents 25 per cent of the GDP, and more than 60 per cent of the population lives in the rural areas. Yet rural development only received 13 per cent of the 2009 budget. Support for the agriculture sector is necessary in order to reduce dependency on food imports (improving balance of payments), increase employment for the rural population and reduce the risk of food shortages. Diversification is also essential so that if harvests are destroyed, other forms of economic revenues can compensate for them. This diversification entails the creation of new economic activities that are less exposed to external shocks.[6]

Most small islands have reached some degree of diversification through tourism, handicraft industries and various service industries, all of which are possibilities for Haiti. Mauritius is an excellent example of a small-island developing state with a high GDP per capita, an island that has overcome many obstacles to reach its present status as a middle-income country. Haiti needs a sustainable growth model. In this regard, the international community has also been criticized for enforcing a predesigned model which may not be the most favourable for Haiti's long-term development.

The imposition of a neo-liberal economic agenda may be self-defeating. It focuses on a minimalist state when Haiti needs a robust and functioning state. The balancing of fiscal accounts has been a major concern of the international financial institutions towards Haiti. Although some of their structural adjustment policies have tolerated higher government expenditure to improve public services and to strengthen governance, they privilege a market-oriented strategy which has, in the past, been harmful to the country. And in a time of financial crisis, there is a danger that coherent, constructive and long-term involvement in fragile states be replaced by more self-centred international policies. International actors should not rule out the possibility that some protectionist measures may be needed in order to insulate developing economies such as Haiti's from the destructive effects of external forces.

In times of crises, the government of Haiti has shown poor leadership, and has missed several opportunities to build ties with its populace. Yet, two important events marked a new form of collaboration with the government: the agreement between the rice importers and the government to subsidize the price of rice by 15 per cent; and the commitment from Digicel, the mobile telecommunications operator, to raise funds for the disaster victims. These are two examples of different sectors working together and re-establishing state/non-state actor ties. The international community could be more involved in creating incentives for the population and the state to work together, and providing conditions to promote oversight, evaluation and follow-up, especially through the Parliament. Haiti's future depends on a meaningful social contract. International actors need to think how they will gradually diminish their involvement and impact on the government while leaving in place a stronger society.

An energy policy for Haiti must also become a national and international priority. Energy and the environment are linked, as deforestation is widespread and charcoal is the main source of energy. The naked mountains amplify the effects of hurricanes and natural disasters by hill slides and flooding. Reducing the dependence on wood and providing the population with affordable electricity would help reduce deforestation. Donors have implemented many projects aimed at breaking the dependency on charcoal, but have thus far not succeeded. As such, the environment has become a lost cause and a forgotten priority. New technologies could be used, such as solar panels, to protect what is left of the "pearl of the Antilles".

## Conclusion

Over the last two decades, efforts to break the poverty cycle and implement state reforms have come from abroad. Seven international missions have attempted to establish a liberal democratic state, a culture of human rights, a professional police force and functioning rule of law institutions. Since 2004, the United Nations Stabilization Mission in Haiti (MINUSTAH) has made it possible to fulfil some basic government tasks, particularly in areas relating to security, both through a large military presence, and other initiatives. International actors have also become the protagonists of the major decision-making in the country – something that has become more acute since the earthquake – and which is seen by some Haitians as a violation of their basic state sovereignty (Castor, 2008).

The international community has tried to strengthen the Haitian state's capacity to perform its functions and responsibilities through an ambitious development and security agenda. Yet, foreign involvement can undermine the social contract in two senses: first by damaging its legitimacy, and second by risking its long-term effectiveness. On the one hand, by being proactive in pressing for rapid political and social development, international actors may inadvertently discourage national actors from taking responsibility for their own fate. Francis Fukuyama (2005: 85) argues that a state structure established by outsiders "often undermines the ability of domestic actors to create their own robust institutions". In essence, international actors are privileging the form of the state rather than the substantive social and political relations that undergird its legitimacy and authority (Shah, 2009: 17).

The absence of a real debate between national actors on the nature of the state and its relation to society is a major deficiency. The irony, however, is that in situations of fragility and vulnerability, where there is a lack of state capacity to provide security and basic services, the basic functions are fulfilled by the international community, which in turn can have the undesired effects of undermining the state–society relationship and delegitimizing the very institutions that are so essential to Haiti's recovery in the post-earthquake era. Haiti's future rests on solving this conundrum.

## Notes

1. Based on the authors' calculation: US imports of apparel: 327,796 versus total US imports: 487,792. (US Census bureau, US Value of imports for the year 2007, accessed on http://www.census.gov/foreign-trade/statistics/product/enduse/imports/c2450.html)
2. Note on the clothing sector: One study of "a decade's worth of hard data" found an almost uniform wage meltdown in the apparel industry in underdeveloped countries, having arguable effects on the long-term and sustainable development of a country. See Tonelson, 2002. For more information see Wade, 2005: 25.
3. United States, 72.9 per cent; Dominican Republic, 8.8 per cent; Canada, 3.3 per cent (CIA, 2007).
4. Interview in Port-au-Prince with UNDP representative. Haiti is unable to reach recovery and development stage because of the constant falling back into a humanitarian crisis.
5. The definition of statebuilding we refer to in this research is the OECD-DAC: "An endogenous process to enhance capacity, institutions and legitimacy of the state driven by state-society relations. In its simplest form, state building is the process of states functioning more effectively. Understood in this positive context, it can be defined as an endogenous process to develop capacity, institutions and legitimacy of the state driven by state–society relationships" (OECD-DAC, 2008: 1). Furthermore, statebuilding is often the central objective of peacebuilding. In the case of Haiti, local actors disagree on this term, because it implicitly refers to a conflict that to them is erroneous analysis.
6. "In the economic history of Mauritius, for example, diversification from the sugar monoculture materialized with the rapid development of the textile industry, continued with a significant acceleration of the tourism industry and culminated more recently with the emergence of a successful offshore financial sector. This pattern of diversification has been described as a unique success story, and a rare case of structural strengthening among small-island developing states" (UNCTAD, 2007: 7).

## REFERENCES

Annabi, Hédi (2008) "UN Security Council, Sixty-Third Year, 5862nd meeting", 8 April, S/PV5862, New York: United Nations.

Borgatti, Lisa (2006) "A New Tariff Database for Selected Least Developed Countries", *HEI Working Paper No: 12*, Geneva: Graduate Institute of International Studies.

Carment, David and Stewart Prest, Yiagadeesen Samy (2004) "Assessing Small Island Developing State Fragility", prepared for Lino Briguglio and Eliawony J. Kisanga, (eds), *Economic Vulnerability and Resilience of Small States*, London: Commonwealth Secretariat. Available at http://www.carleton.ca/cifp/app/serve.php/1020.pdf

Castor, Suzy (2008) "La Transición Haitiana: entre los peligros y la esperanza", *Cuadernos de Pensamiento Crítico Latinoamericano*, Número 7, May.

CEPAL (2008) Balance Prelimiar de las Economías de América Latina y el Caribe 2008, December.

CIA (2007) "Haiti: Country Profile", World Fact Book, Washington, DC: Central Intelligence Agency.

CNSA (2008) *Haiti Flash Report*, November.

Cooper, Andrew F. and Paola Subacchi (eds) (2010) *Global Economic Governance in a World of Crisis*, special edition of *International Affairs*, 86(3): 607–757.

Dupuy, Alex (2007) *The Prophet and Power. Jean-Bertrand Aristide, the International Community and Haiti*. Plymouth: Rowman & Littlefield.

EIU (2008) *Haiti Country Report*, Economist Intelligence Unit, November.

Fukuyama, Francis (2005) "Stateness First", *Journal of Democracy*, 16(1), January.

Gauthier, Amélie (2008) "The Food Crisis in Haiti: Exposing Key Problems in the Stabilization Process", FRIDE Commentary, April.

Geldof, Bob (2008) "Remember the Bottom Billion in Our Brave New World", *Financial Times*, 14 November.

George, Josiane (2004) "Trade and the Disappearance of Haitian Rice", *Ted Case Studies*, No. 725, June. Available at http://www1.american.edu/TED/haitirice.htm.

IMF (2008) "Haiti: Financial System Stability Assessment", International Monetary Country Report No. 08/112, March.

Jimenez, Manuel (2010) "Donors Plan to Put Up $3.8 Billion for Haiti Rebuilding", *Washington Post*, 18 March.

OECD-DAC (2007) "Principles for Good International Engagement in Fragile States and Situations", Organisation for Economic Co-operation and Development Development Assistance Committee, April. Available at http://www.oecd.org/dataoecd/61/45/38368714.pdf

OECD-DAC (2008) *State Building in Situations of Fragility*, Organisation for Economic Co-operation and Development Development Assistance Committee, August.

Pierre, Jose (2008) "A Conversation with Haitian Economist Kesner Pharel", Children's Heritage Foundation, August. Available at http://www.childrenheritage.org/Editorial_082008.htm

Shah, Kamil (2009) "The Future of State-Building and the Promise of State-Failure: Reinterpreting the Security-Development Nexus in Haiti", *Third World Quarterly*, 30(1): 17–34.

Te Velde, Dirk Willem (2008) "The Global Financial Crisis and Developing Countries", ODI Background Note, October.

Thompson, M. and Gaviria, I. (2004) *Weathering the Storm: Lessons in Risk Reduction from Cuba*, Boston: Oxfam America.

Tonelson, Alan (2002) "There's Only So Much That Foreign Trade Can Do", *Washington Post*, 2 June.

UNCTAD (2007) "'Structurally Weak, Vulnerable and Small Economies': Who Are They? What Can UNCTAD Do for Them?", Background note, Trade and Development Board, fifty-fourth session, Geneva, 1–11 October, TD/B/54/CRP.4.

UNDP (2007/2008) *Country Profile: Haiti*, Human Development Report. Available at http://hdrstats.undp.org/countries/data_sheets/cty_ds_HTI.html

UNDP (2010) *Disaster Reduction Unit*, Overview, Country profile. Available at www.reliefweb.int

United Nations (2009) *Revised Flash Appeal 2008: Consolidated Appeal Process*, New York: United Nations.

Wade, Robert Hunter (2005) "Failing States and Cumulative Causation in the World System", *International Political Science Review*, 26:17.

# 2

# Haiti's unending crisis of governance: Food, the constitution and the struggle for power

*Robert Fatton Jr.*

More than two decades after the collapse of the Duvalier dictatorship and the massive popular approval of a new and democratic constitution, Haiti remains in a state of crisis. The political system is still extremely fragile, lacking vital and functioning institutions; the economy is incapable of providing the most basic necessities to the population; and the personal safety of Haitians continues to be precarious. Moreover, rampant unemployment and old and obscene patterns of poverty and inequalities are as entrenched now as they have been in the past. Haiti has not moved away from the abyss of utter catastrophe; in fact, the country has moved closer to it under the combined and devastating impact of the recent food riots, four consecutive hurricanes – Fay, Gustav, Hannah and Ike[1] – and the earthquake of January 2010. That President Préval has remained in office since 2006 and re-established a modicum of stability is largely due to the much maligned presence of international forces from the United Nations, the so-called United Nations Stabilization Mission in Haiti (MINUSTAH).[2] Had it not been for the UN's presence, the current situation would have easily degenerated into a chaotic Hobbesian world; in addition, had the Haitian military not been disbanded it is likely that a coup would have materialized.[3]

Not surprisingly, many observers have sought to explain why the country has failed to extricate itself from this unending crisis. In this chapter I will not try to offer a comprehensive answer to this question; I have done so elsewhere (see Fatton Jr., 2002; 2007; see also Dupuy, 1989, 2007; Moïse, 1994, 2001 and Trouillot, 1990). Instead, I will limit my focus to analysing

*Fixing Haiti: MINUSTAH and beyond, Heine and Thompson (eds),*
*United Nations University Press, 2011, ISBN 978-92-808-1197-1*

the current predicament and its most immediate causes. President Préval has argued that the existing constitutional framework and the effects of globalization on food production and prices are the main reasons for Haiti's ailments. While he acknowledged virtual impotence to deal with the latter, he called for revising the former. I will argue, however, that Préval's arguments are flawed. Globalization does indeed impose severe constraints on a poor country like Haiti, but policy choices favouring domestic production are not impossible. And while reforming the constitution may help improve governance, it will not by itself end the zero-sum game politics nor bridge the profound class divisions that have historically characterized Haitian society.

In October 2007, in a speech commemorating the 201-year anniversary of Jean Jacques Dessalines's death, President Préval (2007) declared that political instability was the "violent poison" endangering Haiti's development.[4] He pointed out that establishing stability had been his obsession and single most important goal since assuming power in 2006. Préval contended, however, that the 1987 constitution undermined and indeed threatened this goal. Moreover, he complained that the president is at the mercy of an omnipotent Parliament. Indeed, while the president chooses a prime minister, it is Parliament – both the congress and the senate – that has the power to ratify and fire the prime minister. The process of ratification is not only complicated and burdensome, but it also further strengthens Parliament by giving it the power of approving both the prime minister selected by the president, and the subsequent "general policy" of the government formed by this prime minister. As Article 158 states: "With the approval of the President, the Prime Minister shall choose the members of his Cabinet of Ministers and shall go before Parliament to obtain a vote of confidence on his declaration of general policy." A prime minister could thus be ratified, only to be quickly dismissed by a vote of no-confidence. While Article 129-6 limits Parliament's power by positing that the "Legislature may not pass more than one vote of censure a year on a question concerning a Government program or declaration of general policy", the constitution imposes more obdurate constraints on executive authority.

The president has no right to dissolve Parliament and, not surprisingly, Préval described this parliamentary supremacy as a thoroughly unbalanced division of power that was likely to generate an impotent president and a dangerous political deadlock. In his eyes, therefore, the country was on the verge of permanent ungovernability and thus the constitution had to be amended and reformed.

The problem is that doing so – constitutionally – would take a long time and could paradoxically open a Pandora's box and generate another major political crisis. Moreover, the constitution per se has never been the cause of the recurring systemic breakdowns that have besieged Haiti's recent history. In fact, since the fall of Jean-Claude Duvalier in 1986, the constitution has been consistently violated not only by duly elected governmental officials, opposition groups and state institutions such as the military and the police but also by the imperial intrusion of major foreign powers. While perpetrators of these violations always justified them in the name of the constitution itself, it is hard to see how the constitution was the source of these violations and how amending it would resolve Haiti's problems.

Revising the constitution, moreover, is no easy task: the constitution is itself a major obstacle to constitutional reforms. A reading of some of its key articles makes this abundantly clear: Article 282 declares: "On the recommendation ... of one of the two (2) Houses or of the Executive Branch, the Legislature may declare that the constitution should be amended." The next article requires that "this declaration ... be supported by two-thirds (2/3) of each of the two (2) Houses". Moreover, the declaration "may be promulgated only in the course of the last Regular Session of the Legislative period". And Article 283 stipulates that it is only "At the first session of the following legislative period" that the Houses shall meet in a National Assembly to "decide on the proposed amendment". In addition, Article 284 states that the "National Assembly may not sit or deliberate on the amendment unless at least two-thirds (2/3) of the members of each of the two (2) Houses are present". It specifies also that "No decision of the National Assembly may be taken without a majority of two-thirds (2/3) of the votes cast". And finally, Article 284 decrees that "The amendment passed may enter into effect only after the installation of the next elected President. In no case may the President under the Government that approved the amendment benefit from any advantages deriving there from."

Under these terms, the earliest that any amendments to the constitution could be considered would be January 2010, and if voted into law, they could be effective only after Préval's departure in February 2011. There is no constitutional alternative to this three-year process since the constitution stipulates in Article 284-3 that "General elections to amend the constitution by referendum are strictly forbidden". President Préval's call for amending what he himself called the "*manman lwa*" (the mother of all law) faces huge constitutional barriers. In addition, given Préval's inability to convince Parliament to ratify two of his nominated choices for prime minister,[5] it is very doubtful that he could muster the two third's majority required for any constitutional amendment. Changing the constitution is not just a matter of respecting the constitutional game itself; it is also the ability to forge a huge political majority transcending ideology, class and private interests. Such a task seems to be well beyond Préval's increasingly debilitated statecraft.

This is not to say that the constitution of 1987 is ideal. Far from it; it was elaborated in the aftermath of Jean-Claude Duvalier's forced departure and its purpose was to emasculate the presidency while greatly empowering Parliament, and to a lesser degree the office of the prime minister as well as political parties. The goal was the creation of a systematic framework preventing the personal rule of a new despot; and as such, the constitution was above all an anti-dictatorial charter. As Louis Aucoin (1999) writes: "the drafter's intent [was] to limit executive power by creating a system based upon Parliamentary supremacy" (see also *Le Nouvelliste*, 2007; Moïse, 2008 and Moïse and Hector, 2007). Parliamentary supremacy, however, is not always assured; in fact, under the two abbreviated presidencies of Aristide, the executive was clearly dominant. This was not merely the consequence of Aristide's charismatic leadership and overwhelming popularity, it was also the product of his capacity to "mobilize the streets" to compel Parliament into submission. In other words, constitutional and extra-constitutional means can be used to impose an all-powerful presidentialism (Moïse, 1994: 51–81).

The reality remains, however, that the constitution has a clear and pronounced parliamentary bias. This is problematic because the constitution can lead and has in fact led to political gridlock. Since 1987, successive presidents, prime ministers and parliaments have blocked each other's policy initiatives and paralysed Haitian politics. For instance, in the late 1990s during Préval's first term as president, Haiti had no working government for over a year. It was only after Parliament rejected three of his candidates for prime minister and only when he manoeuvred to introduce some controversial constitutional measures that Préval managed to form an effective government. On 11 January 1999, he declared not only the termination of Parliament's term in office but also that for all practical purposes he would run the country by decree while organizing new elections (Aucoin, 1999).

Thus, the division of power between executive and legislative is a potential source of systemic crisis. A president lacking a working majority in Parliament is simply incapable of appointing a prime minister of his choice and may be compelled to uneasily share the reins of government with one from the opposition. The constitution of 1987 is not merely anti-presidentialist, it fragments authority by engendering regional and local assemblies; power is so dispersed that rational national planning becomes difficult. Moreover, the constitution calls for a system of multiple elections scheduled at different dates that are inordinately costly for a poor country like Haiti. In short, the centre does not hold.

The president can therefore become a feeble figure in spite of being the only governmental official enjoying the legitimacy of having been elected by universal franchise. Furthermore, after serving a five-year term, the president, however popular and effective he or she may be, cannot serve a second consecutive term. The president must exit the seats of power for the next five years before having the opportunity to run for a second and final term. This generates discontinuity rather than continuity and undermines any coherent long-term project of development. Last but not least, the constitution fails to reflect the increasing economic and political significance of the Haitian diaspora whose members are denied double nationality and thus all the privileges of citizenship. The constitution invites therefore political confrontations, instability and ultimately systemic crisis; not surprisingly, Préval has called for amending it, and redressing its multiple flaws.

What I want to suggest, however, is that while the constitution is quite imperfect, as Préval has suggested, it is not the fundamental problem confronting Haiti. In fact, the constitution's many imperfections are not the cause but rather the symptom of a much wider and profound crisis of underdevelopment. This crisis is rooted in the material structure of power, the balance of class forces and the inherited authoritarian *habitus* (Fatton Jr., 2002; 2007). Changing the constitution will not alter these obdurate realities. Constitution-making requires knowledge, engineering skills and political imagination, but such faculties do not obliterate the fact that there is a fundamental difference between writing a *manman lwa* and adhering to its norms and rules.

There is a profound chasm between constitution and constitutionalism. Constitution-making takes place in what might be termed a "moment of exception". This moment enshrines on paper a framework of governance reflecting a balance of power between contending social classes and actors, or the total victory of a particular social segment of society. It expresses nothing more than this immediate reality; constitution-making, therefore, is no guarantee that the conditions under which it materialized will persist. While a constitution may ultimately frame for the *longue durée* patterns of political behaviour and the "rules of the game", there is good reason to believe that it is more likely to be short lived and have no lasting impact on structures of governance. Constitution-making morphs into constitutionalism when it comes to embody an enduring balance of power, compelling political actors into conforming to an institutionalized set of practices and behaviours. Constitutionalism habituates the key players into accepting limits to both defeat and victory. On the one hand, defeat leads neither to jail, exile nor death; it merely forces the defeated into the sidelines with the full expectation that in the next round they will have the opportunity to become full players and winners. On the other hand, victory does not imply absolute power or the annihilation of the opposition; it is a temporary capacity to "run the show" which is always contested at future regular electoral intervals. Constitutionalism, therefore, minimizes the potential for arbitrary and personalized authority as well as the tyranny of the majority. It embodies civility which is the basis on which democratic stability is established.

Any type of democratic constitutional governance rests ultimately on a peaceful but vibrant balance of power between contending social forces. Constitutional knowledge, civic competence and the desire for a good society are important in democratic transitions and consolidations; but they cannot obliterate class interests, dependence on foreign power and the privileged groups' quest for maintaining their dominant position in the existing order.

In the Haitian context, the fundamental question then is whether the constitution of 1987 or a new one can engender constitutionalism. By itself, amending the constitution cannot achieve this objective; or to put the matter more clearly: a revised constitution may be necessary but is not a sufficient condition for the establishment of constitutionalism. Constitutionalism requires the regulated political unpredictability of democracy – a form of uncertainty contained within and structured by a predictable system of rules. Most critically, political actors have – at a minimum – to be convinced that the uncertainties of defeat do not outweigh the gains of a possible future victory. The precondition for the establishment of such convictions is the institutionalization of uncertainty within a predictable framework within which electoral outcomes would neither be permanent nor arbitrary.

Elections can prove, however, to be a source of great instability and dangerous political calculations when they are deemed dishonest or flawed. In Haiti, in the aftermath of virtually every election, losing parties have cried foul and challenged the fairness of their defeat while the victors have always asserted the absolute legitimacy of their triumph. These disputes have undermined governmental authority, invited foreign interference and nurtured political conflicts. In fact, the exacerbation of such conflicts has fuelled violent and chaotic "regime change"; for instance, the forced exit of President Aristide in 2004 had its origins in the capacity of the opposition to transform the irregularities of the legislative elections of 2000 into a major systemic crisis. Aristide's initial reluctance to reach a compromise with his foes, and increasing reliance on his *chimères* to defend his regime, enabled the opposition to enlist international support and mobilize its domestic constituencies. The resulting stand-off precipitated a crisis of governability which was exacerbated when dubious characters of the disbanded Haitian army launched a violent insurgency against Aristide. The crisis was ultimately "resolved" when the United States, France and Canada engineered Aristide's departure into his second exile (see Dupuy, 2007; Hallward, 2007).

The very prospect of holding elections can also trigger institutional dangers. So, for instance, the incapacity of President Préval to have his first two choices of prime minister – Ericq Pierre and Robert Manuel – ratified by Parliament in the aftermath of the sacking of Jacques-Édouard Alexis's government, was not merely a matter of alleged constitutional technicalities and policy differences; it was above all a matter of *la politique politicienne* and the early struggle to shape *l'après Préval*.[6] The intense bargaining and drama surrounding the subsequent ratification of Michelle Pierre-Louis[7] as prime minister were clearly part of this type of politics which generated among political parties and legislators a thoroughly unprincipled struggle for booty and public office.[8]

Already weak and unstructured, political parties have tended to disintegrate into a coterie of individual "big men" who join and abandon new groupings and alliances in an incessant and Machiavellian *sauve qui peut*. Their constant moves are motivated by the acute competition for prebendary gains and the spoils of public office; their vote is increasingly subjected to patronage whatever its source may be. In fact, Ericq Pierre contended that his rejection by Parliament was largely due to the dishonesty of the legislators whom he accused of representing the "forces of corruption". As he put it:

> From the beginning of the process, I ran up against the forces of corruption. My refusal to make a deal with them resulted today in my being rejected by the Chamber of Deputies. The words "homeland" or "interests of the country" were never present in the messages from emissaries who only pressured to negotiate for ministerial posts for their protégées, envelopes of money, or projects that could facilitate their re-election. I've always said that I would not be prime minister at any price. And I could not make any commitments involving the resources of public coffers before even becoming Prime Minister. I also wanted to play with my cards on the table, refusing to fall into the game of those who think they can hide indefinitely behind an anti-neoliberal mask. (quoted in Pierre-Louis, 2008)

Thus, in Ericq Pierre's view, there was little doubt that legislators were prepared to sell their vote to the highest bidder. Not surprisingly, they have tended to become opportunistic and have changed their position without programmatic or ideological coherence. How else could Parliament have overwhelmingly rejected a motion of censure removing Jacques-Édouard Alexis's government in late February 2008, only to approve this very motion barely two months afterwards? How else could the majority of legislators have called for the reversal of the general policies of the government when they had supported these same policies 45 days earlier? How else could L'Espaw, the party of President Préval, collapse into contradictory pieces and join the so-called Concertation des Parlementaires Progressistes (CPP) to reject two of Préval's very own choices of prime minister? And how else could the CPP pretend to suddenly espouse an anti-neo-liberal program when its members had never voiced any credible alternative to it?

Therefore, *la politique politicienne* played a decisive role in blocking the respective ratifications of Ericq Pierre and Robert Manuel. But there was more to it. The food riots of early April 2008 precipitated the opportunistic volte-face of the legislators; afraid of losing everything and positioning themselves for both forthcoming elections and *l'après Préval*, they called for a departure from neo-liberalism and the adoption of a new economic programme. While they voiced a nationalistic and populistic rhetoric, they failed to provide a clear alternative. The legislators' immediate objective was to distance themselves from the increasingly contested leadership of President Préval without abandoning it altogether.

Preval's term in office was supposed to end in February 2011 and legislators knew that he would soon become a lame-duck president, and that a new and powerful prime minister could easily become the logical heir. This is one of the key reasons why the ratification of Michèlle Pierre-Louis as prime minister involved such high stakes and hard bargaining. Parliamentarians have thus started to be involved in a balancing act to keep some room for manoeuvring but also to begin positioning themselves behind a prospective presidential candidate while simultaneously increasing their own electoral chances and prebendary gains. This is a complicated game with a vast potential for perilous miscalculations and unforeseen and unpredictable consequences, especially in a context of a critical series of forthcoming elections. Senatorial, congressional and presidential elections are supposed to take place over the next two years as well as indirect elections for local assemblies which should culminate in the appointment of a Permanent Electoral Council (CEP).[9] The peaceful and orderly unfolding of these complicated political processes is by no means guaranteed; ultimately, it requires political actors to begin accepting the rules of constitutionalism. Such acceptance, however, is thoroughly dependent on a relative equilibrium of power between the major competing political and social blocs of civil society.

Thus, constitutionalism is not merely a set of normative institutional constraints on majority rule, a binding limit to "passions" and arbitrary power; it is above all a pattern of predictable and civil behaviour generated by a balance of class forces. The making of the constitution and the incentive to obey it are both dependent on power relations. Moreover, power relations can undermine constitutionalism when a privileged or ruling minority persistently manipulates the constitution to preserve its interests in the face of overwhelming popular opposition. In this condition, constitutionalism is nothing but the defence of the status quo and a legal obstacle to any meaningful democratization. It leads to a dangerous political immobilism that is likely to engender chaos or the exercise of brute force, even if the contending parties make vain appeals to constitutionalism.

Constitutionalism is safe only when the parties are convinced that their respective weaknesses and strengths are such that if either of them violates the basic "rules of the game", the other would have enough power to launch a mutually detrimental war of all against all. Thus, an equilibrium of power conducive to civility is decisive for strengthening constitutionalism, but unless the coercive apparatus of the state is relatively independent from all major social forces, constitutionalism itself is unlikely to survive coups and counter coups.

Not surprisingly, the constitution of 1987 implied neither "extrication" from authoritarianism nor a successful democratization. Indeed, democratization failed miserably with the violence that erupted during the aborted 1987 presidential elections, the 1991 coup and the recurring crises of the past 10 years, culminating in the second forced departure of President Aristide and another international occupation. The constitution has thus been violated consistently since 1987. Its written and rhetorical celebration has done little to insure its practical and effective implementation. The mere existence of a constitution does not necessarily lead to constitutionalism.

A constitution cannot transform political actors into democratic agents on its own; in conditions of extreme social polarization, it can only offer the fragility of written codes and regulations, which are unlikely to withstand the ferocious zero-sum game of politics. Constitutional stability is likely to function effectively only when subordinate and dominant classes perceive themselves as equally armed or disarmed; only such conditions create the incentives for the surrender of weapons to the moral force of written pacts and documents. A Haitian proverb expresses this reality well: "*Konstitisyon se papye, bayonèt se fè*" (a constitution is made up of paper, but bayonets are made up of steel). In Haiti no civil equilibrium of forces exists, but the presence of MINUSTAH has insulated the political system from implosion. In spite of nationalistic calls to the contrary, the country is not yet ready for ending MINUSTAH's presence, lest it descends into a new period of anarchy. While MINUSTAH has occasionally used dubious methods of repression, it has established a modicum of security and order.[10] This is far from saying that MINUSTAH itself, the international community and particularly the United States, France and Canada have had a consistently stabilizing influence on the country. On the contrary, in many critical instances the policies of all these actors have simply been reckless.

In fact, the international community has had little interest in long-term solutions for Haiti; for instance, the most recent American and French military intervention following Aristide's forced departure from office in 2004 was brief, opportunistic and self-serving. While the two powers played a significant role in undermining and ousting Aristide, they quickly exited the country and left it under the control of an initially small and disorganized MINUSTAH contingent that seemed accountable to no one. Moreover, they selected a new prime minister, Gérard Latortue, who had neither the domestic constituency nor the financial means to govern effectively. Parachuted into his new position from abroad and lacking legitimacy, Latortue's administration soon lost whatever popularity it may have had. The international community had thus created a political system that was unaccountable to the local population, and had no capacity to stop, let alone reverse Haiti's crisis (see Dupuy, 2007; Hallward, 2007). After two years in power, the Latortue–MINUSTAH regime had accomplished little but a poorly organized election that was saved only because of the determination of Haitian voters.

To that extent, it is extremely unlikely that the international community will ever come to Haiti's rescue; and if it does, there is no reason to believe that it would unleash economic development, establish democratic rule and promote social justice. If the foreign community is really interested in improving conditions in Haiti, its main objective should be alleviating poverty by developing policies that would privilege rural areas and increase domestic production for domestic needs. At the moment, however, the record of international financial institutions bodes poorly for such an outcome.[11] What Haiti needs is the construction of a legitimate state capable of reconciling the contradictory interests of conflicting social actors. Such a construction requires in turn new and effective institutions and the expansion of state capacity; unfortunately, this huge task is not a process springing from mid-air, nor is it the product of administrative will. In fact, the construction of a legitimate state mirrors the configuration of class power and the time-horizon of ruler – that is, it reflects how such rulers value the future given their present strategic situation and calculations. The more secure their political positions, the more likely will they be to invest in long-term projects. In short, the creation of effective institutional structures is dependent on the rulers' capacity to go beyond their immediate, narrow, corporate interests. Only then can the rationalization of politics occur, and only then can progress be "routinized".

This is a long-term process fraught with difficulties requiring resources that seem to be beyond existing international commitments and Haiti's treasury. In fact, the material costs of setting up the mere electoral machinery needed for establishing the elementary basis of constitutionalism are so high that they might severely undermine democracy itself.[12] By diverting scarce funds to an interminable series of dubious elections, critical sectors of society such as education, infrastructure and health may be left starving for resources. In this "zero-sum" environment, the implantation of democratic electoralism in Haiti may well co-exist uneasily with the improvement of social welfare.

Thus, a constitution does not make for an effective form of constitutionalism. Reflecting the balance of forces governing class relations and interests, constitutions simply do not soar above the material and political structures of society. Their effective workings are severely constrained by the material environment within which they operate. This reality became quite evident with the food riots of April 2008. The riots were precipitated by rising costs of living, especially basic necessities. For instance, the price of a 55-lb bag of rice more than doubled between January and April 2008, from US$13.90 to US$28.20. Similarly, during the same period the cost of a 50-kg bag of sugar went up from US$31.50 to US$44.70 and that of flour from US$31.50 to US$53.00 (Loney, 2008). This inflationary spiral has generated a hunger that cannot be exaggerated given that 80 per cent of the population struggles to survive on less than US$2 per day. Not surprisingly, Haitians began talking of a "Clorox" hunger so dreadful that it felt as if their stomachs had swollen with bleach or battery acid. In fact, in their efforts to stop their hunger, the poor, especially in the slums of the capital, filled their empty bellies with "mud cakes". These cakes, which are nothing but watered and buttered dirt left in the sun to harden, have become "a staple for entire families" (Carroll, 2008).

The tragic irony of the Haitian situation is not merely declining domestic food production but also the reality that food, albeit imported, is available, but most people simply do not have the purchasing power to buy it. The crisis constitutes what Amartya Sen (1982:1–7) has called a crisis of "entitlement". As he put it: "Starvation is the characteristic of some people not having enough food to eat. It is not the characteristic of there being not enough food to eat ... [Starvation] statements translate readily into statements of ownership of food by persons. ... [Starvation] is a function of entitlements and not of food availability as such."

And indeed, as Prospery Raymond, country director of Christian Aid, explained to the *Guardian* in July 2008: "Food is available but people cannot afford to buy it. If the situation gets worse we could have starvation in the next six to 12 months" (Carroll, 2008). These are the harsh realities behind the "Clorox" riots and looting which expressed popular outrage against the savage inequalities of Haiti's existing entitlement structures. The riots were also the inevitable by-product of the global neo-liberal regime, and the incompetence of successive Haitian regimes which did little to stop the alarming deterioration of both the environment and the rural infrastructure, especially in the Artibonite – the breadbasket of the country. This sense of general decay exacerbated further the already precarious existence of most Haitians and provoked them into rioting.

It is true that once unleashed, the riots were manipulated by conflicting political "entrepreneurs" and exploited by different forces for their own purposes. The destruction of property that they caused might well have been "targeted", but the anger and resentment of hungry people were very genuine; the protesters were not mere puppets controlled by "invisible" hands.[13] The riots were not unique to Haiti; Burkina Faso, Egypt, Senegal and Cameroon had seen similar popular responses to declining living standards and rising food prices. The question really ought not to be why did poor people riot, but rather how come they had not rioted more frequently, and how did they put up for so long and so silently with these conditions?

The government and the international financial agencies supporting it finally realized that an emergency programme of food delivery and temporary subsidies was necessary to avoid greater instability and popular revolt (Seelke and Hornback, 2008). In the aftermath of the riots, Préval, with the cooperation of the Haitian business community, announced a momentary 15 per cent price reduction in the cost of a sack of rice. The World Bank and the Inter-American Development Bank (IDB) provided US$10 million and US$12.5 million grants respectively, while the World Food Programme appealed for US$54 million. In addition, the United Nations pledged US$131 million to assist Haiti's short- and mid-term programme to increase domestic food production (Seelke and Hornbeck, 2008). Given that the United Nations Food and Agriculture Organization estimated that Haiti's food import bill would increase 80 per cent in 2008 – the fastest in the world – and that donations were lagging, it is highly unlikely that such funding and programmes will extricate the country from its present predicament. They will, at best, constitute a short-term palliative.

What the government and the international financial agencies have offered are pious rhetorical commitments to increase "domestic production", rather than a viable alternative to the current neo-liberal regime. While they promised to provide a long-term strategy for a systematic programme of rural development bent on servicing the needs for local food production, they have so far failed to do so. Moreover, there is virtually no plan for the short term except the good will of international charity. In fact, Préval argued that his government was next to impotent to deal with the bleak immediate conjuncture; he argued that the crisis was the product of globalization and the explosion of oil prices. Haiti, he contended, had limited resources and could not waste them in short-term solutions. If there was hope it was for the future, since increasing domestic food production and revitalizing the rural sector were long-term objectives (Radio Kiskeya.com, 2008a).

It is difficult, however, to contemplate an increase in domestic food production without a major policy shift from the neo-liberal regime imposed on Haiti by the major international financial institutions. In turn, the great dependence of Préval's government on these institutions makes such a shift unlikely but not impossible. Paradoxically, the very failure of neo-liberalism in Haiti and the fear that this may cause political instability and chaos may leave some room for an alternative economic strategy.[14] The country cannot afford to continue its disastrous economic liberalization lest its domestic economic base disintegrate completely. This is the lesson of the neo-liberal regime exported to Haiti.

Indeed, the collapse of domestic food production and particularly rice can be traced back to the policies of trade liberalization introduced in the mid-1980s and 1990s under the guidance of the International Monetary Fund and the World Bank. These policies have resulted in the massive reliance on imported food and the utter neglect of the rural sector. In fact, in 2006–2007 the entire budget of the Ministry of Agriculture was a measly US$1.5 million that contrasted sharply with the US$69 million spent on the UN World Food Programme (WFP). Instead of reconstructing its rural sector and promoting domestic food production, Haiti has remained a country of malnourished and hungry people alarmingly dependent on external assistance and charity. The consequences are dire, as Charles Arthur has remarked:

> Food aid shifts consumption patterns away from locally produced goods in favor of imported goods. For example the distribution of surplus US wheat has fostered a taste for products that can only be produced with this imported staple. As Haitians incorporate these products into their diets, growers of local grains such as corn (maize) – which grows well in Haiti's mountainous terrain – have seen shrinking demand for their products. This breeds dependency, undermines food security and creates an unsustainable reliance on imported food.
>
> The massive amount of aid spent on the purchase, transport, and storage of imported food could instead be spent on helping Haitian farmers meet the WFP's demand and, in so doing, have a tremendous positive impact on agricultural production in Haiti itself, thereby ultimately solving the food problem and reducing the need for food aid. (Arthur, 2008)

While there are other factors, such as governmental incompetence and political instability as well as globalization, that fuelled Haiti's food crisis, the neo-liberal regime imposed on the country is the single most critical cause of that crisis. Josiane Georges shows convincingly how this regime contributed to the drastic decline of rice production in Haiti:

> In 1994 the Haitian government entered into a new agreement with the IMF that contained a "medium-term structural adjustment strategy" which "included sweeping trade liberalization measures." In 1995 when this agreement went into effect, Haiti's tariffs on rice imports were cut dramatically from 35% to the current level of 3% (the bound tariff on rice imports is 50%). By comparison, the Common External Tariff on rice in the CARICOM (Caribbean Community) zone for rice in 1999 was 25%. Haiti's extremely low import tariff on rice is part of the trade liberalization policies which earned it a score of 1 on the IMF's 1999 Index of Trade Restrictiveness, making Haiti the least trade restrictive country in the Caribbean. Yet, in the almost 10 years that have passed, Haiti has also remained the least developed country in the Caribbean ... Following the adoption of these policies local production of rice in Haiti dropped dramatically. (Georges, 2004: 3–4)

Not surprisingly, the collapse of domestic rice production provoked a growing dependence on imports that has had devastating consequences for the country. In barely 20 years Haiti was transformed from a virtually self-sufficient rice producer into a major importer of the staple. As Michael Dobbs (2000) pointed out:

> Over the past two decades, a period of growing IMF tutelage over the Haitian economy, exports of American rice to Haiti have grown from virtually zero to more than 200,000 tons a year, making the poverty-stricken country of 7 million people the fourth-largest market for American rice in the world after Japan, Mexico and Canada. According to US and Haitian economists, the result has been a massive shift in local consumption habits, with many Haitians now choosing cheap imported rice at the expense of domestically grown staples, including rice, corn and millet.

Haiti is now at the crossroads; it must reverse these disastrous trends lest it descends into violent anarchy and deeper poverty. It must abandon the neo-liberal extremism that has drastically undermined domestic production for domestic needs and created an economy that imports virtually everything consumed locally. The state has to regain its central place in society, and policies of development cannot bypass it; privileging "outsourcing" assets and resources to private interests and non-governmental organizations is an invitation to market failures and social disintegration. This does not imply an attack on the market but rather a rejection of an utterly extraverted and unregulated integration into a devouring process of globalization. The current crisis is an opportunity to change course, protect and reinvigorate production that satisfies basic needs and privileges the development of the rural areas. Such a strategy would stop obscene class and regional inequalities from growing further and provide a sense of national cohesion.

These changes require, however, an effective, accountable and regulating state. The state must be placed at the centre of any strategy of development because it plays a fundamental role in organizing social life as well as public and private production. This is especially the case if the country is to rebuild the infrastructure and enhance the life chances of the population that have been destroyed by the most recent natural disasters. While NGOs and other forms of private assistance might offer some needed relief to those without shelter and suffering from hunger, only the state can provide collective protection and create the conditions for self-sustaining growth.[15] Such a state is a precondition for more equitable life chances, more civil relationships among citizens and more stable politics. I am afraid that continuing to accept an unprotected and unregulated participation in globalization while amending or rewriting the constitution will not generate such a state. In conclusion, Haitian rulers and the international community would do well to embrace Adam Przeworski's (1995: 111–112) forceful injunction on the centrality of the state:

> The state is crucial in constituting social order, in enabling regular and peaceful private relations among groups and individuals. If state institutions are unable to enforce rights and obligations in large geographic areas or for significant social sectors, private interactions lose their predictable character. When the state is reduced to the point that it cannot provide physical protection and access to basic social services, public order collapses: material survival and even physical safety can be only privately secured. Private systems of violence are then likely to emerge; violence is likely to become decentralized, anomic, and widespread. Under such conditions, it is not only democracy that is threatened, but the very bases of social cohesion.

## Postscript (October 2010)

On 12 January 2010, Haiti was devastated by a major earthquake which killed more than 220,000 people in the Port-au-Prince area as well as Leogane and Jacmel. Beyond this horrible toll and the atrocious pain and trauma Haitians endured, is the reality that politically, economically and socially the country is no longer the same. In fact, Haiti is at ground zero; every reasonable assumption conceived before 12 January is now undermined; it is likely that nothing will be quite the same after this fateful day.

The analysis that precedes this postscript was written a year ago; some arguments still hold, but others have become more problematic. With the earthquake Haiti is confronting a systemic crisis that portends the danger of an utter catastrophe. Paradoxically, however, the crisis may be an opportunity to create a new and more democratic society in which Haitians treat each other as equal citizens. In its immediate aftermath, the earthquake became a relative equalizer; but it soon became clear that the small, well-off minority was extricating itself from this crisis far more quickly and easily than the poor majority. While death and devastation affected all irrespective of class or colour, old divisions and social reflexes soon reasserted themselves. In the midst of the cataclysm, however, Haitians showed a new sense of solidarity and citizenship that offered a glimpse of an alternative order; whether they can reignite this fleeting solidarity and finally understand that a better future requires the demise of the old ways of governing and producing, remains an open question. It is not unthinkable to imagine that a more inclusive social pact between the privileged few and the poor majority may rise from the ghastly dust of the earthquake, but the travail of past history and the hard realities of severe material constraints, entrenched class interests and foreign intrusions (Nairn, 1994; Renda, 2001) do not bode well for such a happy vision.

In fact, in the aftermath of the earthquake such foreign intrusions have turned Haiti into a virtual trusteeship (Vorbe, 2010). The idea of transforming Haiti into a trusteeship is not new (Bohning, 2004; Marcella, 2005), but it is becoming a reality under a wave of humanitarian interventionism and plans of reconstruction. Haiti's government, however weak it was before, has been completely displaced by a civilian supranational body called the Interim Haiti Recovery Commission (IHRC) (2010). Before dissolving itself in April 2010, the Haitian Parliament voted for a state of emergency law giving the Commission complete authority to determine the country's future over the next 18 months (Ibid.; Bylaws IHRC, 2010; Préval, 2010).

According to Article 9 of its constitution the Commission's mandate is "to conduct strategic planning and coordination and implement resources from bilateral and multilateral donors, non-governmental organizations, and the business sector, with all necessary transparency and accountability" (Ibid.: 5). In addition, as Article 10 stipulates, the Commission "shall be responsible for continuously developing and refining development plans for Haiti, assessing needs and gaps and establishing investment priorities" (Ibid.). Finally, Article 12 makes the Commission unaccountable to any Haitian representative body (Ibid.), as it "shall operate within the framework of the State of Emergency Law. Consequently, it shall be vested with the powers necessary to conduct its activities."

The Commission is co-chaired by the Haitian prime minister – currently Jean-Max Bellerive – and "a prominent foreign official involved in the reconstruction effort", who at the moment, happens to be former US president Bill Clinton. All decisions made by the Commission "shall be deemed confirmed" unless vetoed by Haiti's president within 10 business days after formal notification. Thus, the Commission preserves a legal façade of ultimate Haitian authority, but in reality it clearly places Haiti under a de facto trusteeship. Indeed, the voting members of the Commission are equally divided between a number of representatives of Haiti's government and civil society on the one hand, and foreign powers and institutions on the other. Apart from the representative of the Caribbean Community (CARICOM), the other foreign voting members are representatives of institutions or countries that have "pledged to contribute at least US$100,000,000 (one hundred million US dollars) for the reconstruction of Haiti as a gift over a period of two consecutive years or at least US$200,000,000 (two hundred million US dollars) in debt relief". In addition, MINUSTAH, which has approximately 13,000 foreign troops, is the only functioning peacekeeping and coercive force operating in the country.

Conceived with very little national debate or discussion, the Interim Commission is at best problematic. At worst, it is unconstitutional, undemocratic and a portent of future political challenges. In the first place, the Commission has neither a peasant nor a refugee camp representative on its board, in spite of the rhetorical commitment of the government and international community to develop the rural areas and alleviate the plight of the displaced and homeless. The Commission is instead an urban, elite and foreign phenomenon attempting to speak for the countryside and the poor. Moreover, the continued "invisibility" and managerial incompetence of the president and of the Haitian state in the aftermath of the earthquake has damaged both seriously. If the chaos and unending delays in the reconstruction effort persist, and if the more than a million displaced and homeless inhabitants continue to feel marginalized and ignored, political instability is likely to be the outcome, an outcome with unpredictable consequences.

It is in this charged political climate that the presidential and parliamentary elections of November 2010 will take place. Moving forward with this regular electoral ritual bodes well for the political life of the country and the possibility of the consolidation of more accountable forms of governance. However, elections may unleash generalized instability. Historically, as I have argued above, elections in Haiti have entailed dramatic displays of popular struggles, political confrontations and disputed outcomes. Elections in Haiti are therefore moments of great uncertainty and dangers. They open a Pandora's box, releasing political consequences that can be difficult to control. More than two decades after the fall of the Duvalier dictatorship, Haiti is still mired in an unending transition to democracy.

It is difficult to see how the elections of November 2010 can successfully bring that transition to a close. They will take place in a thoroughly devastated land, and in the context of a virtual loss of national sovereignty and utter state incapacity. In fact, it remains unclear how an elected Parliament will function in an environment dominated by the IHRC. Can these two bodies coexist, or are they bound to generate instability? Furthermore, how can free and fair elections occur when a state of emergency is in place, and when opposition parties do not trust the impartiality or competence of the electoral council?

Préval has not only managed to appoint a Conseil Electoral Provisoire (CEP) – Provisional Electoral Council – of his liking, but he has also weakened the opposition by recruiting some of its major figures into his party, Inité. It seems clear that in spite of his "invisibility" in the aftermath of the quake, Préval has imposed, in the words of Le Nouvelliste, his "mastery of political time" (Alphonse, 2010). However unpopular he may be, he is likely to play a critical role in the November elections as he has manoeuvred to concentrate power in his own hands. Préval's lack of leadership in the aftermath of the earthquake may have contributed to his growing estrangement from the people, but so far no credible alternative has filled the political vacuum.

The traditional opposition forces have been unable to capitalize on the crisis to advance their own objectives; they have been largely irrelevant and absent in the current drama. It remains to be seen whether they will muster the strength to use this exceptional moment in Haitian history to unite and mobilize behind one or two presidential candidates to challenge Préval's chosen "dauphin", Jude Célestin. But even if they do, there is absolutely no guarantee that they would win the elections, let alone change the zero-sum politics that has characterized Haitian history. Their programme does not seem to go beyond a feeling of utter opposition and contempt for the president. They lack a comprehensive political strategy and they are themselves fractured by personal and ideological divisions. Such opposition is ultimately opportunistic and incapable of offering a credible and popular alternative to the existing order.

On the surface it appears therefore that 12 January has not dramatically changed the political landscape; prior to the catastrophe, Préval and his party, Inité, were the powerful masters of the immediate future; they seem to have remained so in spite of their manifest failures in the face of the reconstruction challenge. Moreover, Inité should overcome its internecine divisions because of its members' hunger for both electoral success and controlling the vast resources reconstruction will bring.

Unforeseen but far from implausible events such as a popular uprising from the refugee camps, another natural catastrophe or a further deterioration in the global economy and its ensuing consequences for food and oil prices, could provoke the collapse of Préval's coalition and chosen *dauphin*. Significant elements of uncertainty persist. The gross inability of the Commission and the government to deliver in any significant, let alone effective, way on the promised foreign assistance amounting to more than US$5 billion over the next three years is quickly nurturing a sense of despair that could easily turn into anger and revolt. The political landscape could thus change dramatically in a flash.

I should add also that the sudden emergence of a messianic candidate could unsettle the conventional political calculus since ties of political affection are unprincipled, patronage networks unstable and alliances opportunistic and "gelatinous". In fact, the eruption as a presidential contender of the well-known entertainer and *compa* singer Michel Martelly – "Sweet Micky" – could unravel the plans of older, established but increasingly discredited members of the traditional political class. Despite his lack of preparation, Martelly seems to have a popular base in the urban youth because of his celebrity status and vast musical appeal. Whether these attributes could transform Martelly into a new messianic figure remains an open question, but what is clear is that he represents a wild card in the political chess board.

Finally, if the evangelical Protestant movement manages to coalesce around a single candidate, it could challenge secular political forces. It is worth remembering that an unorganized and divided Protestant movement did well in the elections of 2006. This religious alternative with its manifold networks of churches and NGOs could surprise traditional forces, particularly if the country suffers another round of riots or natural catastrophes. In fact, religious groups, particularly those connected to the rescue efforts, may well attract popular support by emphasizing a struggle against "*les forces du mal*" and embracing spiritual submission to God as the means to Haiti's salvation (Sontag, 2010). Jean Chavannes Jeune will seek to unify fundamentalist sects and win the evangelical Christian vote as the candidate of Alliance Chrétienne Citoyenne pour la Reconstruction d'Haïti. If he were to succeed, he could well develop into a potent political force.

In any event, virtually all the "serious" candidates who will fight for the presidential office offer little programmatic vision of the future, let alone a political and economic rupture with existing policies. In fact, excepting Célestin and Martelly, they are all a part of the political generation of the 1980s and 1990s. Haitian society seems to be fractured between an aging and increasingly disconnected and self-serving elite of rulers and politicians and a growing lumpen youth with little hope for a better future (Dumas, 2010). This presidential political season is unlikely to heal this severe fracture; it is prone to signal continuity with, rather than a major departure from, past and failed practices. As Haitians put it, this will be a "*bouillon rechauffé*" – a reheated soup.

And yet, the earthquake has let loose an unpredictable and confusing political climate fuelled by a widespread sentiment that the existing state is incompetent, self-serving and unaccountable. The vast majority of Haitians, especially those living amid the rubble and the stench of excrement, no longer want to put up with "*leta enkapab sa a*" – this incapable state – but they have yet to find the means to replace it. The old is still dominant, but the new may well erupt from the subterranean political terrain created by the earthquake and ultimately unleash a political tsunami of unforeseen consequences.

## Notes

1. In 2008, and in less than a month, four devastating tropical storms and hurricanes ravaged the country and left 800,000 people – about 10 per cent of the total population – without shelter and food. This human catastrophe came on the heel of food riots and aggravated an already acute systemic crisis. As one Haitian put it: "In Haiti, we live in a constant cyclone."

2. According to MINUSTAH's own web page, as of May 2008 its peacekeepers comprised "9,055 total uniformed personnel, including 7,174 troops and 1,881 police, supported by 499 international civilian personnel, 1,167 local civilian staff and 206 United Nations Volunteers" (See MINUSTAH, 2010).

3. The fact that the military has been disbanded does not mean, however, that they no longer represent a danger. When in July 2008, former members of the Haitian army occupied old military barracks in Cape Haitien and Ouanaminthe, they remind us that the problem posed by their uncertain status is a potential threat to the survival of the Préval administration.

4. Préval's speech was inspired by a report on the "Constitutional question" written in March 2007 by two prominent Haitian intellectuals, Claude Moïse and Cary Hector. The report submitted to President Préval criticized the anti-presidentialism and parliamentary supremacist tendencies of the Constitution of 1987.

5. On 12 April 2008, in the aftermath of major food riots, the senate voted to oust the government of Prime Minister Jacques-Édouard Alexis. In his subsequent search for a new prime minister, President Préval nominated Pierre Ericq Pierre and then Robert Manuel for the office, but both were rejected by Parliament. His third nominee, Michelle Pierre-Louis, ultimately won ratification and became Haiti's second woman prime minister.

6. President Préval first nominated Ericq Pierre, an economist at the Inter-American Development Bank, who won the approval of the senate only to be rejected by the lower house. After this defeat, Préval chose his close confident and friend, Robert Manuel, for the position. Manuel suffered a similar fate and his nomination was overwhelmingly turned down by the house.

7. Pierre-Louis, 61, a leader of civil society and close friend of President Préval, was ratified by the senate and the house after both engaged in prolonged negotiations with

legislators and political parties about the distribution of cabinet positions in the future Pierre-Louis administration. The ratification was complicated further by allegations that Pierre-Louis was a lesbian and thus "morally unfit" to become prime minister. It was only after Pierre-Louis publically denied her homosexuality that she secured the votes of socially conservative Christian parliamentarians. The ratification process, however, had a second round requiring the approval of Pierre-Louis's government's "general policy". This approval was ultimately won only as a result of the fears that the country could not be left without a functioning administration in the middle of the massive natural catastrophe brought about by hurricanes Gustav, Hannah and Ike. The ratification of Pierre-Louis ended a four-month stalemate that started with the sacking of Prime Minister Alexis and his government.

8. When the newly elected Parliament convened for the first time in 2006, the model of cars and the legislators' per diems were among the first matters debated. Recently, a report about Parliament's management of its resources pointed out that its members had hired a plethora of aides; the report indicated also that one legislator had allegedly grossly abused his tyre allowance, managing to rack up charges for 87 tyres in one year, 82 more than the allowance (see Desrosiers, 2008).

9. The significance of the creation of a Permanent Electoral Council replacing what has historically been a profoundly politicized Provisional Electoral Council cannot be underestimated. Not surprisingly, the stakes in the indirect local elections are high precisely because the winners of these elections will be responsible, in conjunction with the president, for appointing the members of the Permanent Electoral Council. In a country where the organization of elections and the alternation of power have always been controversial and uneasy, the creation of a Permanent Electoral Council can be disquieting to powerful interests. This is especially the case given the growing number of potential presidential candidates within and outside Parliament. Most Haitian commentators assume that some key senators such as Yuri Latortue or Rudolph Boulos, as well as Mirlande Manigat, the General Secretary of the Rassemblement Des Démocrates Nationaux Progréssistes (RDNP), and the fallen Prime Minister Jacques-Édouard Alexis who declared that the country will always be able "to count on him", are already positioning themselves to succeed President Préval.

10. Some observers have accused MINUSTAH of using unnecessary and deadly violence against residents in the slums of Port-au-Prince. In their efforts to fight criminal gangs, the international forces have caused what Edmond Mulet, the Special Representative of the United Nations Secretary-General in Haiti, has himself called "collateral damage". Opponents of MINUSTAH have argued that these troops' mission is "to consolidate George Bush's *coup d'etat*" against President Aristide (see Joseph and Concannon Jr., 2007). On the other hand, other organizations and anti-Aristide forces have asked MINUSTAH to engage in more drastic interventions. For instance, Refugees International recommended in 2005 that the government of Brazil "allow its troops to use deadly force, if necessary, to stop those who [committed] violence with impunity in Haiti" (see Gantz and Martin, 2005). Refugees International did acknowledge, however, the alleged sexual exploitation of Haitians by some MINUSTAH peacekeepers. The organization called for sanctions against perpetrators of such crimes and the establishment of a clear code of conduct and ethics (see Martin and Gantz, 2005).

11. It is difficult to envisage how Haiti can embark on a systematic programme of agrarian transformation without significant investments in the rural areas. These investments, in turn, are virtually impossible without a cancellation of Haiti's debt, whose service compels the country to pay between US$5 and US$6 million every month. For instance, in his visit of October 2008 to Port-au-Prince, Robert Zoellick, the president of the World Bank, misled Haitians into believing that half of their external debt of US$1.7 billion

had been forgiven and that the other half would soon be cancelled. In fact, international financial institutions have not cancelled Haiti's external debt. As the Haiti Support Group (2008a) emphasized:

> Haiti's total external debt stands at $1.7 billion, compared to $1.36 billion in 2005, when it was told it was eligible for the World Bank and IMF's Heavily Indebted Poor Countries debt relief initiative (HIPC).
>
> Under HIPC and the Multilateral Debt Relief Initiative that follows completion of HIPC, as well as an associated agreement by the Inter-American Development Bank, Haiti stands to receive approximately $1.2 billion of debt cancellation, but only when it reaches HIPC "Completion Point".
>
> At the World Bank and IMF annual meetings in Washington [of October 2008], Haiti's expected Completion Point date was put back from "last quarter 2008" to "first half 2009" – a delay of six months.
>
> The only debt relief Haiti has so far received under the HIPC scheme has been limited relief on its debt service payments since entering the scheme in 2006 – estimated by the IMF as $19.8 million. However, no debt stock is actually forgiven under HIPC until a country reaches Completion Point. Haiti's budgeted debt service payments in 2008 have continued to be more than $1 million every week.
>
> Some $400 million to $500 million of Haiti's debt will not be cancelled under HIPC even when the country reaches Completion Point because they are not covered by the cut-off dates for the scheme. World Bank debts are only cancelled up to the end of 2003 and IMF debts up to the end of 2004. (See also Haiti Support Group, 2008b)

12. For instance the Provisional Electoral Council estimated that organizing the forthcoming elections for a third of the senate seats would cost US$16 million. This sum represents more than 10 times the Ministry of Agriculture's annual budget.

13. For instance, the former prime minister Alexis blamed drug traffickers for the riots, while anti-Lavalas observers argued that Aristide was fomenting the instability from South Africa. See Radio Kiskeya.com (2008b) and Côté-Paluck (2008). Etienne Côté-Paluck, "Haïti – Derrière les Emeutes, le Spectre d'Aristide", *Le Devoir.com*, 12–13 April 2008.

14. The major international financial organizations expressed their willingness to exercise some flexibility in shaping the country's new economic policies. For instance, Andreas Bauer (2008), the IMF mission chief for Haiti, issued the following statement:

> As a large net importer of food, Haiti has been particularly affected by the sharp rise in international prices, which continues to impose enormous hardship on the country's population. This shock has also had a significant impact on domestic inflation and caused a widening of the trade deficit.
>
> The IMF is deeply concerned about the social impact of higher food prices and firmly committed to support efforts to ease this burden, while safeguarding economic stability and maintaining focus on continued economic and social progress in Haiti. . . . The IMF supports the government's response strategy that seeks to provide immediate relief from higher food prices and to boost agricultural output. We are working closely with donors and the authorities to review Haiti's need for increased financial assistance, and will adapt the macroeconomic framework of the PRGF-supported program to reflect the external shock.

15. Currently, Haiti is "La République des ONGs (Organisations Non-Gouvernementales)". The result of these NGOs' work is at best mixed. While NGOs can be effective at a

community level, they tend to undermine any comprehensive national strategy of development. As Nikolas Barry-Shaw (2008) has pointed out:

> NGOs have come to blanket Haiti. According to the World Bank, there are today over 10,000 NGOs working in Haiti, the highest per-capita concentration in the world. These organizations occupy every possible sector of activity, their budgets sometimes dwarfing those of their governmental counterparts.

## REFERENCES

Alphonse, Roberson (2010) Haïti: "Le Temps n'est Plus au Dilatoire, Selon Préval", *Le Nouvelliste*, 30 June. Available at http://www.lenouvelliste.com/article. php?PubID=1&ArticleID=80918

Arthur, Charles (2008) "The WFP and Food Aid", *Haiti Support Group*, 17 July.

Aucoin, Louis (1999) "Haiti's Constitutional Crisis", *Boston University International Law Journal*, 17: 116–117 (Summer).

Barry-Shaw, Nikolas (2008) "Haiti's new PM and the power of NGOs", *HaitiAction.Net*, 30 September. Available at http://www.haitiaction.net/News/ HIP/9_30_8/9_30_8.html

Bauer, Andreas (2008) "Statement by the IMF Mission Chief for Haiti on the Impact of Higher Food Prices", International Monetary Fund Press Release No. 08/91. Available at http://www.imf.org/external/np/sec/pr/2008/pr0891.htm

Bohning, Don (2004) "An International Protectorate Could Bring Stability to Haiti", 23 November, *Miami Herald*. Available at http://www.lecontact.com/ archives_of_editorials_7.htm

Bylaws of the Interim Haiti Recovery Commission (IHRC) (2010), June 20. Available at http://www.cirh.ht/resources/20100615_IHRC_Bylaws.pdf

Carroll, Rory (2008) "Haiti: Mud Cakes Become Staple Diet As Cost of Food Soars Beyond a Family's Reach With Little Cash and Import Prices Rocketing Half The Population Faces Starvation", *Guardian*, 29 July.

Côté-Paluck, Étienne (2008) "Haïti – Derrière les Émeutes, le Spectre d'Aristide", *Le Devoir*, 12 April. Available at http://www.ledevoir.com/international/ 184765/haiti-derriere-les-emeutes-le-spectre-d-aristide

Desrosiers, Jacques (2008) "Chambre des Députés, Une Affaire de Pneus qui Sent le Roussi", *Le Matin*, 4 April.

Dumas, Pierre-Raymond (2010) "Deux Haïti face à face", *Le Nouvelliste*, 24 August. Available at http://www.lenouvelliste.com/article.php?PubID=1& ArticleID=82752

Dupuy, Alex (1989) *Haiti in the World Economy*. Boulder: Westview Press.

Dupuy, Alex (2007) *The Prophet and Power*. New York: Rowman And Littlefield.

Fatton Jr., Robert (2002) *Haiti's Predatory Republic*. Boulder: Lynne Rienner.

Fatton Jr., Robert (2007) *The Roots of Haitian Despotism*. Boulder: Lynne Rienner.

Gantz, Peter H. and Sarah Martin (2005) "Haiti: Brazilian Troops in MINUSTAH Must Intervene to Stop Violence", *Refugees International*, 18 March. Available at http://www.unhcr.org/refworld/docid/47a6eeb80.html

Martin, Sarah and Peter H. Gantz and Sarah Martin (2005) "Haiti: Sexual Exploitation by Peacekeepers Likely to be a Problem", *Refugees International*, 7 March. Available at http://www.unhcr.org/refworld/docid/47a6eeb40.html

Georges, Josiane (2004) "Trade and the Disappearance of Haitian Rice", *Ted Case Studies*, 725, June. Available at http://www1.american.edu/TED/haitirice.htm

Haiti Support Group (2008a) *Haiti News Briefs*, 30 October. Available at http://haitisupport.gn.apc.org/fea_news_index.html

Haiti Support Group (2008b) "Open letter from the people of the Caribbean calling for the cancellation of Haiti's external debt – 24 October 2008" Available at http://www.haitisupport.gn.apc.org/CaribbeanCSOdebt.html

Hallward, Peter (2007) *Damning the Flood*. London: Verso.

Interim Haiti Recovery Commission (2010) 20 July. Available at http://www.cirh.ht

Joseph, Mario and Brian Concannon Jr. (2007) "Haiti, MINUSTAH, and Latin America: Solidaridad?", Americas Policy Program, Center for International Policy (CIP), 9 April.

Loney, Jim (2008) "Haitians Say their Hunger is Real", *Reuters*, 12 April.

Marcella, Gabriel (2005) "The International Community and Haiti: A Proposal for Cooperative Sovereignty." Paper presented at the National/International Symposium: "The Future of Democracy and Development in Haiti", 17–18 March, Washington, DC.

MINUSTAH (2010) "MINUSTAH Facts and Figures", United Nations Stabilization Mission in Haiti. Available at http://www.un.org/Depts/dpko/missions/minustah/facts.html

Moïse, Claude (1994) *Une Constitution dans la Tourmente*. Montreal: Les Editions Images.

Moïse, Claude (2001) *Le Projet National de Toussaint Louverture*. Port-au-Prince: Editions Memoire.

Moïse, Claude (2008) "Le Bicamérisme Parfait est-il un Danger?", *Le Matin*, 11 July.

Moïse, Claude and Cary Hector (2007) *Rapport Sur La Question Constitutionnelle*. Available at http://www.radiokiskeya.com/spip.php?article4295&var_recherche=Claude%20Moïse

Nairn, Alan (1994) "Behind Haiti's Paramilitaries: Our Man in FRAPH", *Nation*, 259(3): 458–461.

Pierre-Louis, Yves (2008) "Ericq Pierre Charges Corruption Sank His Nomination", *Haitianalysis.com*, 23 May. Available at http://www.haitianalysis.com/2008/5/23/ericq-pierre-charges-corruption-sank-his-nomination

Préval, René (2007) "Diskou Prezidan Repiblik la, 17 October, Anivèsè lanmò Anperè Jean Jacques Dessalines. Available at http://www.radiokiskeya.com/spip.php?article4295&var_recherche=Claude%20Moïse

Préval, René (2010) *Decree of Interim Haiti Recovery Commission (IHRC)*, 21 April. Available at http://www.cirh.ht/resources/IHRC_Decree.pdf

Przeworski, Adam (1995) *Sustainable Democracy*. Cambridge: Cambridge University Press.

Radio Kiskeya.com (2008a) "Pas de Politique de Subvention des Prix des Produits Importés", 10 April. Available at http://radiokiskeya.com/spip. php?article4919

Radio Kiskeya.com (2008b) "Rapport du RNDDH Sur les Emeutes de la Faim d'Avril 2008", 17 April. Available at http://radiokiskeya.com/spip.php? article4941

Renda, Mary A. (2001) *Taking Haiti*. Chapel Hill: The University of North Carolina Press.

Seelke, Clare Ribando and J.F. Hornbeck (2008) "Haiti: Legislative Responses to the Food Crisis and Related Development Challenges", *Congressional Research Service, CRS Report RS22879*, 15 May.

Sen, Amartya (1982) *Poverty and Famines*. Oxford: Clarendon Press.

Sontag, Deborah (2010) "Amid Rubble, Seeking a Refuge in Faith", *New York Times*, 17 January. Available at http://www.nytimes.com/2010/01/18/world/americas/18church.html?scp=47&sq=us+earthquake+aid+to+haiti+government&st=nyt

Trouillot, Michel-Rolph (1990) *Haiti: State Against Nation*. New York: Monthly Review Press.

Vorbe, Charles (2010) "Earthquake, Humanitarianism and Intervention in Haiti", *Latin American Studies Association Forum*, 41(3): 16–19.

3

# The legacy of the 1987 constitution: Reform or renewal?

*Mirlande Manigat*

## Introduction

The 1987 constitution is the last of a series during two centuries of Haitian national history. From the first one issued in May 1805, one year after the 1804 independence celebration, to today, 22 different constitutions have seen the light of day, with durations ranging from 10 months (1888) to 29 years (1889). Haiti has a long history of developing and negotiating its democratic credentials (see Kretchik, 2007). The Haitian constitutions laid the foundations for distinct normative layers which give rise to a unique situation. In this chapter two approaches are combined to examine the legacy of Haiti's constitutions: an exegetic one, which places each constitution in its political and sociological context, and an historical one, which regards them as successive and different steps in the search for the best and most appropriate instrument.

Haiti's constitutional heritage is impressive. Haiti was the third country where a modern constitution was forged, after the United States (on 17 September 1787) and France (on 3 September 1791). Despite its failure to build a stable political system, there is a Haitian contribution to constitutionalism which is often overlooked. After all, in the United States there has been only one constitution with 27 amendments, while France has had 16 of them between 1791 and 1958.

The danger in assessing the "legacy of the 1987 Constitution" – the task assigned to me by editors of this volume – is that it implies that the document already belongs to the past. While this logical interpretation

*Fixing Haiti: MINUSTAH and beyond, Heine and Thompson (eds),*
*United Nations University Press, 2011, ISBN 978-92-808-1197-1*

justified by the grammar is intellectually appealing, it must be recognized that as long as the constitution is not abolished or amended, it is still organizing Haiti's public and private life.

My main field of expertise since I returned to Haiti in 1986 is the constitutional *problematique*. I did not take part in the making of the constitution, but on behalf of the party I belong to, the RDNP (Rally of the National and Progressive Democrats), I was instructed to follow the work as it was proceeding, and to convey our observations, critiques and suggestions. For instance, the party was given credit for the preamble which was spontaneously and fully accepted, notwithstanding the references to the 1804 Declaration of Independence and the 1948 UN Universal Declaration of Human Rights, which were wisely introduced. But the Assembly disregarded some advice, the most important being the complex procedure which governs the appointment of a prime minister, as the 2008 controversies surrounding the appointment of Mme Pierre-Louis have revealed.

A third motivation stems from the assumption which pervades this edited volume, and places the theme of my chapter in the general background dedicated to examining the governance challenges and, more specifically, the effectiveness of multilateral, regional and bilateral approaches to peacebuilding in Haiti since February 2004. How can the constitution facilitate the realization of specific objectives now underway by the forces operating in Haiti – bilateral, regional (namely OAS) and international (the peacekeeping by MINUSTAH imposed by the UN Security Council)? In the autumn of 2008, the UN secretary-general requested MINUSTAH's extension for one more year, a request that subsequently has been and will undoubtedly continue to be repeated. This decision offended Haitian nationalism, for such a presence is an anomaly in a sovereign country – even though MINUSTAH serves an important function in certain circumstances, such as during the 2008 hurricane season and the earthquake of 2010. Competing needs between Haitian sovereignty and the need for external assistance in the face of grave difficulty must be addressed.

From a conceptual and practical point of view, how can a national law serve such diverse interests? The subject seems to put the two on an equal footing, although such a perspective reveals an inequality, for it is assuming that the international forces are coherent, logical and driven by the same interest within and about Haiti – something that remains to be proven.

In other words, it raises the following question: how does a specific legal text favour or impede the proper governance of a country? The role assigned to the constitution is twofold: it is a tool for achieving Haiti's governance as well as international expectations of what this governance is about. By itself, a constitution cannot achieve the goals anticipated by a society, particularly in a post-dictatorship context, and/or by the international community. Moreover, there is no evidence that those interests coincided when the charter was drafted nor is there evidence that they have coincided since its ratification. Finally, we have to keep in mind that the principle of governance encompasses both the rules and the society in which they are applied. Governance exists as a necessary articulation between them. The challenge is to discover the nature of that liaison, and the forces driving it. This means assessing the compatibility between society at a certain moment (in this case the immediate period after the end of Duvalierism), and the given constitutional instrument.

Is a constitution capable of changing society by imposing principles, methods and behaviours? Or is it that a constitution has to be crafted so that it can keep abreast of social changes, taking into account that the law does not always have a prospective character, and any society evolves more rapidly than legal principles? The problem goes back to the compatibility between the role of the law and its useful integration into social structures. In a country like Haiti, plagued by so many challenges in terms of inequalities, prejudices and social injustices, the role of a constitution is bound to be exaggerated, for it is assumed that it will help resolve those problems merely by its very existence. Haitian President René Préval once accused the constitution of being responsible for the dysfunction of the political system and has described it as "the single greatest threat to Haiti's long-term stability" (quoted in Perito and Jocic, 2008), but he could not convince Parliament that this was true. A more balanced view must identify the strengths and the weaknesses of the 1987 constitution. The observance of the latter depends upon its appropriateness to social and political conditions and, above all, to the will of those who govern the country to abide by the law. This has not been the case in Haiti since 2004.

## The making of the 1987 constitution

The origin of the initiative and the conditions in which it was conducted affected the nature and the qualities of the text but also its weaknesses. The Constitutional Assembly was composed of 62 personalities, 42 of them elected, 20 appointed by the Military National Council of Government, which took power after President Jean-Claude Duvalier was overthrown. The post-Duvalier climate was propitious for the making of a new constitution. It was expected that this could build democracy or at least lay the groundwork for it, and promote social justice and further sustained economic development.

In order to understand the conditions in which the Assembly proceeded, it is useful to keep in mind the following:

- For the first time in Haitian history, the government combined two traditional mechanisms, election and nomination, to select the persons who were endowed with responsibility for drafting the text;
- Those participants who were chosen had impressive intellectual credentials, but they were not all constitutional lawyers and that affected the quality of the deliberations, despite a valuable effort to minimize the effects of this limitation;
- The country also went through a unique experience: for 15 months, from Jean-Claude Duvalier's departure on 7 February 1986 and the publication of the new constitution in the *Official Journal* on 28 April 1987, the country did not have a constitution. Such a situation had never occurred in the past, and in seven separate occasions, the provisional government, in order to avoid a vacuum, brought into force a former constitution while the new one was still being drafted;
- As a consequence, the Military National Council of Government enjoyed for two years the totality of executive and legislative powers, a privilege which was ultimately codified in the constitution itself, in Article 285-1.

The new constitution was approved overwhelmingly by popular referendum on 29 March 1987. The popular support was not the expression of genuine appreciation of the text – the majority of the population did not even read it. The constitution was welcomed warmly simply because it existed and also because of widespread approval of Article 291, which forbade for 10 years the Duvalierists, that is those responsible for the 29 years of dictatorship, from taking part in any election.

The first original sin of the constitution was this contradiction between the deficiencies of a document which did not deserve this massive and unrealistic approval and the weight of the conjuncture, which compelled the citizens to do so. That contradiction led me to undertake an historical and exegetic study of the 21 previous constitutional documents in order to assess the general belief that the new text was the best that the country had produced. I came to the professional conclusion that this was not the case. Nonetheless, it would have been unwise to bring one of the previous versions into force again, for any restoration of a past text would not have been an acceptable response to the 1986 conditions.

In many ways, the constitution fulfilled contemporary aspirations, in terms of human rights. The text is in keeping with historical traditions and experiences. Those who drafted it were inspired not only by the Haitian normative legacy but also by the French experience as embodied in the 1958 constitution. Not surprisingly, the elites who were educated mainly in France tried to reproduce legal principles which were positively applied elsewhere. For more than 20 years after its independence Haiti relied on the Napoleonic Code. There existed "the temptation of mimesis" (*mimétisme*), as Haitian lawyers tried to reproduce, with some adaptations, the principles which were implemented in France, and, to a lesser extent, in the United Kingdom. As was the case in all Latin America, the US experience also inspired the drafters, particularly on matters relating to the office of the president.

In spite of these influences, the constitution was a Haitian product, and, to the best of my knowledge, there was only limited interference from foreign observers or advisers acting on behalf of the international community. Still, foreign governments followed the work with great attentiveness, and expressed satisfaction with the result, even though in private circles they stressed the dangers stemming from certain legal provisions. It is also obvious that for many Haitian observers, it was impossible at that time to anticipate the evolution of the chaotic Haitian political situation. Indeed, in 1988, President Leslie Manigat tried his best to eagerly and faithfully apply the constitution, and for that reason, among others, was overthrown by a military coup after four months in power (see Rotberg, 1988; and Manigat and Rotberg, 1988). After he was forced out of office, political life in Haiti did not follow constitutional paths. The constitution by itself cannot be made accountable for that; it was, after all, a feeble protection against political forces operating in defence of private interests.

Now, after more than two decades, it is admitted that the ideals articulated in the constitution have not been realized, such as those relating to fundamental liberties and freedom of speech. The institutional framework is still in need of being reinforced; however, even if this were to happen, Haiti would still not be considered among the most vibrant democracies. Although the constitution by itself is not responsible for the country's political difficulties, there is a general assumption that the constitution needs to be amended or drastically changed (see Perito and Jocic, op. cit.). The actual debate is based on this alternative: draft a new constitution or amend the existing one?

I find myself in a peculiar situation. As a scholar, teaching constitutional law for many years, I have been able to study the constitution in great detail. Thirteen years ago, I wrote a rather unorthodox book entitled *Plaidoyer pour une nouvelle constitution* (A plea for a new constitution), in which I tried to demonstrate its positive and the negative contents (Manigat, 2000a). Since then, in other books, particularly *Traité de droit constitutionnel Haitien* (Haitian constitutional law treaty) (Manigat, 2000b), through my teaching, in articles and regular interventions on radio and TV, I have tried to convince my fellow citizens about the compatibility between two apparently contradictory arguments: as a constitutionalist, I am claiming the liberty to criticize the constitution, but as a citizen committed to the building of a democratic system based on the rule of law, I stand for the respect of legality that is embodied in a constitution which governs the social and political life of the country.

Yet, the present circumstances are not conducive to the convocation of a Constitutional Assembly or to the transformation of the actual Parliament into a constitutional body that will draw up a new charter. The geneses of previous constitutions were the following:

- Eleven of Haiti's constitutions were issued by an ad hoc Constitutional Assembly: 1805, 1806, 1807, 1816, 1843, 1867, 1874, 1888, 1889, 1950, 1987;
- Eight were issued by the Parliament's National Assembly: that is, a joint meeting of the senate and the Chamber of Representatives, a non-permanent body extant since 1843: 1879, 1918, 1932, 1935, 1946, 1957, 1964, 1983;
- One was issued by solely the senate: 1846;
- One was issued by the two chambers acting separately: 1849;
- One was issued by a State Council: 1811.

Now, one can discuss the most appropriate procedure on the basis of technical and political arguments. But the present conjuncture is not favourable for either option because of the lack of stability and popular confidence in the neutrality of the government. Besides, the 1987 constitution does not anticipate this role for the Parliament. Therefore, some political and limited reforms may be the best we can hope for under the present circumstances.

## A reasonable plea for revision

The first and most immediate problem in the current constitution lies in the semi-parliamentary regime in place. There is a diarchy established in the executive, with an elected president who enjoys popular legitimacy, and an appointed prime minister approved by what the constitution identifies as a "majority in Parliament". This arrangement arose originally in 1985 by an amendment to the 1983 constitution, when the international community tried to make the regime more palatable, offering an alternative to President Jean-Claude Duvalier: to renounce to the presidency-for-life clauses or to agree to share executive responsibility with a prime minister. Duvalier chose the latter but never appointed a prime minister. After 29 years of presidential dictatorship, the instinctive tendency shared both by the Constitutional Assembly and a large part of the population was to limit the power traditionally invested in a president. From 1988

Table 3.1 List of Haitian prime ministers (since 1987)

| | |
|---|---|
| Martial Célestin | (9 February 1988–20 June 1988) |
| René Garcia Préval | (13 February 1991–11 October 1991) |
| Jean-Jacques Honorat (interim) | (11 October 1991–19 June 1992) |
| Marc Louis Bazin | (19 June 1992–30 August 1993) |
| Robert Malval | (30 August 1993–8 November 1994) |
| Smarck Michel | (8 November 1994–7 November 1995) |
| Claudette Werleigh | (7 November 1995–27 February 1996) |
| Rosny Smarth | (27 February 1996–20 October 1997) |
| Jacques-Édouard Alexis (1st time) | (26 March 1999–2 March 2001) |
| Jean Marie Chérestal | (2 March 2001–15 March 2002) |
| Yvon Neptune | (15 March 2002–12 March 2004) |
| Gérard Latortue | (12 March 2004–9 June 2006) |
| Henri Bazin (acting for Latortue) | (23 May 2006–9 June 2006) |
| Jacques-Édouard Alexis (2nd time) | (9 June 2006–5 September 2008) |
| Michèle Pierre-Louis | (5 September 2008–11 November 2009) |
| Jean-Max Bellerive | (11 November 2009– ) |

*Source*: BioScience (2010)

to 2010, 14 prime ministers have occupied the office, reflecting a high turnover (see Table 3.1). The procedure for their appointment is highly cumbersome (as evidenced by the turmoil surrounding Mme Pierre-Louis's appointment in 2008, which took five months), and if the office of prime minister is to be kept, a streamlining of this process will be necessary.

The constitution states that the prime minister must be approved by the majority in Parliament. According to parliamentary law, a single party must enjoy a clear majority (half of the body plus one) in the senate as well as in the Chamber of the Representatives, something different from any kind of majority that can be engineered through coalitions. The current procedure was inspired by the French system. However, there are two important differences: first, only the Chamber of Representatives intervenes in the selection of a prime minister (not the senate). Second, confusion was created between what the Haitian Constitution identifies as the "National Assembly" – that is, the reunion of the two legislative bodies – and the French legal terminology which, since 1792, has equated the national assembly with the Chamber of Representatives.

Finally, there is the problem of the possible human, political and ideological incompatibility between "two personalities". This is particularly so since the constitution codifies a situation, which in France is called "cohabitation" between the president and the prime minister, which in practice can be quite damaging if they each represent different political parties. This situation can lead to political deadlock and even paralysis. Contrary to a common belief, the president still holds considerable powers. He is the head of the state; he is not accountable to Parliament except if he behaves in such a way that he could be judged and impeached by the High Court of Justice (the senate), but only while he is in power; he has the authority to nominate ambassadors, consuls, the army and Police Chief of Staff and members of the Supreme Court, even though these nominations must be approved by the senate. Above all, in keeping with Haitian mentality and traditions, he is the boss. In contrast, the prime minister appears to be "an expendable fusible": she is vulnerable to a censure vote issued by one of the chambers and she enjoys authority for appointing only minor posts. Of course, one has to take into account the personality of the men involved; for instance, Prime Minister Gérard Latortue exercised more power than the Provisional President Boniface Alexandre from February 2004 to April 2006. Still, the president cannot get rid of the prime minister, who can only be removed from office if she either renounces her position or, as mentioned above, is censured by one of the chambers. France has experienced such circumstances and, as a result, two presidents requested from a prime minister a signed but undated letter of resignation. Such behaviour is not advisable and does not represent a reliable solution.

The present system thus combines the shortcomings of the presidential and the parliamentary systems without the advantages of either. It should still be possible to go back to presidentialism, which Haitians lived with for more than two centuries. Such a system should not be thought of as inherently undemocratic; any absence of democracy is not the fault of the system but rather of the individuals in power who used their office for personal gain. Parliamentarianism, on the other hand, does not have a track record in developing countries that do not belong to the Commonwealth where the Westminster system has a long history.

Bicameralism has existed in Haiti since the creation of the Chamber of Representatives in 1816. This system lasted throughout Haiti's history with only two interruptions: first, from 1918 to 1930, when the two chambers were replaced by an appointed Council of State which performed all the parliamentary duties; and, more recently, during the Duvalierian era from 1957 to 1986, which imposed a single chamber. This formula was rejected as akin to dictatorship. For that reason, the advantages of "unicameralism" have never been seriously discussed since, even though observers agree that a poor country cannot afford the financial burden of a 30-member senate and a 99-member Chamber of Representatives (according to the Constitution there should be 142 members, one for each commune).

It is not reasonable to have a system according to which Parliament is granted the power to dismiss a minister, even the prime minister, without recognizing the equivalent right of the president to dissolve the chambers. The latter impinges upon the necessary balance of powers between the executive and the legislature.

The election calendar for selecting people's representatives at different levels, from the 565 CASECs (Administrative Council of the Rural Sections) to the 30 senators, 99 deputies and the president forces the electorate to cast a ballot practically every two years. The problem is not the principle of universal suffrage (an irreversible democratic achievement) but the preparedness of the population and its lack of civic training. And even if the number of elections were reduced, the necessary matching of this democratic activity with the ability of the population to rationally choose its representatives must still be resolved.

In Haiti and elsewhere we favour elections as being the paramount instrument for monitoring democratic progress. It grants legitimacy to the individual or the group which gathers the majority expressed in the formula 50 per cent plus 1, while leaving the other half in a precarious position, all the more so since, in a country like Haiti, the basic notions of pluralism and alternation in power are not yet fully assimilated. Thus, sayings like *"Ote toi que je m'y mette"* (now, leave the place for me; it is my turn) are common. Clientelism, meaning the desire to secure privileges by the group that takes power, is thus more powerful than the fight for civic rights. A mere constitutional change cannot erase such practices, but it could help to develop a different conception of public service in Haiti. Two prospective temptations must come into consideration. The first one is to disregard popular voting as being unrealistic on the basis that a non-educated population cannot wisely select its representatives, and replace it by an indirect vote, at least for the presidential election. The second is that election itself is not a standard of democracy. In many circles in Haiti, a stimulating debate is underway about the primacy of electoral legitimacy, as compared to other forms of permanent validation based on achievements – and that can lead to a perversion of the concept of democracy itself. What is needed is a redefinition of the notion of decentralization conceived mainly in institutional terms, with the creation of various bodies integrated in a hierarchical order into a system which, for lack of previous conceptualization and means, remains "empty shells". I propose a reassessment of the decentralization process that could help build a kind of *"légitimité de proximité"*, a closer relationship between the people and the local representatives.

Another badly needed constitutional reform is the creation of a Constitutional Court, composed of well-prepared, courageous and independent citizens, tasked with assessing the constitutional validity of any decision coming from the executive and legislative bodies. The absence of this body has led to very difficult situations as regards, for instance, the problems of nationality (what constitutes "Haitian"?). And more recently, only a Constitutional Court could have said *"le mot du droit"* (what the law says), during the long process of approving Prime Minister Michèle Pierre-Louis in 2008.

A proper recognition of the role of political parties beyond what is said in a laconic way in Article 31.1 of the 1987 constitution is needed. In theory, some hundred political parties officially exist in Haiti, most of them coming to life only during election time and not having a permanent existence. One explanation lies in the fact that Haiti did not experience a succession of fair and reliable elections which, in any country, will weaken the political party system.

In the nineteenth century there were just two parties, the liberal one and the national one. Their respective slogans were: *"the power to the most competent"* for the liberals; "the greatest good for the overwhelming majority", through which they expressed their social, political and international opposing visions for the national party. Each alternated in power for about 20 years before disappearing from the scene. In 1946, during the so-called revolution, over 40 political parties were formed in order to take part in the elections, but except for the Communist Party (created in 1934 with the famous writer Jacques Roumain, better known for his book *Gouverneurs de la rosée* (the masters of the dew), and the populist Mouvement d'Organisation du Peuple, the leader of which was Daniel Fignolé, none survived this exceptional period.

Haiti's political life could be organized into four or five large ideological and political formations that would structure the population's various sensibilities. However, there are two types of populism that have pervaded the system: the Duvalierian one, which did not survive except in residual terms and, up to now, the Aristidian one. The effects of the latter still influence the behaviour of the popular masses and even governing circles. The result is that the citizens who are still fighting for democracy deem it necessary to organize themselves in groups, the majority of them leading a very difficult existence. There is a strong case to be made for helping the most serious groups to strengthen their organizations, not only at election time. But they currently do not have the financial means to fulfil their responsibilities, either in power or in opposition. It should be the duty of the state to help the reliable parties. Moreover, this should be a constitutional requirement.

Whenever there is a constitutional crisis in Haiti, one realizes that the international community is rather tolerant of the constitutional manipulation or even violation. We have witnessed this kind of reaction, or absence of reactions, when the international community deems it necessary not to criticize too openly those deviations in the name of realism, because they back the Haitians who appear to serve their interests, and above all, because they claim the necessity to abide by the law, a principle that they eagerly defend in their own national system. They criticize, sometimes openly, the 1987 constitution as being too complicated and too advanced in its principles, a kind of sterile luxury for the illiterate and poor Haitian people. For example, we have seen that during the 2006 presidential elections when applying a formula proposed by Brazil, the Provisional Government, the Electoral Council and some members of the international community improperly shared the "blank votes" among the candidates in order to grant the presidency to the one they favoured, René Préval, depriving the Haitian population of what Leslie Manigat, the victim of this combination, called "the pedagogy of the second ballot". They would never have accepted that in their own country and it is useful to recall that some months later the Brazilian president submitted himself to a second ballot while in the first one he got more than 47 per cent of the votes. Indeed, in those circumstances, the *raison d'état*, which is the contrary to the *état de droit*, was put forward in order to accept the legally unacceptable solution. Therefore, one has to point out a contradiction between the selection of the constitutional factor as a basis of governance and the fact that, for international purposes, it is not permanently defended by the same international community.

What is a good constitution? One which includes coherent normative principles? The one which lasts and proves its efficacy? The one which expresses some basic requirements in keeping with the aspirations of the people, as well as universal ones shared by the majority of states? What are democratic achievements? If you ask a Haitian peasant what democracy is about, he will not answer by recalling the etymological roots, *demos kratos*, but he can clearly identify the basic conditions of life, security, health, education, respect for human life – in other words all the fundamental topics listed in the United Nations Universal Declaration of Human Rights. The 1987 constitution encompasses all of these conditions, but the problem is that they are not implemented. There exists in Haiti a "two-wheel legality", one of which is known and advocated for by a minority, and another one – shared by the majority who are overwhelmed by daily problems – for which the constitution is a kind of foreign body, an inaccessible luxury, even though the preamble solemnly states: "The Haitian people proclaim the present Constitution."

## REFERENCES

BioScience (2010) "List of Prime Ministers of Haiti", *BioScience Encyclopedia*. Available at http://www.bioscience.ws/encyclopedia/index.php?title=List_of_Prime_Ministers_of_Haiti

Kretchik, Walter E. (2007) "Haiti's Quest for Democracy: Historical Overview", in John T. Fishel and Andrés Sáenez (eds) *Capacity Building for Peacekeeping: The Case of Haiti*. Dulles, Virginia: Potomac Books, pp. 8–34.

Manigat, Leslie F. and Robert I. Rotberg (1988) "Haiti's Past", *Foreign Affairs*, 67(2): 169–172.

Manigat, Mirlande H. (2000a) *Plaidoyer pour une nouvelle constitution*. Port-au-Prince: Université Quisqueya.

Manigat, Mirlande H. (2000b) *Traité de droit constitutionnel Haïtien*. Port-au-Prince: Université Quisqueya.

Perito, Robert and Jasenka Jocic (2008) "Paper versus Steel: Haiti's Challenge of Consitutional Reform", *USIPeace Briefing*, January. Available at http://www.usip.org/files/resources/1.PDF

Rotberg, Robert I. (1988) "Haiti's Past Mortgages its Future", *Foreign Affairs*, 67(1): 93–109.

# 4

# Haiti: Malversive state and teetering nation

*Patrick Sylvain*

As a former slave colony with a multifaceted and difficult heritage of so-cial exclusion imposed by various governments and reinforced by foreign entities, Haiti has experienced a variety of contradictory politics and poli-cies that have rendered it structurally vulnerable. The harsh stratification of Haitian society during slavery and the years that followed created massive social chasms along race and colour lines. The 1825 indemnity imposed by the French Imperial Government and the subsequent long-term annexation of Santo Domingo exacerbated a fragmentation of the state that eventually led into the formation of two distinct republics. However, it is politics that have led to Haiti's diminished capacity for sur-vival. Haiti is a tropical island and, as such, the occurrence of naturally occurring disasters is unavoidable. The dearth of cultivated natural re-sources is also a strong contributor to Haiti's economic underdevelop-ment. Time and time again its leaders have failed to create policies that were/are aligned with the patterns of natural occurrences (hurricanes, drought, earthquakes) that could potentially lead to disaster.

The 12 January 2010 earthquake, the most catastrophic in Haiti's his-tory, presented a unique set of challenges and opportunities: how to create an integrated and productive civil society and secure long-term in-vestments in human capital. A striking parallel can be drawn between this earthquake and another event in Haitian history. The devastating earthquake of 1842 coincided with a socio-political revolution against the government; it exposed the weaknesses of the state led by then president Jean-Pierre Boyer and ushered in a stealthy fight for democratic free-

*Fixing Haiti: MINUSTAH and beyond, Heine and Thompson (eds),*
*United Nations University Press, 2011, ISBN 978-92-808-1197-1*

dom. The conditions exposed by the 2010 earthquake could likewise fuel a desire for political and social renewal and may result in the creation of a model for post-colonial and post neo-colonial politics. This would require the establishment of an integrative and decentralized political system where corporations and imperial powers cease to continue to subjugate the masses. If, however, the status quo remains and the international community continues to apply exploitative policies, Haiti will descend into chaos while becoming ever more vulnerable to natural disasters.

The effects of massive fires (1820, 1822, 1827, 1832), hurricanes (1827, 1831, 2008) and earthquakes (1842, 2010) have marked Haiti's political landscape over time and contributed to the nation's deficit in institutional capacity building. One could argue that Haiti's unpreparedness for handling natural and other disasters is rooted in the lack of forward thinking by its many apathetic leaders and malevolent dictators who have turned a blind eye towards sustainable development.

There are strong similarities between former Haitian president Jean-Pierre Boyer (1818–1843) and the current president, René Préval (1996–2001, 2006–2011). They relate to the lack of institutional progress during their respective terms and the entrenched nature of the political struggle for power between the executive and the legislative branches of government under their watch. Both men were educated in Europe and returned to Haiti in order to serve the interests of the "masses". They saw themselves as public servants rather than career politicians. Both inherited decades of divisive national politics and the after-effects of revolt that derailed structural growth and cemented class and colour animosities. (Somehow, perhaps due to their pragmatism and fluidity with the ruling class that earned their trust, both were able to superficially reconcile most political differences for the benefit of national stability.) Both leaders created a level of cultural democracy that allowed freedom of the press and the circulation of free and critical thought to flourish. Yet, despite their accomplishments and minor visions for a stable, democratic and prosperous Haiti, each succumbed to international pressure, and in so doing, undermined national sovereignty and the very essence of democracy that they once promised. For Boyer, it was his acceptance of the terms of France's indemnity. For Préval, it is his constant renewal of the United Nation Mission of Stability in Haiti (MINUSTAH).

Both men were 66 years old and in charge of the nation when the two most catastrophic earthquakes in the island's recent history struck. To the surprise of even their staunchest defenders, both men remained silent in the calamitous days following the earthquakes and their support from that point on plummeted. It seemed as though each was more concerned with maintaining institutional stability than addressing the needs of the masses.

## Historical implications

Haiti's tragic history has not been the result of natural evolution. It emerged from territorial insecurity, economic subjugation imposed by Western powers in order to satisfy market needs and the propagation of certain policies dictated by post-colonial rules. The country failed to redress the imbalances created by France in the years following revolution, owing to divisive class and race politics and the politics of integral territoriality that became psychologically embedded in the draconian policies of nationhood. As Robert Fatton Jr. (2006) points out: "Haiti's predicament is not rooted in the absence of a nation, but rather in the ruling class's incapacity to construct an 'integral' state." By that he means "a state that is capable of organizing both the political unity of the different factions of the ruling class and the 'organic relations between ... political society and civil society'". The emancipatory modernist project of the Haitian state was an aborted project that failed to usher in the promises of "Liberty, Equality and Fraternity" and that Haitians "shall remain the masters of [our] soil" as Dessalines often uttered.

## Territorial security

Regional security, homeland security and international security are important considerations in the maintenance of a continuous and stable functioning of Western democracy as nations seek to sustain free markets vital to their national growth in the twenty-first century. However, in the beginning of the nineteenth century, Haiti was consumed by its own efforts at territorial security as it tried to guarantee freedom for the black majority. As David Nicholls (1979: 5) remarked, "Haitians in the nineteenth century saw their country not merely as a symbol of black regeneration, but as an effective proof of racial equality". Embedded in the idea of establishing racial equality was the notion of democracy and human respectability.

The 1803 Haitian slave revolution brought independence but also established a nation plagued by its security obsessions. Provoked by slave-owning nations with goals of imperial expansion, Haiti stood up to those who sought to thwart its independence and stance against slavery. Thus, the early days of Haiti's security pursuits entailed aggressive acts of territorial integrity. It succeeded in annexing Santo Domingo, wrested from the Spanish crown, and brought it into the cadre of independent nation states that sought to keep slave-owning nations at bay. Security, in the Haitian political mindset, implied an institutional commitment to nation-building and the establishment of an island-based common market and currency. Ensuring security also meant the systematic exclusion of the French because of their practice of slavery and insistence of maintaining Haiti under the colonial status quo.

## Economy and structural imbalance

Despite the early successes of the nation in productivity and prosperity achieved through the harvesting and marketing of its abundant natural resources, these did not translate into sustainable economic development. The harsh reality remained that Haiti existed as two separate and com-peting entities.

Haiti's inept politics of territoriality ultimately resulted in a cata-strophic mismanagement of the land, exhausting the very resources that gave it economic advantages in the first place. As Jared Diamond (2005: 340) puts it, the "elite identified strongly with France rather than with their own landscape, did not acquire land or develop commercial agricul-ture, and sought mainly to extract wealth from the peasants". Let it be noted that the elite did acquire land; yet, they did not work the land. In-stead, they created a quasi-sharecropping system that further exploited the poor and contributed to the migration of the peasants towards urban areas where zoning codes were ignored as the population expanded.

## The Boyer government and the annexation of Santo Domingo

While Boyer was instrumental in developing Petion's 1807 constitution and economic policies, he was also responsible for the establishment of a compensation policy in order to appease the elite of the south (including former colonists) who lost property and lives during Dessalines's massa-cres that occurred from August to the middle of September 1806. "To for-tify his position with the important people ... Pétion quickly got the Senate to pass laws annulling Dessaline's despoliations and reimbursing owners of crops lost while their plantations had been expropriated. As further sweeteners for the elite, Pétion at the same time repealed the 25 per cent share on every crop, ordained originally by Toussaint" (Heinl and Heinl, 1996: 135). Whether this form of disbursement without arbitration set a precedent for the later French indemnity is not clear. However, it was the first case in the Americas where the government compensated a group of victims for a previous administration's actions. Coincidentally, as Mimi Sheller (2000: 57) indicated, the French had established detailed plans to recapture Saint Domingue "by force in 1814, 1817, 1819 and 1822, in addition to more explicit attempts to negotiate French sovereignty with President Pétion in 1816 and with President Boyer in 1823. Although France finally recognized Haitian independence in 1838, it backed the breakaway of the Dominican Republic in 1844, and was involved in secret negotiations for use of the port of Samana."

By transferring territorial control over to the Haitians and becoming Spanish-Haitians, (the first case of cultural and political hybridization in the world) the people of Santo Domingo wanted to achieve security with the hope of building political and military institutions, and to achieve economic prosperity. Despite the divisions generated by Christophe, Pétion and the others, Haiti was still at this time a modern state that had established the first fully democratic republic in the world. The country's prosperity was evident in its grandiose symbols of power such as the Citadel, and the Palais Sans Souci. The latter, completed in 1813 by King Henry Christophe, "had floors of marble mosaic, walls of polished mahogany, tapestries and drapes imported from Europe. It also had bathrooms. Under the floors, conduits carried a cold mountain stream – ancestor of air conditioning – which emerged below as a fountain" (Rodman, 1968: 287). Sans Souci, today in complete ruins, was an imaginative and architectural feat of the nineteenth century.

Having annexed Santo Domingo, a partnership was sealed with the hope that such an entrusting act would bring Spanish-Haiti into modernity. The voluntary annexation to the Haitian republic represented an aspiration to establish a sovereign territory with functioning institutions that would usher in security for its people. The project placed an emphasis on the state as an evolving and progressive entity that would ensure its legitimacy by providing general welfare and a sense of freedom.

Boyer thus forged an inclusive political entity that promised a prosperous future, albeit one constrained by external forces, internal aspirations and the permanent challenge of the force of nature.

## The indemnity and post-unification aspirations

The catastrophic infighting between ruling classes and the international exclusion of Haiti from international trade placed the island in a precarious position. Twenty-one years after the revolution that created the first black republic, President Boyer's administration was driven to bankruptcy as he accepted a gun-boat-imposed French indemnity of 150 million francs. From that moment, a sequence of disasters was in motion and each policy from then on was a response to these repayment needs. By then, Boyer had to contend with the aspirations of the French-inspired aristocratic class on the west, and the Spanish-favoured aristocratic class to the east. The indemnity-induced impoverishment presented problems as well.

A draconian militarization took place in order to repel future attacks. It also served to enforce Boyer's *étatique* decree of 1826, a rural code that forced people to work the land, reattaching themselves to specific estates and "plantations". This action served to reverse the democratic and economic progress made between 1820 and 1825. The 1826 Rural Code reintroduced the notion of large-scale sharecropping and assigned the people to landless peasantry, bound to the land to increase cash crop production, so that the state might make up for the 70 per cent indemnity-related loss of revenue. By the mid-1830s, the impact of the French indemnity on the country's agricultural production and legislative politics was substantial and essentially usurped any territorial and political gains.

Boyer's policies alienated many and fostered hatred and significant chasms among the Dominicans who had been subjugated to harsh treatment. Under Boyer, full or partial military training was required for all males. Forced militarization without institutional benefits contributed to numerous revolts and Boyer eventually capitulated. Between 1836 and 1838, Boyer came under pressure to democratize the Haitian political system, and many young black and mulatto intellectuals formed alliances, arranged political debates, created newsletters and demanded greater participation in state affairs. These new radical practices created an "anti-authoritarian intersection of educated liberalism and popular association that democracy in Haiti became a possibility" (Sheller, 2000: 130). However, these aspirations could not be sustained owing to the economic strains that France's indemnity had placed on the feeble governmental institutions and the devastating 7 May earthquake that violently traversed the entire island. This earthquake, with its potent epicentre fixed in the north, brought in the August 1842 revolution that commenced Haiti's path toward perpetual revolt and strong-man politics. As reported by the Haitian historian Beaubrun Ardouin, who held a prominent post in the Boyer's government, quoted in Sheller (2000: 120–121):

The mobilized opposition swept the elections of 1842, but Boyer garrisoned twelve armed regiments in the capital when the deputies tried to meet, 'he stationed at the door of the House a guard of 180 men with strict orders to admit those men only who were declared supporters of the government' … Those excluded in 1839, along with their supporters, were not allowed to take their seats. Altogether almost one third of the deputies, including most for the capital, all from Santo Domingo, and most of the representatives of the south were forced out. To make matters worse ... the country was not only awash in worthless paper money, but the public trust was by now completely destroyed.... Following Boyer's crackdown on the elected representatives of the people, the liberal opposition formed the secret society for the Rights of Man and the Citizen, which in September 1842 signed a call to arms and catalogue of grievances that came to be known as the Manifeste de Praslin.

Towards the end of 1842, Western inhabitants and rulers of the French-speaking side of Haiti were, in the eyes of the Eastern inhabitants of Spanish-speaking Haiti, seen as dictators and eventually became more despised than the Spanish colonialists. Haiti's loss of the eastern part of the island in February 1844 would accelerate social and political tensions, leading to a series of military coups and civil wars. As a result, Haiti would later be forced to accept the 1860 Concordat signed by the Vatican and France that ordered the recognition of Christianity as the national religion and the acceptance of French education and social norms. Haitians would thus become further divided along lines of class, colour, education and religion.

## The 1842 earthquake and rupture

The internal contradictions that the indemnity triggered erupted on 7 May 1842, when Boyer was unable to rally the nation following its worst natural disaster of the nineteenth century. His inability to respond to the 1842 earthquake caused the wrath of a destitute population clamouring for change. According to Saint-Rémy (1846: 212), the flourishing city of Cap-Haitian was totally devastated with half of its population perished under the rubble and many buildings burnt to the ground. The people were left to fend for themselves; looting, ransacking and fighting went on for two weeks, including a raid on the public treasury. The Boyer government stood by the older generations and the mulattos who supported his regime but further alienated the young lycéens who sought to move beyond colour lines.

It is the historian and former Senator Beaubrun Ardouin (1860) who provides the most vivid details of the earthquake and notes the bravery and kindness of the population despite the looting that took place in Cap-Haitian, where 5,000 people died. Pertinent for this analysis of the 1842 earthquake are the following key points that I have drawn from Ardouin's historical narrative chronology (ibid., Chapter V):

1. Only one million gourdes were ever distributed to Cap-Haitian, a location that at one point Boyer considered vital due to its political and commercial importance.
2. Relying primarily on local authorities, Boyer did not visit the affected localities, nor did he send on his behalf any members of his government to express his condolences.
3. Boyer failed to delegate tasks, even in advanced age.
4. After long administrative delays in Port-au-Prince, only two officers were arrested and charged for ransacking the treasury in Cap-Haitian (Colonel Bobo and Captain Moreau).
5. Daily discords were recorded between the population and the executive due to inefficiency of the latter and its failure to reconstitute the disillusioned nation, particularly the in the northern and eastern regions of the country where banditry and theft increased over time.

An inappropriate response to the vital affairs of the nation demonstrated the regime's incompetence. In a sense, it held the country hostage by its inaction and selectively tangential leadership, and destroyed the potential for national cohesion. The Spanish-Haitians responded by forming their own representative republic after the entire nation erupted in fervent revolutionary determination to unseat Boyer on 13 March 1843.

## The modern state

The modern Haitian political system is widely considered to be dysfunctional. Since 1986, changes of government have been violent or the result of brokered deals and electoral fraud. Thus, the endless process of democratization has never succeeded in establishing a consolidated state.

Prime Minister Jean-Max Bellerive, in a speech given on 18 February 2010, ably stated: "We share one dream: to see Haiti as an emerging country by 2030, a society of simplicity, equitable, just and unified, living in harmony with its environment, its culture and a controlled modernity where the rule of law is established, the freedom of assembly and of expression and the development of the territory are established ..." [author's translation]. Implicit in the prime minister's speech is the notion that the nation is not currently viable nor democratically ruled. Hence, the restoration of governmental authority following the 12 January 2010 earthquake must have public safety and security as a prime objective for constituting a democratic and representative state.

President Préval reacted to the 2010 earthquake in a similar fashion to that of Boyer. The difference is that in 2010, with the presence of MINUSTAH as a buffer and a stabilizing force, President Préval's power was not threatened. Since he is cognizant of the political weight of the disarrayed population vis-à-vis the international force, he really does not have any incentive to be responsive to the fragmented population whose future rests with external actors who are attempting to reshape Haitian politics and problematic institutions where priorities often run counter to the population's needs.

## Préval's leadership and natural disasters

After 20 years of violence, kidnappings, coup d'états and popular protests, René Préval's second term in office was marked by the promise of political stability, democratization and constitutional order. On 8 January 2007, during his "State of the Nation" speech given in front of Parliament, he stated that what he said was common knowledge: that both the state and private sector were incapable of providing solutions to the structural ills of the nation. He further declared that "contraband was destroying the national product while preventing the state from earning much needed tax revenues that could go towards development" [author's translation] (PrimaInfo, 2007: 2). He decried the dangers that kidnapping and narco-trafficking posed for stability and much needed development. Without assigning blame, he proclaimed that the solutions to Haiti's problems had been readily discussed on the streets and radio. He declared a prime constitutional duty that: "politicians, president, senators, deputies, the government, [must] unite in order for the country to move forward. That's what the people demand. It is difficult, but it can be done. It is starting already" (ibid.). In that speech, Préval was cognizant of his limited power but engaged in the political game of making demands via request. He sidestepped the folly of nationalism by naming what was undeniable. He then proceeded by presenting to members of the Parliament a reminder of what he had said during his January 2001 speech, that drugs were and still are the greatest obstacles to the nation's security.

Préval had learned from his differences with Parliament during his first term. Although he had a majority-member party (OPL), they quickly switched sides and formed a legislative opposition to the president, refusing to confirm any of his proposed prime ministers. As a result, most of his progressive social and economic policies were blocked. With his much needed developmental funds in remission, Préval's administration ultimately gave in to the opposition's demands.

As Préval became more savvy, he became more of a broker. He abandoned Jacques-Édouard Alexis, his first prime minister, after the March 2008 hunger protests. He sacrificed his second prime minister, Michèle Pierre-Louis, a former business partner and close family friend, whom

President Préval enlisted to rescue his government in 2008. A year later, without constitutional due process, and no popular protests against her, Préval gave in to three of his senators' demands and relieved her from her post. Préval, it seems, became more enshrined in the power of the executive than the moral principles behind the democracy to which he so often referred.

While it is true that political instability, drugs and violence were key forces, challenges and constitutional transgressions by the executive are equally as dangerous. The November 2009 legislative coup against Prime Minister Pierre-Louis, who wanted to maintain a clear line of governance, was an executive exercise of democratic repression. Préval, like all other Haitian heads of state, never fully accepted the constitutional principles of the republic that the three branches of government must be separated, and that the executive cannot be the central distributor of power. Thus, the contradiction at the heart of Haitian politics lies in the challenge to achieve a real democracy within a stable republic, and not just an electoral one. The government should remain committed to an institutionally substantive democracy, based on respect for the rule of law, human dignity and rights.

While Préval's political reading of Haiti's challenges is judicious, measured and realistic, he fails at institution-building as a result of his personal trajectory. Even his ascent to power through five different political parties and/or platforms (Respé, Lavalas, OPL, Lespwa and his recently formed political party, Unité) is indicative of Préval's quest – not in any political loyalty – and a national culture that lacks established political parties.

Despite Préval's unassuming and low-key behaviour, he is sometimes cynical in his remarks. Préval will not hit back at his enemies or detractors, though he will cut their access to power. He often refers to Alexis as "Ti" Alexis ("ti" is short for "piti" meaning small). After that he will smile and then move on to more serious matters. President Préval knows how to form alliances and to dissolve them. And as Phillip Girard (2010: 212) accurately remarked: "Reaching out to one's foes is highly unusual in Haiti's winner-takes-all political culture, but Préval's conciliatory tactics bore fruit."

Préval is a master of the Haitian political balancing act but has little connection to the masses. Despite his fundamental knowledge of the streets, he failed to listen to the very same people that he wanted members of Parliament to listen to. In September 2000, he once told a delegation of women to "*naje pou sòti*" (swim their way out) of their difficult situations. In March 2008, while thousands of people were protesting against high food prices, he indicated that he too was paying the same amount for a cup of rice. For this he is seen as aloof and cynical.

In the aftermath of four hurricanes in 2008 (Fay, Gustave, Hanna and Ike), that buried Gonaïves and many other towns and provinces, Haiti's vulnerability to natural disasters became evident. The country sank to its lowest level of poverty, with the collapse of major roads and bridges, a thousand deaths and over 800,000 homeless. A CRS Report for the US Congress stated, "the Haitian government [sic] needs $400 million over the next 18 months for hurricane recovery and reconstruction" (Taft-Morales and Sullivan, 2008: 1). A total 84,625 houses were damaged with "nearly 70% of the internally displaced persons living in shelters in the wake of the storms were in the Department of Artibonite, known as Haiti's rice bowl. In the departmental capital of Gonaïves, at least 80% of the city's 300,000 residents were affected" (ibid.: 2). The government did not respond to the people's needs and relied entirely on international assistance. In January 2010 in Gonaïves, Préval reminded the population of the importance of security, stability and continuity to achieve progress. He went on to elaborate on the progress made despite the setbacks encountered in 2008 but feared a return to the instability of 2001 to 2006. He reminded them that it was "stability and unity that brought about 1804, and instability that gave us the divisions in 1806 ... Our work today, and even after 7 February 2011 when I leave office, is for us to work in unity to reinforce and maintain stability" [author's translation] (Haitian Embassy).

Preval's insistent emphasis on stability and security places him above the average political figure in Haiti. However, his silence and public absence after the 12 January earthquake have compounded the people's indifference toward him. President Préval knows that common citizens play an inconsequential role in the country's public policies. As Prime Minister Bellerive remarked when asked by the US Public Service Broadcasting's Martin Smith to comment on the executive's silence after the quake despite protests, "It's a choice. There is so much to do. There is so much to organize. There [are] so few people to help you to do the job. And time is very rare commodity for the government right now" (PBS Frontline, 2010).

Préval's silence after the quake, his deficiencies as an institution builder and the constant renewal of MINUSTAH's mandate means he will go down as just another languid president, despite the fact that he has claimed "our priority right now is that democracy must be strengthened by economic progress" (PBS NewsHour, 2006). Haiti under Préval has made substantial economic progress, but he has not been able to end the country's instability. Furthermore, the cholera outbreak that has killed over 1,000 people in the north of the country and spurred violent protests from Cap-Haitian to Port-au-Prince is allegedly associated with the UN's Nepalese base whose new members are accused of bringing the disease to Haiti. What the cholera reveals is Haiti's structural vulnerability to the global circulation of disease.

As a result of the country's violent past, natural disasters and institutional neglect Haiti's leaders are unable to respond to the nation's many demands. Unfortunately, Préval's view for capacity building and stability was only externally supported.

## Préval's political legacy and political strategy

The spate of violent protests that started in 2004 and disrupted the relative stability that had been gained under the first Préval administration resurfaced in 2008 with the food riots. A weak state, safeguarded by MINUSTAH, entered into a dance of power with the protesting public. Préval criticized the economic impacts of expanded international trade that highlighted the diminished local rice production and agricultural products. In an interview with PBS's NewsHour, President Préval stated: "We cannot continue to rely on giving food to the population that comes from abroad, because we're competing against our own national agriculture. What has to happen right away is to create labor-intensive jobs to give money to the population to buy national products" (PBS NewsHour, 2010). Since the removal of both Aléxis and Pierre-Louis as successive prime ministers, it has been the president who sets the national agenda for development and the reorganization of the state. Despite President Préval's statement, the fact remains that the country is vulnerable to serious food insecurities and "a majority of Haitians live in rural areas and depend on agricultural livelihoods, but neither the government nor the international community has paid sufficient attention to agriculture, leaving the countryside increasingly marginalized" (Oxfam, 2010).

Constitutionally, it is the prime minister who sets the agenda of the government and all of the ministers that fall under his purview. However, since 1987, not a single government has respected the legal parameters of the constitution. While the current crisis has significantly weakened its institutions, the power of the president has overtaken the prerogatives of the prime minister.

The president remains the commander-in-chief in a bureaucratized system that favours the president while the prime minister acts as an executive shield in times of crisis. In such a setting, President Préval is much more powerful and entrenched in his executive power than the constitution intended. Haiti has had a domineering presidency and a legislative branch of government that either sought power for itself or functions as an extension of the executive branch. The Haitian Parliament historically, and more poignantly, since 1986, has been not only a body of lawmakers but a political space where money and power are a form of investment. Furthermore, the weakness of the legislative body and its potential for corruption is due to the fact that while members are highly politicized, they have no political party experience, and certainly no legal or political education. Such an unfortunate reality marred Préval's first presidential tenure.

Since democracy was established in 1987, one can argue that Préval has impacted democratic rules in Haiti and offered some stability. He is the only president who succeeded in completing his full electoral terms. He was also very influential not only as an activist for democracy in the late 1980s but served as a prime minister, the head of government, under the first democratically elected populist government led by President Aristide. As Reginald Dumas (2008: 257) points out: "Préval came to office bearing the heavy burden of his country's socio-economic underachievement and political turbulence." President Préval can be seen partly as an architect and partly as a builder of the Haitian house of "democracy", and the extent to which the house is viable or unsustainable is a major determinant of his presidential legacy. In 2000, Haiti was a party to the Community of Democracies, "Warsaw Declaration: Toward a Community of Democracies", pledging its adherence to democratic rule and human rights. However, at the same time, Haiti's most prominent journalist, Jean Dominique, was assassinated and the electoral process was tainted by allegations of fraud under the weak leadership of the Electoral Council (CEP).

President Préval is not corrupt and indeed cares about the promotion of democracy, but he will not ruffle the feathers of the corrupt elite in order to ensure the growth of this desired democracy. "Préval's low-key style, however unimpressive, had the advantage of facilitating national reconciliation and cooling the process" (Girard, 2010: 212). Préval's sights are set upon the long term, on the delivery of services to the population and to democracy promotion. Girard further remarks on Préval's Social Appeasement Plan, whose goal was "designed to placate potential critics, [as he] also decided to keep paying Aristide bureaucrats and former army members their salary – in other words, he bought out his enemies on the far left and right" (ibid.). Préval's priority was to eliminate the violence that kept Haiti insecure and unattractive for foreign investment. His priorities are security, education, health and agricultural developments under government control but not constrained by the bureaucracy, so that partnerships can be formed with NGOs without further incapacitating the state.

The stability and strength of the state are so central to Préval's politics that his "conciliatory manners extended to the international community,

which he did not attack in the strident tone Aristide had employed before his downfall; in turn, the international community responded generously to his call for continued assistance" (ibid.: 213). In a sense, Préval's
"tactical" selection of a successor in the current political context is to ensure the structural continuity of governance. He chose Jude Celestin not
only as the representative of the newly established INITE party but also
as the heir of the executive to ensure a stable government and ensure
that his legacy is perpetuated through a hand-picked leader who seems,
thus far, to have the support of the international community and a large
part of the Haitian elite. In an interview given to Al Jazeera's Juliana
Ruhfus, Haitian presidential contender and entertainer Michel Martelly
said: "people would tend to say that Jude Célestin [will win], but I would
say that he is the one with more money. He is the one who has the power
with him and he has the system, he has the electoral council, so he probably would definitely get close; but I don't think anybody wants to deal
with him for belonging to the system" (interviewed by Al Jazeera, 2010).
With an emphasis on maintaining "continuity" and "stability of governance" by the international donors and the Préval government, there is
indeed a preference for stability. Haiti's legal counsel in the United States
under President Aristide, Ira J. Kursban, is correct in asserting that: "the
current Provisional Electoral Council, hand-picked by President Préval,
has fabricated a new eligibility requirement to disqualify Fanmi Lavalas
from the presidential elections. This new rule requires that the head of
each party register presidential candidates in person" (Kursban, 2010).

While Préval is far from being dictatorial or overtly retaliatory, his
pragmatic politics is imbedded in the Haitian culture of patronage. This
approach to democracy is best expressed by the Haitian journalist
Michelle Montas, wife of the late Jean Dominique, who, in an interview
with the *Los Angeles Times'* Joe Mozingo, claimed that: "I've never seen
a political figure as shrewd as René Préval ... Can you imagine a politician who gets to power and he didn't even campaign?" (Mozingo, 2010).

## Misreading Préval

The claim often made by Préval's critics is that he is too shy for his own
good. This couldn't be further from the truth. Préval is certainly not a social exhibitionist, nor is he an inspiring leader. However, he is a sharp
politician with a sound understanding of the Haitian people and culture.
Ambassador James Dobbins remarked, "when in office, I think those in
the United States government who dealt with him found him personally
to be honest and accessible if rather undynamic" (PBS Online News-
Hour, 2006). In his former role as minister of the interior, Préval was

known for disguising himself as an old man in order to get the pulse of the street. He has the reputation for being an excellent listener with a sharp memory for detail, and prefers to observe instead of being observed. He is also a pragmatist who easily refutes contrary advice and will eschew radical paradigm shifts. Instead he will gradually rearrange the paradigm to render it anew. Again in referring to Préval's politics of appeasement in the context of insecurity, Girard (2008: 213) poignantly writes:

> Préval characteristically resorted to the carrot as well as the stick. Rather than attacking gang leaders as political extremists and drug warlords, he described criminality as a sad by-product of poverty and created the National Commission for Disarmament, Demobilization, and Reintegration (CNDDR) to foster small-scale social projects in the slums. Faithful to his strategy of defusing opposition, Préval even went as far as appointing gang leaders implicated in the murderous 'Operation Baghdad' as members of the commission.

Préval's goal seems to be the establishment of an enduring democracy that slowly chips away at corruption and violence while the government slowly builds institutions for people to comfortably adjust to their new bureaucratic environment. Préval is a new brand of Haitian nationalist leader who is candid about expounding upon the weaknesses of the state but aims to establish his economic and political vision. Through his politics of appeasement and desires to maintain political stability and the effective continuity of governance, he has silenced his competition through political action: for example, the abrupt removal of his best friend, Michèle Pierre-Louis, from the office of prime minister, or the sidestepping of former Prime Minister Alexis as a presidential candidate.

The unconstitutionality of the prime minister's censure preceded any formal debate on the senate floor while several senators were pronouncing their opinions on various radio stations a few days earlier. Senator Joseph Lambert from Lespwa declared on 29 October that his party had secured 18 votes to topple the prime minister. Through it all, the president remained silent and never intervened on behalf of the woman who had brought order and fiscal responsibility to the state in the eyes of the World Bank and the International Monetary Fund.

Under Prime Minister Pierre-Louis all parliamentary requests had to be written, and her government was the only one that delivered a line item budget of the government's expenditures to Parliament as mandated by the constitution. Pierre-Louis's governmental approach was a threat to certain members of Parliament who benefited from past uncertainties and a relaxed rule of law. Nancy Roc's investigative reporting revealed that:

In December 2008, Senator Joseph Lambert's name was linked to the case of Monique Pierre, the wife of Gonaïves Police Commissioner Ernst Bouquet Dorfeuille, who was abducted and murdered on November 29 in Port-au-Prince. The official registration plate 00332 used by the kidnappers corresponded to the vehicle in Senator Joseph Lambert's name. This assassination was linked to drug traffickers and Kelly Bastien referred to "a plan to destabilize parliament" and called for the top commanders of the Haitian National Police to be summoned to give explanations. This summons never took place. (Roc, 2009: 7)

With corruption in all branches of government, and under pressure from the IMF's Article VI Consultation for Poverty Reduction and Growth Facility, President Préval conceded and declared in May 2007: "we are fighting against corruption in order to stabilize the country ... and all parties who are involved in corruptions are traitors to the nation. Those who take part in corruption are enemies of the country because they are preventing the return of investors" (Radio Métropole, 2007).

In June 2007, Judge Claudy Gassant, the Government High Commissioner, also declared war on corruption and promised to eradicate its practices. Unfortunately, corruption persists. Nancy Roc points out in her article "Haiti: the Bitter Grapes of Corruption" that:

The Corruption Perception Index (CPI), published in November 2006 by Transparency International (TI), highlighted the fatal link between corruption and poverty. Haiti was at the bottom of the list where corruption was most widely perceived, scoring below Burma, Iraq and Guinea. In 2007, the Corruption Perception Index again showed that corrupt practices had not been mitigated despite the stated intentions of the Haitian government to combat this scourge. In fact, Haiti's score shifted downward slightly (from 1.8 to 1.6) owing largely to a very weak "confidence gap" between 1.3 and 1.8 out of 10. TI underscored that corruption affects both public institutions and the private sector. In 2008, the result was no better: Haiti came 177th out of 180 countries. (Roc, 2009: 6)

With the appointment and parliamentary approval of Michèle Pierre-Louis as prime minister in September 2008, people felt hopeful and optimistic about Haiti's future, given her track record and commitment to progress. She had earned the trust of the people and the international community by decreasing the rate of kidnappings in the country by 90 per cent. UNICEF indicated that there was "a significant decline in reported kidnappings of children from 89 cases in 2008 to only 21 cases (15 girls and 6 boys) in 2009" (UN Secretary-General [A/64/742-S/2010/181] Report). There was a significant improvement in security, due in part to the expanded presence of the police in various corners of the capital. In addition, there were economic benefits enjoyed at this time, as there was an increase in GDP from 2.3 per cent in 2008 to a 3.6 per cent in 2009. According to the IMF Executive Board, Haiti's growth "reached 2.9 per cent in 2009, one of the highest rates in the Western Hemisphere, fueled by stronger agricultural and manufacturing output" (IMF No. 10/XX). According to several prominent Haitian politicians (ex-Colonel Himmler Rébu, Édouard Paultre and others), the removal of Prime Minister Pierre-Louis was a pre-emptive electoral manoeuvre by President Préval who wanted to curtail her popularity prior to the 2010 electoral process. The country was moving towards stability, and as Joseph Guyler Delva reported: "Clinton had surprised some analysts early in October by telling an investor conference in Port-au-Prince that Haiti's political risk was lower than it had ever been in his lifetime" (Delva, 2009). Indicative of systemic institution frailties and lack of due process within the legal system in Haiti was the parliamentary process in itself; and as Delva accurately observed:

> Haiti won $1.2 billion in debt relief from the World Bank, the International Monetary Fund and other creditors in July [2009], freeing up an estimated $50 million a year to spend on other projects. . . . In April, donors pledged $324 million over two years to help rebuild Haiti. The Inter-American Development Bank said in June it would provide $120 million in grants next year to improve infrastructure, basic services and disaster prevention ... Senate opponents of the resolution to fire Pierre-Louis called it unconstitutional and said lawmakers had no power to remove the head of government in a special session without explicit instructions from Préval. (ibid.)

Préval's neo-nationalist and patriarchal view of governance is anchored in the reality that Haiti is a weak state. He also knows the limits of his power against the Haitian bourgeoisie, drug dealers, corrupt officials and the international community. He wants to assure that his democratic legacy is preserved at all costs. Préval's formula and vision for Haiti's democratic governance are relevant to his constituencies and international supporters who see in him a trustworthy partner. In US Secretary of State Hillary Clinton's view, he "is reliable, but he is a partner who has very serious challenges when it comes to capacity" (PBS Frontline, 2010).

Despite this, Préval seems to be implementing a long-term goal of having his political party in democratic control of all branches of government in order to fulfil the major developmental goals expressed in the government's 2008–2010 DSNCRP (Document de Stratégie Nationale pour la Croissance et la Réduction de la Pauvreté; MPCE, 2007). These are to decentralize the country, increase agricultural production, decrease the rate of illiteracy, make improvements to infrastructure, buttress governmental institutions and increase tourism (MPCE, 2007).

I would argue that President Préval's executive legacy will be viewed as one that strove to establish a "dignified" state under significant constraint, one that nurtured democratic power but failed to distribute it and to promote accountability. However, he is still a product of a recalcitrant political environment. Hillary Clinton observed, "[Préval] has a government and a political system and a social structure which is very entrenched in the way it has always done business" (PBS Frontline, 2010). Democracy is not only a function of governmental institutions; it is also a byproduct of culture, the sacred soil for its implementation. Hence, there is the desire for social justice in Préval's vision, even though his political tactics and apparent indifference to the plight of the people at times place him at odds with the Haitian polity. Nevertheless, he seems to understand what it is that Haitians need: "we must deal with the need of rebuilding Haiti, thanks to an effective decentralization policy – namely, offering health care, education, jobs to all Haitians, men and women, regardless of where they live in the country, in order to prevent migratory flows toward the big cities, towards Port-au-Prince, and that will help avoid that disasters such as the earthquake would cause so many victims" (The White House, 2010). Préval's broad vision is to be lauded, but the obstacles to his goals now depend on Haiti's rapprochement with donor countries and the nation's continuous ability to maintain democratic order and equitable governance.

## REFERENCES

Al Jazeera (2010) "Haiti: Seismic Election", People and Power, 18 Nov. Available at http://english.aljazeera.net/programmes/peopleandpower/2010/11/20101117839903761.html

Ardouin, Beaubrun (1860) *Études sur l'histoire d'Haiti*, 11 vols. Paris: Dezobry, Magdeleine et Ce.

Delva, Joseph Guyler (2009) "Haiti: Senate Ousts Prime Minister Pierre-Louis", Reuters, 30 October. Available at http://in.reuters.com/article/2009/10/30/idINIndia-43554220091030

Diamond, Jared (2005) *Collapse: How Societies Choose to Fail or Succeed.* London: Penguin Books.

Dumas, Reginald (2008) *An Encounter with Haiti: Notes of a Special Adviser.* Trinidad and Tobago: Medianet Limited.

Fatton Jr., Robert (2006) "Haiti: The Saturnalia of Emancipation and the Vicissitudes of Predatory Rule", *Third World Quarterly*, 27(1): 115–133.

Girard, Philipe (2010) *Haiti: The Tumultuous History – From Pearl of the Caribbean to Broken Nation.* New York: Palgrave Macmillan.

Heinl, Robert and Nancy Heinl (1996) *Written in Blood: The Story of the Haitian People, 1492–1995.* Lanham, MD: University Press of America, Inc.

International Monetary Fund (IMF) (2010) *Haiti Staff Report*. Washington, DC: IMF.

Mozingo, Joe (2010) "Haitian Quake Shook Leader to His Core", *Los Angeles Times*, 15 August. Available at http://articles.latimes.com/2010/aug/15/world/la-fg-haiti-preval-20100815

MPCE (Ministère de la Planification et de la Coopération Externe) (2007) *Document de Stratégie Nationale pour la Croissance et la Réduction de la Pauvreté 2008–2010: Pour Réussir le Saut Qualitatif*. Port-au-Prince: Ministère de la Planification et de la Coopération Externe, Républic D'Haiti.

Nicholls, David (1979) *From Dessalines to Duvalier: Race, Colour and National Independence in Haiti*. Cambridge: Cambridge University Press.

Oxfam (2010) "Planting Now: Agricultural Challenges and Opportunities for Haiti's Reconstruction", Oxfam Briefing Paper 140, October. Available at http://www.oxfam.org/sites/www.oxfam.org/files/bp140-planting-now-agriculture-haiti-051010-en_0.pdf

PBS Frontline (2010) *The Quake*. Documentary, 30 March. Available at http://www.pbs.org/wgbh/pages/frontline/haiti/

PBS NewsHour (2010) "Haiti's Preval Striving for Normalcy Amid Chaos", 28 January. Available at http://www.pbs.org/newshour/bb/politics/jan-june10/haiti2_01-28.html

PBS Online NewsHour (2006) "Haiti in Turmoil", 15 May. Available at http://www.pbs.org/newshour/bb/latin_america/haiti/

PrimaInfo (2007) "Batay Jodia se Batay pou Devlopman", *PrimaInfo*, 4, 15 January. Available at http://caraibesfm.com/primature/PrimaInfo_04.pdf

Rodman, Selden (1968) *The Caribbean*. New York: Hawthorn Books.

Roc, Nancy (2009) "Haiti: the Bitter Grapes of Corruption", FRIDE (Fundación par alas Relaciones Internacionales y el Diálogo Exterior) Comment, March. Available at www.fride.org/descarga/COM_Haiti_bitter_grapes_ENG_mar09.pdf

Saint-Rémy, Romuald de Lepelletier (1846) *Saint-Domingue: Études et solution nouvelle de la question Haïtienne*. Paris: Arthus Betrand.

Sheller, Mimi (2000) *Democracy after Slavery: Black Publics and Peasant Radicalism in Haiti and Jamaica*. Florida: University Press of Florida.

Taft-Morales, Maureen and Mark P. Sullivan (2008) *CRS Report for Congress. Haiti: Post-Hurricane Conditions and Assistance*. 27 October. Available at http://www.policyarchive.org/handle/10207/bitstreams/18885.pdf

UN Secretary-General (2010) *Children and Armed Conflict: Report of the Secretary-General*. New York: United Nations.

The White House (2010) "Remarks by President Obama and President Préval of the Republic of Haiti", Office of the Press Secretary, 10 March. Available at http://www.whitehouse.gov/the-press-office/remarks-president-obama-and-president-preval-republic-haiti

5

# Reforming the Haitian national police: From stabilization to consolidation

*Timothy Donais*

Passing judgement about success, failure or even progress amid "the fog of peacebuilding" is never easy (Barnett et al., 2003). It is especially difficult in the case of contemporary Haiti. The country's recent past has been marked by both hope and despair; periods of relative stability have been punctuated by episodic crises, the most dramatic of which was the devastating earthquake of January 2010 which left over 200,000 dead and more than two million displaced. As Haitians struggle to recover from the most devastating natural disaster in their history, the longer-term implications of the quake in terms of political stability, economic recovery and peacebuilding remain difficult to predict. On the security side as well, recent trends have been anything but clear. While gang violence and kidnapping, the most visible manifestations of Haitian insecurity, have been reduced in recent years, overall levels of criminality remain high, spoilers continue to threaten the tentative and uncertain advance of the rule of law and the escape of half the country's prison population in the immediate aftermath of the earthquake remains cause for concern.

Within this broader context, this chapter will assess police reform both as the cornerstone of security sector reform and as a vital component of stabilization and peacebuilding in Haiti. Several years into the second attempt to establish a professional national police force in Haiti, it remains possible, on balance, to be guardedly optimistic about the state of reforms. Recruitment and training have slowly repopulated the ranks of the Haitian National Police (HNP), and gradual if uneven progress is being

*Fixing Haiti: MINUSTAH and beyond, Heine and Thompson (eds),*
*United Nations University Press, 2011, ISBN 978-92-808-1197-1*

made in removing the corrupt and the criminal from the force. While widespread doubts about the HNP's ability to enforce the law persist, recent developments have at least eroded the widespread public sense of the force itself as a source of *insecurity* (see Refugee International, 2005). For its part, the international community appears to have learned the right lesson from its premature withdrawal of the late 1990s, and now seems committed for the long haul in Haiti. Combined, these factors have of late contributed to the emergence of a discernible if still tenuous security dividend in which even formerly no-go areas, such the notorious Port-au-Prince suburb of Cité Soleil, are now relatively safe. Balancing these hopeful signs, however, are fears that the police reform process has lost momentum, as well as the reality that while the ability of the HNP to carry out basic policing functions has improved, it remains years away from being able to tackle complex criminal problems such as the country's illicit drug trade.

In terms of both the overall security situation and the reform of the HNP, Haiti currently stands at a crossroads between stabilization and consolidation. It has been here before. In the years following the US-led restoration of President Jean-Bertrand Aristide in 1994, the initial effort to stand up the HNP produced what was seen, for a time, as "the most honest and effective component of the Haitian bureaucracy" (Dobbins, 2003: 77). In subsequent years, however, Haiti's political crisis eroded and ultimately overwhelmed the gains made in police reform, and the HNP effectively disintegrated in the lead-up to the 2004 uprising/coup which drove Aristide from power. While current circumstances differ considerably from those prevalent in the late 1990s, Haiti remains a fragile, unstable state, and the key challenge now lies in consolidating the security gains made over the past several years in order to ensure a definitive break from the country's recent cycle of violent instability.

While examining both progress made and progress still to be made with regard to transforming the HNP into a professional, impartial guardian of public security, this chapter will also locate the police reform process within the broader context of ongoing efforts to build sustainable peace in Haiti. It will suggest that, in Haiti as elsewhere, the success and sustainability of police reform processes are ultimately dependent on broader political developments, and on the willingness of key local actors to take ownership over the process. Thus, while international police reform efforts – manifest in the work of the civilian policing element of the UN Stabilization Mission in Haiti (MINUSTAH) – have without question played a role in helping Haiti emerge from its latest security crisis, the Haiti case also points to the inherent limits of externally driven security reforms as a tool of political and social transformation.

## The political context

The most striking feature of Haiti's recent past is the radically different political climates that existed before and after the country's 2006 elections. Prior to the elections, the country was in turmoil, deeply divided between pro- and anti-Aristide forces, governed by a dysfunctional and widely despised interim government and overseen by UN peacekeepers who were simultaneously viewed as incompetents and occupiers. More than 800 Haitians died in sporadic violence between September 2004 and the end of 2005, and the paramilitary-style police response to the ongoing insecurity was seen by many Haitians less as an effort to restore law and order and more as an organized assault on Aristide supporters, carried out with the tacit blessing of MINUSTAH (see Griffin, 2004). Under such conditions, developing and implementing a coherent police reform strategy proved next to impossible, while MINUSTAH itself was more focused on electoral preparations than on restoring the rule of law; MINUSTAH's first two years on the ground were, therefore, lost years as far as police reform was concerned (Mobekk, 2008).

Given the violence and despair that prevailed across Haiti in mid-2005, the transformation of the political environment following the election of René Préval to the presidency in February 2006 was nothing short of miraculous. The election of the former Aristide protégé tempered, at least somewhat, the conflict between pro- and anti-Aristide forces, while the emergence of a legitimate, democratically elected Haitian leader fundamentally changed the dynamic among the Haitian public, its government and the international community. The most visible manifestation of change was the anti-gang initiative of late 2006 which led to the arrests of some 750 gang leaders and produced near-immediate results in terms of enhanced security, particularly in the capital (see Dziedzic and Perito, 2008). In the aftermath of the campaign, Haitian attitudes towards MINUSTAH softened considerably, with polls suggesting that nearly three in four Haitians held a positive impression of the mission. In the words of Gary Pierre-Paul Charles, a prominent Haitian radio host: "MINUSTAH is now becoming part of the society, and is increasingly accepted as having an important role to play here."[1]

While there are dangers in over-estimating the impact of a single individual, it is clear that Préval, through the injection of both legitimacy and domestic political will into the current peacebuilding process, was a key factor in Haiti's post-election peace dividend. His election, and the subsequent appointment of Mario Andrésol as the director general of the HNP, also gave the international community a credible local partner in police reform. Under Andrésol, the HNP has been making a gradual comeback. Through new recruitment, the force grew from approximately 3,500 personnel in 2005 to 9,250 in March 2009, with the ultimate goal to reach 14,000 by 2011 (UNSC, 2009: 7). Some 540 officers were dismissed for corruption in the first year of Préval's mandate – although Andrésol himself has gone on record as saying that up to one-quarter of his officers are corrupt – and the process of vetting currently serving officers has finally begun.[2] While Haiti's security forces have traditionally been public oppressors rather than public defenders, there have been indications of growing public confidence in the HNP. The anti-gang campaign, for example, pushed many gang leaders out of their slum strongholds and into the countryside, and tips provided to either the HNP or MINUSTAH by local residents led to the arrest of many of those who fled. Similarly, recent polls suggest that two in three Haitians consider the HNP to be the most reliable state institution (cited in Crane et al., 2010: 63.)

Given Haiti's troubled history, and the fact that the first attempt at building a national police force failed largely as a result of circumstances beyond its control – the HNP, in the words of James Dobbins, was "slowly sucked into the culture of corruption, incompetence and politicization in which it was embedded" (Dobbins, 2003: 77) – it is impossible to underestimate the importance of political stability as a prerequisite for sustained and sustainable police reform. In this sense, the current Préval administration has provided a critical window of opportunity for reform; with a new round of elections on the horizon (in which Préval himself will not be eligible to run), and with structural reforms at least temporarily sidetracked by the massive humanitarian, clean-up and rebuilding effort required in the aftermath of the January 12 earthquake, it is unclear how long this window will remain open, or whether it has in fact already closed.

## CIVPOL and the HNP

The basic model through which international police assistance is delivered in post-conflict contexts has changed little over the past two decades. Some institutional strengthening has taken place within the UN system – particularly within the Civilian Policing (CIVPOL) Division of the Department of Peacekeeping Operations. There has also been a shift towards the deployment of formed police units, paramilitary-style formations specializing in operational tasks such as riot and crowd control; indeed, currently in Haiti more international police serve in formed police units (which play, at best, a minimal role in police reform) than in traditional CIVPOL roles. Beyond this, however, international assistance geared specifically at police reform continues to follow the so-called

SMART model, which emphasizes supporting, monitoring, advising, reporting and training; in other words, international police are neither expected nor mandated to enforce the law but rather to support local law enforcement in their efforts to do so (Hartz, 2000: 31). At its core, therefore, the CIVPOL model is based on an effort to transform both the structures and the mindsets through which policing functions are carried out in post-conflict contexts. In contrast to the military side of peacekeeping, which has become increasingly robust and assertive in recent years, "policekeeping" remains highly dependent on the cooperation and buy-in of local police counterparts. As Charles Call and William Stanley have argued, "no amount of training or institutional development will produce positive results where domestic actors are not really interested in changing the status quo" (Call and Stanley, 2001: 170).

MINUSTAH's civilian policing arm also labours under additional structural constraints endemic to multilateral civilian policing missions. At present, 49 countries contribute policing resources to MINUSTAH, and cobbling together a multiplicity of different officers, representing a multiplicity of different policing cultures, into a coherent force for reform remains an ongoing challenge. Similarly, international civilian policing has long been supply-driven rather than demand-driven, with missions forced to work with what they are given, in terms of resources and expertise, rather than with what they need. Police officers with experience in institutional reform and change management are in chronically short supply, as are francophone officers available to serve in French-speaking nations such as Haiti (Creole-speaking CIVPOL are an even rarer commodity).[3] Moreover, as David Beer, MINUSTAH's first police commissioner, has noted, "many of the contributing countries sent representatives with no more formal training or appropriate experience than the Haitian National Police they are mandated to develop" (Beer, undated). Finally, as discussed in more detail below, coordination across the range of interconnected justice and security sub-sectors remains more an aspiration than a reality; even MINUSTAH, formally an "integrated" peace support mission, has struggled to fit the various components of its mandate together in a coherent manner (Mobekk, 2008).

While police reform can be viewed both in political and in technical terms, the combination of structural constraints and on-the-ground realities has meant that police reform in Haiti, as it has unfolded over the past several years, has followed a relatively narrow, technical agenda, emphasizing training and vetting/certification. On the one hand, the precipitous decline in the HNP's human capacity in the run-up to the 2004 political crisis required, and continues to require, urgent attention. The HNP's own reform plan suggests that a minimum of 14,000 uniformed officers are required to provide basic policing duties across Haiti, although it is increasingly clear that delays in recruitment and training – which have been exacerbated by the earthquake – mean that the 2011 target date for reaching this goal can no longer be met.[4] On the other hand, in terms of both operational effectiveness and the HNP's reputation vis-à-vis the public, addressing questions of corruption within the force remains a pressing priority. The appointment of Andrésol – once described by the *Los Angeles Times* as "a rare Haitian hybrid of Frank Serpico and Eliot Ness" (Fineman, 2001) – to the post of HNP director-general was an important signal in this regard, but the hard work of purging the force of the criminal, the incompetent and the corrupt continues. While new recruits are vetted as part of basic training, the process of vetting and certifying existing officers really only began in earnest in mid-2007; as of March 2009, more than 5,400 individual files had been reviewed, or were under review, by joint MINUSTAH–HNP teams (UNSC, 2009: 8).

While getting new recruits into the HNP and simultaneously weeding bad apples out are eminently defensible priorities, and essential to the broader process of restoring the HNP's capacity to provide basic policing services, it has also produced a police reform process that is inherently inward-looking. As with past international interventions in Haiti, the civilian policing component remains "a mission within the mission," incompletely integrated into the broader peacebuilding project. Similarly, the HNP remains, in the words of a recent report by the North-South Institute (NSI), "impervious not only to its own members but also to the broader public, to civil society organizations, and to certain state institutions" (Fortin and Pierre, 2008: 27). Given the interconnected nature of the security challenges facing Haiti, overcoming this state of affairs represents a key challenge as the peacebuilding task shifts from stabilization to consolidation. Three sets of linkages – horizontal, upwards and downwards – are particularly important if police reform is to be an integrated component of a broader social and political transformation in Haiti.

First, it continues to be the case that the various components of security sector reform – including police reform, disarmament, demobilization and reintegration (DDR), and justice reform – are following largely separate tracks. Indeed, with regard to the police/justice nexus, one of the key lessons of Haiti's police reform experience of the 1990s was that successful reform requires sustained and parallel progress in all areas of the justice sector, including police, the judiciary and the penal system.[5] Unbalanced development across the justice sector can in fact be destabilizing; the ongoing crisis in Haiti's penal sector – a consequence of over-crowded prisons, a surfeit of inmates languishing in pretrial detention, and now insecure, earthquake-damaged facilities – is partly attributable to the reality that the ability of police to arrest suspects once again far outstrips the ability of the justice system to process them. While more attention has been paid to judicial and penal reform in recent years, and the Haitian government has recently adopted several key laws and a multi-year justice reform plan, the reality is that judicial reform is by its very nature more complex, politically sensitive and time-consuming than police reform. This leads to a fundamental dilemma: while the pressure to calibrate the pace of reforms to ensure balanced progress across the justice sector suggests a more coordinated, deliberate and inevitably slower approach to reforms, there continues to be pressure to push the police reform envelope as far and as fast as possible to take advantage of the current window of political stability. While there is no easy resolution to this dilemma, a basic prerequisite to addressing the coordination challenge involves confronting the ongoing animosity between the HNP and the judicial system, which has long constituted a serious obstacle to broader progress on the rule of law front in Haiti.[6]

The relationship between DDR and police reform in Haiti has been equally distant. It is now generally acknowledged that DDR in Haiti started off on the wrong foot by applying a conventional DDR process – focusing on the disarming and retraining of "combatants" – to a highly unconventional conflict, and was largely disconnected from broader rule-of-law reform efforts (Muggah, 2005). Of late, the DDR process has been reoriented and relaunched, and now focuses on a broad-based agenda of community violence reduction, aimed at strengthening the rule of law and local governance while at the same time providing opportunities for former gang members and at-risk youth.[7] While the jury is still out on whether this new approach will be any more effective than the old one, it seems clear that any sustainable programme of community violence reduction will require an effective partnership with the HNP, ideally through the renewal of community policing programmes. Such a partnership has been slow to develop, however, and ironically there may now be a danger of DDR being unsustainably ahead of the police on basic issues of community engagement.

Second, the linkages connecting the operational mechanisms of public security upwards to the executive and legislative arms of government need to be strengthened and enhanced if the promise of democratic policing is to be fulfilled in Haiti. This is especially crucial given the historic role of Haitian security forces as instruments of oppression rather than protection, and the manner in which the first incarnation of the HNP was drawn into, and decimated by, the country's broader political conflict. More generally, one of the overarching principles of security sector reform is that reforms must ensure not only the effectiveness of security structures but also their accountability. To date in Haiti, the preoccupation with achieving a basic level of operational effectiveness within the HNP has come largely at the expense of building mechanisms of democratic accountability. This means, in part, equipping parliamentary oversight bodies with the skills and resources to hold the police accountable for their actions. It also means ensuring that while the police are subject to appropriate ministerial oversight, they are also insulated from *in*appropriate political influence. While this is politically sensitive terrain, and inevitably subject to the idiosyncrasies of personality, in Haiti's case the challenge of effective political oversight is further complicated by the realities of Haitian parliamentary politics. As the NSI has noted, the Conseil Supérieur de la Police Nationale, which includes the prime minister and other key public security ministers and has direct responsibilities for HNP oversight, is not operational, while senate oversight commissions are understaffed and over-tasked. At the same time, the fact that no legal mechanism exists through which Haitian parliamentarians can access government files and documents seriously undermines their ability to carry out effective oversight (Fortin and Pierre, 2008: 22–23). While some bilateral initiatives, such as the four-year Haiti Parliamentary Support Project, implemented by Canada's Parliamentary Centre, are focusing on legislative capacity-building,[8] a much more concerted effort is needed to meet the challenges of democratic security governance in Haiti.

Third, any sustainable policing strategy for Haiti must take seriously the challenge of transforming the climate of fear, suspicion and mistrust that has long characterized police–society relations in Haiti. For the vast majority of Haitian citizens, the presence of police in their communities has been a source of dread rather than comfort. In the current climate, transforming police–society relations depends in large part on operational effectiveness: the HNP's ability to demonstrably enhance public security, while at the same time addressing corruption and criminality within its own ranks, would go a long way to unsettling long-standing and well-justified public perceptions about what the police do and whose interests they serve. Ideally, however, placing police–society relations on a different foundation will also require at least some blurring of the line separating the police officer as the agent of security and the citizen as the object to be secured. Not only should the police be more active in, and engaged with, the communities they serve, but citizens need to see themselves as participants when it comes to the provision of public security. What is needed, in other words, is a model of community policing that speaks directly to the particular security concerns of Haitian communities.

Community policing is not a new concept in the Haitian context, and was incorporated into the first HNP development effort in the 1990s. However, in the face of limited international support and deteriorating political conditions, community policing never really got off the ground (Davis et al., 2003: 293); indeed, the failure of these first tentative efforts may have done little more than generate scepticism among Haitians and internationals alike about the applicability of generic community policing models in the Haitian context. Nevertheless, a commitment to community policing reappears in the 2006 HNP Reform plan, and elements of community policing are currently being reintroduced. However, as the International Crisis Group has noted, the absence of a nationwide strategy for community policing has meant that recent efforts to strengthen police–community links have been piecemeal, uncoordinated, and under-resourced and therefore of questionable utility and sustainability (International Crisis Group, 2008: 15). While community policing is no panacea for overcoming legacies of distrust between providers and recipients of policing service, it does offer at least the promise of improving community–police relations and changing public perceptions about the police and vice versa (Davis et al., 2003: 299). In Haiti's case, using community policing as a mechanism for social cohesion has yet to be seriously attempted.

## Achieving local ownership

In the context of the broader transition from stabilization to consolidation, there is no avoiding the issue of local ownership. From its origins in international development thinking, the notion of local ownership has in recent years come to occupy an increasingly prominent role in discussions of both peacebuilding and security sector reform. The growing emphasis on the agency of local actors has emerged in large part as a consequence of the underwhelming results of outside-in, top-down reform processes which view local actors and structures as targets *of* reform rather than partners *in* reform. Indeed, the recent history of Haiti itself provides ample empirical evidence of the inherent limits on the ability of international actors to transform troubled states into stable liberal democracies.

While the notion of local ownership remains contested and ambiguous – both in terms of the identity of "the locals" and the meanings of "ownership" – the underlying premise is that reform processes lacking meaningful local involvement are unlikely to be sustainable. At issue, of course, is how meaningful such involvement needs to be. Laurie Nathan, for example, argues that local ownership means that reform processes must be "designed, managed and implemented by local rather than international actors" (Nathan, 2007: 4). Others, including Simon Chesterman, tend to equate local ownership with local "buy-in," suggesting that while local ownership may be a key goal of reform processes – especially in post-conflict transitions – it cannot realistically be the means through which reform goals are achieved (Chesterman, 2007: 7). While there are important differences between the view that local actors should drive the reform process from conception to implementation and the contrasting view that local ownership is about encouraging, socializing or even coercing local actors to embrace externally defined means and ends, both positions accept – whether implicitly or explicitly – that local ownership matters to the long-term success of reform.[9]

In Haiti, three categories of local owner are of particular relevance to police reform: political elites, the police themselves and civil society. While there have been signs of progress towards local ownership in recent years, it is also clear that police reform processes in Haiti have yet to reach the point where they could be self-sustaining in the absence of ongoing international support.

As noted above, the election of Préval and the subsequent appointment of Mario Andrésol to the post of HNP director general were crucial factors in making recent progress on police reform possible. Both men appear committed to a model of professional, public-service policing in Haiti, and have been willing to work closely with the international presence – MINUSTAH in particular – to move the process forward. At the same time, and in contrast to the interim government period in which MINUSTAH was viewed as an occupying force and interim Prime Minister Gérard Latortue as a puppet of Washington, the emergence of a democratically elected, reform-oriented government has put a Haitian face on the police reform process that has significantly enhanced its domestic legitimacy. More generally, the Préval presidency lowered the political temperature in Haiti and enabled – at least until 2008, when the country was buffeted by a series of crises, including food riots, serial hurricanes and an extended and paralysing prime ministerial crisis – a shift from short-term crisis management to longer-term structural reform. While these have been positive developments with regard to local ownership, the extent to which elite ownership, both of police reform and of the stabilization process more generally, remains individualized rather than institutionalized remains a cause for concern as Haiti heads into a new electoral cycle.

While elite ownership over police reform is crucial, so too is fostering a culture of professionalism across the entire HNP. This is an enormous, long-term challenge, particularly in a country such as Haiti where a position in the public sector has long been viewed primarily as an opportunity for private gain. It has also become clear, however, that there are inherent limits on the capacity of outsiders to instil a professional policing ethos, either through basic training or ongoing in-service mentoring. The experience of the first HNP development effort underscored these limits, as externally driven attempts to transfer norms across the international–local divide foundered on the reality that for individual officers abstract policing principles mattered far less than the exigencies and opportunities of everyday policing in Haiti. In other words, no amount of training and mentoring in democratic policing principles can fully inoculate individual officers against the temptations of corruption and criminality, particularly in a broader context of weak oversight and generalized impunity.

If the development of a locally owned culture of democratic policing is almost necessarily a long-term process, in which the interplay among policing, politics and society at the domestic level matters more than the international–domestic dynamic, a more viable medium-term strategy might focus on modifying incentive structures through developing and strengthening accountability mechanisms. While the importance of such mechanisms between police and the political system and between police and society has already been noted, no less crucial are the HNP's own internal accountability mechanisms. The joint HNP–MINUSTAH vetting process is, for the moment, the centrepiece of the accountability effort; while the unfolding process is removing some of the HNP's bad apples, there is, as noted in reports by both the International Crisis Group and the North-South Institute, ongoing scepticism about whether the process is sufficiently thorough, comprehensive or transparent (International Crisis Group, 2008: 9; Fortin and Pierre, 2008:18–19). On the other hand, the HNP's Office of the Inspector General has shown some promise as a locus around which a culture of accountability within the HNP can be developed and promoted (Mobekk, 2008: 13). Concurrently, however, much work remains to be done to institutionalize mechanisms of everyday accountability and oversight within the HNP. One ongoing challenge in this regard is the HNP's hourglass-shaped organizational structure, as the absence of a cadre of experienced middle-level managers presents a key obstacle in achieving adequate control, supervision and oversight over what remains an inexperienced force operating in a volatile environment.[10] More generally, in the context of Haitian policing the core work of institution-building must include a local ownership strategy focused on supporting and insulating key reformers located at strategic positions within the HNP hierarchy.

Finally, in a troubled and fragile society such as Haiti's, the argument that police reform is far too important to be left in the hands of the police themselves remains compelling. It is cause for concern, therefore, that to date the bulk of the police reform process has been about police reforming police, largely in isolation from the communities they are supposed to serve. If local ownership of police reform – and of policing more generally – is to be taken seriously, then the focus must not be solely on the providers of security but on the consumers of security as well. As noted above, the reinvigoration of community policing may provide part of the answer to the broader problem of police–community relations, at least insofar as it encourages dialogue between police and citizens and gives communities and their representatives a voice in how public security is delivered. However, there is a danger in equating community policing with community ownership, particularly if the former is conceived narrowly in terms of co-opting communities into supporting a top-down law-and-order agenda, in which citizens are valued more as informers than interlocutors.

It is, of course, unsurprising that civil society has to date played at best a marginal role in Haiti's police reform process. The priority given to restoring basic policing capacity, the country's historically strained relations between police and civil society, and the fact that CIVPOL as an institution has tended to define police reform narrowly have all worked against the view that police reform in Haiti is as much about social repair as about law and order. Nevertheless, as Marina Caparini has noted, "the involvement of civil society groups is vital to the success of police reform and democratic policing because they serve to link the police to the broader community" (Caparini, 2004: 57). Indeed, Haitian civil society as a whole represents a potentially crucial source of domestic support for the broader vision of a professional, democratically accountable and public-service oriented national police force. As police reform in Haiti continues to unfold, therefore, it makes sense for the international community to seek out and support allies within Haitian civil society, both in terms of promoting local ownership and in support of the even longer-term goal of democratizing public security provision.

## Security after the earthquake

The magnitude-7.0 earthquake that levelled large parts of Port-au-Prince and the surrounding region on the afternoon of 12 January 2010 plunged Haiti back into crisis in a matter of seconds, and represented, in the words of the UN's Nigel Fisher, "a disaster of a magnitude that would have set any country reeling" (United Nations, 2010: 3). With hundreds of thousands killed, and nearly one in four Haitians displaced, the Port-au-Prince region immediately became the site of the world's worst humanitarian crisis.

While the availability and provision of food, water and shelter were the immediate preoccupations of both survivors and aid providers in the immediate aftermath of the disaster, there were also genuine fears about the impact of the earthquake on the broader security situation. Despite some predictions of chaos and anarchy, however, the security situation in the quake zone in the days and weeks following the disaster was relatively calm, and the overwhelming impression of observers on the ground was that Haitians were weathering the crisis with dignity, equanimity and patience (Pilger, 2010: 20; Dupuy, 2010: 198). Incidents of theft – particularly of food and water – emerged as a security issue in the quake's aftermath, while the number of sexual assaults, especially within displaced persons' camps, also increased. Potentially more destabilizing, however, was the fact that the earthquake liberated – directly or indirectly – more than 4,000 prisoners, representing half of the country's prison population. Among the escapees were an estimated 300–500 gang members, including many of those rounded up as part of the anti-gang initiative of late 2006 (ICG, 2010: 9). In recent months, there have been disturbing signs that some of the more notorious Haitian gangs are beginning to reorganize in the devastated landscape of Port-au-Prince (Roig-Franzia, 2010).

From the perspective of security provision, the HNP was also a victim of the earthquake, losing 77 officers, while the UN lost more than 100 personnel. Infrastructure, including police stations, judicial buildings and prisons, was also seriously affected by the quake; while the police training school survived, it was quickly reassigned as the temporary home of the Haitian Parliament. Despite the losses, the HNP was a visible presence on the streets of Port-au-Prince in the immediate aftermath of the earthquake (even though the magnitude of the disaster meant the police could not be everywhere they were needed), while the United Nations quickly authorized an additional 3,500 troops and CIVPOL to help shore up the security situation.

As of mid-2010, despite growing frustration among many Haitians who have seen few concrete manifestations of the billions of dollars of aid and reconstruction assistance they were promised as part of the initial outpouring of international solidarity, the political situation has stabilized to the extent that the word "reform" is now back on the political agenda in Haiti. At the New York donors' conference in March 2010, the Haitian government presented its Action Plan for National Recovery and Development, which attempts to chart a path from disaster response to a renewal of longer-term structural reform efforts. On the security and justice side, the plan lists immediate priorities as restoring the operational capacity of security and justice agencies, providing quake-affected communities (including those hosting displaced populations) with access to justice and security and – somewhat more ambiguously – creating "favourable conditions" for the administration of justice and security in the post-crisis period (Government of Haiti, 2010: 45). In short, while the earthquake represented both a major humanitarian crisis and a definite setback to long-term stabilization efforts, the struggle to consolidate the rule of law in Haiti continues. As before, the success of this effort depends in large part on both social stability and a favourable political climate. Unlike the prequake period, however, institutional reforms will now have to compete for both resources and attention with the bricks-and-mortar reconstruction effort, and will eventually have to be tailored to any longer-term strategy aimed at decentralizing government administration and services outside of Port-au-Prince (Crane et al., 2010: 68).

## Conclusion

Police reform in Haiti remains very much a work in progress. While there have undoubtedly been advances since the dark days of the 2004–2006 interim administration, and the HNP has been at least partially rehabilitated as the cornerstone of Haiti's security sector, the reform process is not yet self-sustaining and the force's commitment to policing as a public service remains to be proven. More worryingly, perhaps, the reform process appears to have lost momentum of late, as a result, at least in part, to the combination of natural disaster and political crisis: serious concerns have emerged about the rate at which the HNP's basic human capital is being replenished, and about the viability of the process meant to rid the force of those demonstrably unfit for duty. Beyond these basics, much remains to be done to both broaden and deepen progress made thus far. In a 2008 report, the International Crisis Group outlined a laundry list of reforms – in areas ranging from border control to witness protection to intelligence gathering to improving both gender awareness and gender balance – which highlights both the long-term nature of the HNP development project and the ongoing gap between needs and resources (International Crisis Group, 2008: 7–11). The continued focus on the restoration of "basic" policing capacity also underlines how far the HNP remains from being capable of addressing Haiti's most serious and complex security challenges, from marginalizing criminal gangs to reining in the organized networks seeking to solidify Haiti's position as a key transhipment point for illegal narcotics.

At the same time, policing can never be fully insulated from broader political dynamics, and on this dimension the next two years may prove crucial. The year 2008 saw the end of the Préval honeymoon, which was characterized by an extended window of political stability in which longer-term structural reforms, rather than short-term crisis management, became possible. The serial crises of 2008 sent shockwaves through a still-fragile political system, which was still recovering its equilibrium when the January 2010 earthquake struck. It also remains unclear whether sufficient progress has been made on the police reform file to insulate the HNP from a renewed period of political turbulence. Even more fundamental questions persist about the role of the HNP as a key interface between state and citizen: while the international community continues to promote a democratically accountable, public-service oriented vision of policing for Haiti, the alternative in an environment of renewed instability may be a form of policing as "liddism", with the HNP increasingly called upon to suppress chronic social unrest produced by a deeply inegalitarian society. In short, Haiti's socio-political and economic foundations remain profoundly unstable, and the possibility that the entire post-Aristide stabilization process will unravel cannot yet be ruled out.

Precisely because Haiti's future remains uncertain, this chapter has argued that the progress that has been made towards stabilizing the security situation in recent years must now be consolidated and made self-sustaining, in order to ensure that renewed political crisis does not tip over into a more generalized security crisis. While international support will continue to be needed for years in order to solidify the basic foundations of policing in Haiti – a well-trained, disciplined, sufficiently resourced force operating within a coherent institutional framework tailored to the specificities of the country's public security challenges – this chapter has also argued that policing must also be seen as one component of a broader and integrated process of security sector reform. Restoring basic policing capacity is crucial, but so too is working with Haiti's government to ensure that the HNP is both subject to appropriate political oversight and shielded from inappropriate political interference; that the broader justice system – including police, prosecutors and judges – functions as a coherent whole; and that police–society relations are progressively transformed from a relationship of mutual animosity to one of mutual support. Such tasks extend far beyond the current scope of CIV-POL activities; addressing them will therefore require not only greater cross-sectoral coordination within MINUSTAH – giving real meaning, in other words, to the concept of an "integrated mission" – but also a more coherent and comprehensive rule-of-law/security sector strategy on the part of the broader international community. After 12 January, justice and rule of law reform will also have to be located within the broader context of post-disaster reconstruction and the widespread rehabilitation of basic government services.

Consolidating security improvements in Haiti will also require greater attentiveness to the challenge of local ownership. While the local ownership debate exposes serious tensions between outside-in and inside-out visions of reform, on basic questions of security the gap between international and domestic visions of reform has in fact been closing in recent years. Not only have the priorities of the Préval government been more or less aligned with those of the international community, but few dispute the importance of strengthening the HNP as the cornerstone of Haiti's security sector. As ActionAid Haiti reported in 2006, "There is no question in Haitian civil society or the international community that a stable sustainable PNH [the HNP's French acronym] needs to be established and is essential for the future security and stability of Haiti" (Mobekk, 2008:13). That said, questions remain about the depth of the commitment among Haiti's political class to comprehensive police reform, as well as about the extent to which a culture of professionalism and public service is beginning to take hold within the HNP itself. While there are, almost by definition, limits on the ability of outsiders to foster local ownership, the international community can and should accelerate efforts to provide strategic support to key reform-minded constituencies both within and outside the HNP in the name of advancing sustainable local ownership.

There are, ultimately, no shortcuts to the manifold challenges of police reform and public security in Haiti. Rebuilding the Haitian National Police will continue to require both the resources and the political will of the international community for years to come, and donor fatigue may yet risk the sustainability of the broader police reform enterprise. Success or failure, however, will depend on much more than sheer international persistence. It will depend on the pace of post-earthquake recovery, on whether a climate of relative political stability holds through Haiti's next electoral cycle and even more profoundly on the achievement of a new social contract between Haitians and their government which offers at least the promise of alleviating the misery in which the majority of Haitians continue to live. It will depend as well on whether police reform can be effectively integrated into a long-term rule-of-law strategy that can demonstrably deliver both security and justice to a critical mass of the population. And it will depend, finally, on whether both Haitians and the broader international community take seriously the question of how policing fits into the broader relationship among security, development and democracy.

## Notes

1. Author interview, Port-au-Prince, June 2007.
2. Author interview with Mario Andrésol, HNP director-general, Port-au-Prince, June 2007.
3. In 2006, for example, only 38 per cent of CIVPOL officers in Haiti were French-speaking; see Mobekk (2006).
4. Haiti's recent Action Plan for National Recovery and Development has revised these numbers slightly; the new goal is for the HNP to comprise 16,000 police officers by 2015; see Government of Haiti (2010: 45).
5. For a broader discussion of the police–justice nexus in Haiti, see Donais (2005).
6. For more details on the difficult relationship between the HNP and the broader Haitian justice system, see Fortin and Pierre (2008: 20–22).

7. Information on Haiti's revised DDR process is available on the website of the UN's Disarmament, Demobilization and Reintegration Resource Centre at: http://www.unddr.org/countryprogrammes.php?c=80
8. More information on this project is available at: http://www.parlcent.ca/americas/haiti_e.php
9. For a broader discussion of the local ownership debate in the context of peacebuilding, see Donais (2009).
10. Author interview with Mario Andrésol, HNP director-general, Port-au-Prince, June 2007.

## REFERENCES

Beer, David (undated) "Complex Mandate: The Multifaceted Role of International Policing". Available at http://www.vanguardcanada.com/ComplexMandateBeer

Call, Charles T. and William Stanley (2001) "Protecting the People: Public Security Choices After Civil Wars", *Global Governance*, 7: 151–172.

Caparini, Marina (2004) "The Relevance of Civil Society: Response to 'Security Sector Reform in Developing and Transitional Countries'", in Clem McCartney, Martina Fischer and Oliver Wils (eds), *Security Sector Reform: Potentials and Challenges for Conflict Transformation*. Berlin: Berghof Center for Constructive Conflict Management, pp. 53–61. Available at http://www.berghof-handbook.net/uploads/download/dialogue2_ssr_complete.pdf

Chesterman, Simon (2007) "Ownership in Theory and in Practice: Transfer of Authority in UN Statebuilding Operations", *Journal of Intervention and Statebuilding*, 1(1): 3–26.

Crane, Keith, James Dobbins, Laurel E. Miller, Charles P. Ries, Christopher S. Chivvis, Marla C. Haims, Marco Overhaus, Heather Lee Schwartz and Elizabeth Wilke (2010) *Building a More Resilient Haitian State*. Santa Monica: Rand Corporation.

Davis, Robert, Nicole Henderson and Cybele Merrick (2003) "Community Policing: Variations on the Western Model in the Developing World", *Police Practice and Research*, 4(3): 285–300.

Dobbins, James (2003) *America's Role in Nation Building: From Germany to Iraq*. Santa Monica: Rand.

Donais, Timothy (2005) "Back to Square One: The Politics of Police Reform in Haiti", *Civil Wars*, 7(3): 270–287.

Donais, Timothy (2009) "Empowerment or Imposition: Dilemmas of Local Ownership in Post-Conflict Peacebuilding Processes", *Peace and Change*, 34(1): 3–26.

Dupuy, Alex (2010) "Commentary: Beyond the Earthquake – A Wake-Up Call for Haiti", *Latin American Perspectives*, 37(3): 195–204.

Dziedzic, Michael and Robert Perito (2008) "Haiti: Confronting the Gangs of Port-au-Prince", United States Institute of Peace, Washington, DC, Special Report, 208, September. Available at http://www.usip.org/files/resources/sr208.pdf

Fineman, Mark (2001) "Aristide Foes Decry Lawman's Arrest", *Los Angeles Times*, 24 August, p. A-1.

Fortin, Isabelle and Yves-François Pierre (2008) *Haïti et la reforme de la police nationale d'Haïti*. Ottawa: North-South Institute. Available at http://www.nsi-ins.ca/fran/pdf/INS%20-%20Haiti%20et%20la%20reforme%20de%20la%20PNH.pdf

Government of Haiti (2010) *Action Plan for National Recovery and Development of Haiti*. Port-au-Prince: Government of Haiti. Available at http://haiticonference.org/Haiti_Action_Plan_ENG.pdf

Griffin, Thomas (2004) *Haiti – Human Rights Investigation: November 11–21, 2004*. Coral Gables, FL: Center for the Study of Human Rights, University of Miami School of Law. Available at http://www.lakounewyork.com/rap%F2%20Miami%20law%20school%20human%20rights%20stotzky-griffin.pdf

Hartz, Halvor (2000) "CIVPOL: The UN Instrument for Police Reform", in Tor Tanke Holm and Espen Barth Eide (eds), *Peacebuilding and Police Reform*. London: Frank Cass, pp. 27–42.

International Crisis Group (2008) "Reforming Haiti's Security Sector", ICG Latin America/Caribbean Report, 28, 18 September. Available at http://www.crisisgroup.org/home/index.cfm?id=5681&l=1

Mobekk, Eirin (2006) *MINUSTAH: DDR and Police, Judicial and Correctional Reform in Haiti: Recommendations for Change*. London: Action Aid, 14 July. Available at http://www.actionaid.org/docs/actionaid%20minustah%20haiti%20report.pdf

Mobekk, Eirin (2008) "MINUSTAH and the Need for a Context-Specific Strategy: The Case of Haiti", in Heiner Hanggi and Vincenza Scherrer (eds), *Security Sector Reform and UN Integrated Missions: Experience from Burundi, the Democratic Republic of Congo, Haiti and Kosovo*. Geneva: LIT Verlag and the Centre for Democratic Control of Armed Forces, pp. 113–168.

Muggah, Robert (2005) *Securing Haiti's Transition: Reviewing Human Security and the Prospects for Disarmament, Demobilization and Reintegration*. Geneva: Small Arms Survey.

Nathan, Laurie (2007) *No Ownership, No Commitment: A Guide to Local Ownership of Security Sector Reform*. Birmingham: University of Birmingham Press.

Pilger, John (2010) "The Kidnapping of Haiti", *New Statesman*, 1 February, p. 20.

Refugee International (2005) "UN Civilian Police Require Executive Authority", Press release, 14 March. Available at http://www.reliefweb.int/rw/RWB.NSF/db900SID/HMYT-6AGUHC?OpenDocument&rc=2&emid=ACOS-635P2K

Roig-Franzia, Manuel (2010) "Haiti's Most-Wanted on the Loose after Quake", *Washington Post*, 9 April, p. A10.

United Nations (2010) *Haiti: 6 months after. . . .* Port-au-Prince: United Nations. Available at http://www.un.org/en/peacekeeping/missions/minustah/documents/6_months_after_commemoration.pdf

UNSC (2009) *Report of the Secretary-General on the United Nations Stabilization Mission in Haiti*. United Nations Security Council, S/2009/129, 6 March.

# Part II

# The United Nations at work

# 6

# The "MINUSTAH experience"

*Gerard Le Chevallier*

## International engagement and Haiti's governance challenges since 1989

The first direct international engagement began in 1993 in response to the military coup d'état led by General Raoul Cédras and the Front pour l'Avancement et le Progrès d'Haiti (Front for the Advancement of Progress in Haiti, FRAPH) against the then Haitian president Jean Bertrand Aristide (see Dupuy, 2007). Following the establishment of the joint United Nations/Organization of American States (OAS) Civilian Mission to Haiti (MICIVIH) to monitor the human rights situation in 1993, the UN Security Council established a United Nations peacekeeping operation – the United Nations Mission in Haiti (UNMIH) at the end of 1994. The mandate of the operation was to assist the democratic government of Haiti in fulfilling its responsibilities in connection with: first, sustaining the secure and stable environment that was established by UNMIH, including providing protection for international personnel and key installations; and second, the professionalization of the Haitian armed forces and the creation of a separate police force (see United Nations, 1996). UNMIH was also mandated to assist the legitimate constitutional authorities of Haiti in establishing an environment conducive to the organization of free and fair legislative elections, to be called by those authorities. Following the 1995 elections in Haiti, UNMIH was gradually disengaged and replaced from 1996 to 2000 by what were essentially police training and monitoring operations (UNSMIH, UNTMIH,

*Fixing Haiti: MINUSTAH and beyond, Heine and Thompson (eds),*
*United Nations University Press, 2011, ISBN 978-92-808-1197-1*

MIPONUH), since one of President Aristide's first initiatives upon returning to office was the dissolution of the army.

At the time, observers considered UNMIH, and the subsequent police training missions, to have been peacekeeping successes. And they certainly were, as they accomplished the immediate tasks at hand: namely to help restore the legitimate civilian authorities of the country, assist in the conduct of free and fair elections, and lay the foundations of a civilian police force, the first such in Haitian history. Yet in 2004, less than 10 years later, political instability and violence prompted a new United Nations peacekeeping mission to Haiti, the United Nations Stabilization Mission in Haiti (MINUSTAH).

Short-term operations will not be sufficient to address the many challenges in Haiti. In a joint press conference with President Préval in Haiti in 2006, former Secretary-General Kofi Annan (2006) stated: "nation-building is a long term proposition. It does take time, it is hard it is difficult and it requires everyone to play his or her part." MINUSTAH's fundamental goal is to ensure that it is the last peacekeeping operation in Haiti. In order to do so, we have to address the root causes of Haiti's instability by promoting democratic governance, strengthening the capacity of state institutions and helping Haiti begin a genuine economic recovery process. Clearly, MINUSTAH cannot do this alone – a closely coordinated approach with the rest of the United Nations organizations and other donors is crucial.

We have reasons to be optimistic in Haiti; after all, its problem is a political conflict, which has no ethnic, religious or territorial dimensions. It is also a small country whose neighbours, in a relatively rich hemisphere, wish to assist it in achieving a durable stability. It is also only one-and-a-half hours away by airplane from the United States, still the biggest market in the world. So it should be possible to "fix" Haiti. However, in order to do so, the international community must be willing to provide the necessary resources and make a long-term, concerted and coordinated commitment. In discussions in New York with the member states and donor countries, I have tried to get everyone to understand that nation-building is a long-term proposition. It does take time, it is hard, it is difficult and it requires everyone to play his or her part. Various stakeholders and operations need to work in partnership: the government, the private sector, civil society and all of us. Haitians, both men and women, can now make individual contributions towards the rebuilding of this nation. Still, the obvious question before the international community at large was and still is: what went wrong with our earlier peacekeeping efforts? What is it that MINUSTAH, within that partnership, needs to do in order to help anchor Haiti on the way to lasting stability and thus obviate the need for a new peacekeeping operation in the future?

## What has changed since 1993 to 1996, and what are the current challenges?

*The assertion of Latin America on the global stage*

North American and European engagement in Haiti has traditionally been strong for a variety of historical, geographical and political reasons. The recent strong engagement of Latin America in Haiti, which is explored in Chapter 10 in this volume, is a welcome change. It sets a fine example and precedent for South–South cooperation on peace and security issues. It gives a broader base to international engagement in Haiti, thus enhancing its effectiveness and legitimacy. In this regard, it is critical for the success of Haiti – and therefore of MINUSTAH – that Latin American countries remain engaged and committed to seeing through the current stability consolidation process in Haiti. And, one cannot talk about Haiti and the engagement of the Americas without mentioning the longstanding and significant contribution of the Organization of American States (OAS). The OAS has been a partner of choice for the United Nations in Haiti since the early 1990s. Cooperation between the United Nations and the OAS in Haiti needs to continue and build on the complementarities of the two organizations.

*Haiti has changed*

As the chapters by Fatton Jr. and Manigat demonstrate, the 1987 Haitian constitution was designed to prevent Haiti from returning to a dictatorship through the establishment of a complicated political system which includes an extensively representative series of local councils and assemblies. To date, 22 years after it was adopted, successive governments have been unable to implement the political system as designed. As demonstrated in a 2009 exchange between President René Préval and US Secretary of State Hillary Clinton, discussions today are finally focused on how Haitians themselves must commit to building efficient, transparent and self-sustainable institutions, and are coming to terms with the need to amend the constitution (US Department of State, 2009).

The political disturbances of April 2008, the subsequent ousting of the government and the five months of political impasse over its replacement, combined with the disaster caused by four consecutive tropical storms and hurricanes, have served as a strong wake-up call to both the Haitian government and the international community to examine how to provide for the critical needs of the Haitian population, and put the country on the track to sustainable development. The new government is struggling to become operational. It needs and is welcoming support.

Indeed, the devastation by the hurricanes was extensive: hundreds died, close to 170,000 families (almost a million persons, including 300,000 children) had no access to food and water, more than 400 schools were damaged or destroyed as well as key infrastructure such as bridges (Delva, 2008). A good part of the autumn harvest was lost.

## Peacekeeping has changed

Since the 2000 "Brahimi report" (United Nations, 2000), United Nations peacekeeping has evolved in two particular interrelated areas that are directly relevant to the current engagement in Haiti: (1) consolidating stability in post-conflict situations by not disengaging too soon following elections; and (2) more systemic and holistic efforts for rule-of-law sector reform – police, judiciary and penal. In short, an "exit strategy" for international peacekeeping has evolved; the successful holding of elections is no longer necessarily the milestone that triggers disengagement.

On the first point, elections took place in Haiti in 2006, but, unlike with UNMIH in 1996, the Security Council did not choose to disengage MINUSTAH but rather to maintain it to undertake stability consolidation tasks. In late 2008, MINUSTAH stood roughly at the same strength as in 2006, and in his latest report to the Security Council, the secretary-general recommended that MINUSTAH's current strength and configuration be preserved during the next mandate period, which began in mid-October following the adoption of Security Council Resolution 1840, which authorized renewing the mission for a period of one year with the possibility of subsequent renewals after 15 October 2009 (UNSC, 2008a; see also, UNSC, 2008b).

MINUSTAH's mandate is large in scope. It includes support for the political process and elections; support for the maintenance of public safety and order through operational support to the Haitian National Police; support for police, justice and penal sector development; assistance with strengthening state institutions (especially outside of the capital, including border management); and help in coordinating the activities of the United Nations organizations in Haiti. MINUSTAH is currently comprised of 7,060 military personnel from 18 countries, and 2,091 police officers from 39 countries. The mission has 522 international civilians (of whom 34 per cent are female), 225 United Nations Volunteers and 1,206 national employees. Its annual budget for 2007–2008 stood at US$535 million. Its budget for 2008–2009 was US$601 million (MINUSTAH, 2010).

On the second issue, namely strengthening the criminal justice system, support for rule of law reform is one of the cornerstones of MINUSTAH's mandate. The mission supports national authorities in reforming and building the capacity of the Haitian police, judiciary and penal system, following reform plans that have been developed by the Haitian government with support from the international community. The task at hand is large. On the issue of police reform (see Chapter 5 in this volume), the challenge is for MINUSTAH to assist in vetting and training 14,000 police officers by 2011, of whom 8,500 had already been trained by the autumn of 2008; most specialists agree that 14,000 is the minimum number of officers required for the Haitian police to undertake "essential policing duties". Similarly, with respect to judicial reform, the challenge is to ensure the independence of the justice system and build its capacity. In this regard, much progress has been achieved since 2004: the Haitian Parliament has adopted three essential laws on the independence of the judiciary. The establishment of the Superior Council of the Judiciary has almost been completed. The Magistrates School has been reopened and magistrate training resumed in August 2008 for the first time since 2004, with refresher training for 30 justices of the peace; a second batch of 30 judges is currently under training. The challenges, however, remain daunting: the country needs 350 additional magistrates beyond the current 700, as well as the establishment of 160 new courts, in order for the judiciary to have an adequate coverage of the national territory. Finally, on reform of the prison system, the challenges are to improve the Haitian prison infrastructure, procure the necessary equipment, train prison personnel and enhance the treatment the prisoners. In 2008, MINUSTAH supported the training of 227 new Haitian prison officers, bringing the staffing of the penal system to 752, in addition to providing day-to-day technical advice and support in most of the country's prisons. Improvements in the police and justice sectors are critical for progress in the penal sector as 83 per cent of the current inmates in Haiti are in pretrial detention, and overcrowding in the prisons is severe.

Kidnappings represent a poignant example of the challenges associated with Haitian rule-of-law reform. After a sharp decline in 2006 and 2007, kidnappings rose in 2008, albeit not to the previous levels reached in 2006. From 1 January to 31 August 2008, 162 cases of kidnapping were registered in Haiti for an average of about 20 cases per month (see International Crisis Group, 2007). Comparisons with other countries from the region suggest that there are relatively lower levels of kidnappings in Haiti than elsewhere. Yet, kidnappings are an issue that resonates with the Haitian public and cannot be ignored, especially since they are relatively recent. Higher levels of kidnappings create a feeling of impunity for perpetrators, allow criminal gangs to diversify their sources of income and undermine public confidence in the capacity of the state (and also of MINUSTAH) to maintain a climate of security and safety. Curbing kidnappings is therefore likely to be seen by parts of the Haitian public as a critical test for the effectiveness of police and justice reforms in Haiti.

In order for rule-of-law reforms to be successful, it is crucial to ensure their sustainability in the long term. Increasing the capacity of the police, justice and prison systems requires, at the same time, increasing the capacity of the state to collect revenue, as well as to disburse it in an efficient way. One initiative that MINUSTAH is working on is collaboration with national authorities to build a border management capacity with two objectives: to curb smuggling and thus increase government revenue, and to curb trafficking of illicit goods, such as drugs and weapons (see UNSC, 2009).

## The "missing link": Transition from peacekeeping/peacebuilding to development or to "securing development"

### *The socio-economic dilemma or "securing development"*

Lasting stability cannot take root without a meaningful improvement in the living conditions of the population. The public is much more likely to support a reform process that it associates with improvement to its everyday life. Similarly, it is likely to be indifferent, or even hostile, to a reform process that it perceives as perpetuating extreme poverty and the status quo, or "more of the same". A disgruntled public provides fertile ground to spoilers with hidden agendas designed to undermine efforts to bring stability to a country by manipulating otherwise legitimate and understandable social demands.

MINUSTAH and Haiti recently experienced the linkage between stabilization efforts and socio-economic conditions. Indeed, a rising cost of living in Haiti owing to soaring food and fuel prices on international markets caused social unrest in April 2008 that led to the ousting of Prime Minister Alexis's government by Parliament (Delva and Loney, 2008). The resulting impasse over the designation of a new prime minister, which lasted almost five months, brought to a halt vital civil service reforms, and slowed down equally critical legislative and rule-of-law reforms. Much needed funding was also lost.

The transition from short-term stabilization to long-term stability and development is a key challenge for the national authorities and the international community in Haiti, as in many other post-conflict situations. As World Bank President Robert Zoellick (2008) noted in a speech that he delivered on conflict and development:

These situations require looking beyond the analytics of development – to a different framework of building security, legitimacy, governance, and economy.

This is not security as usual, or development as usual. Nor is it about what we have come to think of as peacebuilding or peacekeeping. This is about Securing Development – bringing security and development together first to smooth the transition from conflict to peace and then to embed stability so that development can take hold over a decade and beyond. Only by securing development can we put down roots deep enough to break the cycle of fragility and violence.

Within that context, there are five pressing factors that are impeding the transition from security (or short-term stabilization) to development and lasting stability in Haiti.

## Pressing factors for lasting stability and development

The first is the need for sustained efforts at the national level. Lasting stability and development require long-term efforts that go beyond the terms of a single national legislature or of a single president. The various sectors of Haitian society should thus establish some sort of stability or governance pact based on agreed upon and shared national objectives and priorities that cut across party lines and electoral cycles. Such a pact would provide the necessary vision and stability, improve the efficiency of international aid and avoid the "starting all over" syndrome following each electoral cycle, which, in itself, is a form of instability.

The second is a greater recognition that international development assistance alone cannot bring about the socio-economic improvements that Haitian society needs. It is only direct investment by the private sector, both national and foreign, that can create lasting development and generate the employment and income that Haitians need. Creating an environment conducive to investment, however, requires a deliberate commitment on the part of the state to provide security to the populace, to strengthen the rule of law and to make foreign markets more attractive and viable by seeking preferential trade agreements for Haitian producers. It also requires strengthening the state's capacity to disburse funds and implement projects, especially in public infrastructure development.

The third is that lasting stability and development require long-term efforts and solutions, but it is difficult to support long-term solutions with one-year budgets. Most of the international assistance is committed on an annual basis; in some cases, it is planned over two or three years. Yet, the basic postulate remains the same: stabilization and development efforts would benefit from more predictable, long-term development assistance.

The fourth is that the difficulties in coordinating international assistance must be overcome in order to ensure project complementarity. Several tools, such as the International Monetary Fund's *Poverty Reduction*

*Strategy Paper* (2008), have been developed to encourage project coordination and complementarity, as well as to ensure alignment of international assistance with national priorities. Yet, donor engagement still follows at times a bilateral logic, based on bilateral priorities. Also, often donors seek engagement in the most "noble" sectors possible to the detriment of other, less visible sectors: for example, it still remains easier to find assistance for the rehabilitation of a hospital or a school than to find support for the equally important rehabilitation of a prison.

The fifth obstacle is donor fatigue. As a result of the devastation brought to Haiti by the hurricanes of the summer of 2008, the United Nations launched a Flash Humanitarian Appeal for US$108 million over six months to fund humanitarian assistance and early recovery activities in Haiti (United Nations, 2008). More than 10 days following the appeal, however, only 3 per cent of the necessary US$108 million had been committed by donors, despite the urgent need for humanitarian assistance. Donor fatigue is a potential danger and a key challenge for the stabilization efforts. Haitian authorities must understand that in order to keep donor interest and engagement in Haiti as well as to attract investment, they must keep making progress and implementing vital reforms, as was the case in 2007. On the other hand, the international community must stay the course and continue to support Haiti in order to protect its initial investment in the country's peace and stability.

## Conclusion

The international community has been trying to learn from its past mistakes in order not to repeat them. But Haitian partners must also learn from past mistakes, and transcend their differences of the moment in order to work, in a spirit of cooperation, for the long-term prosperity and welfare of their beautiful country. If both international and domestic actors were to do so, then both, together, would be paying the ultimate tribute to the memory of all the victims of the recent hurricanes which have once more brought human and material devastation to Haiti, from which it will take a long to recover.

### REFERENCES

Annan, Kofi (2006) "Remarks by the Secretary-General at a joint press conference with President Rene Préval of the Republic of Haiti", United Nations: Office of the Spokesperson for the Secretary General, 2 August. Available at http://www.un.org/apps/sg/offthecuff.asp?nid=913

Delva, Joseph Guyler (2008) "Haiti Hurricane Damage Estimated at $1 Billion", Reuters, 23 October. Available at http://www.insurancejournal.com/news/international/2008/10/23/94906.htm

Delva, Joseph Guyler and Jim Loney (2008) "Haiti's Government Falls after Food Riots", Reuters, 12 April. Available at http://www.reuters.com/article/idUSN1228245020080413

Dupuy, Alex (2007) *The Prophet and Power: Jean-Bertrand Aristide, the International Community, and Haiti.* Plymouth, UK: Rowman & Littlefield.

International Crisis Group (2007) *Consolidating Stability in Haiti.* Latin America/Caribbean Report, 21, 18 July. Available at http://www.crisisgroup.org/~/media/Files/latin-america/haiti/21%20Consolidating%20Stability%20in%20Haiti.ashx

International Monetary Fund (2008) *Haiti: Poverty Reduction Strategy Paper.* Washington, DC: International Monetary Fund, IMF Country Report No. 08/115. Available at http://www.imf.org/external/pubs/ft/scr/2008/cr08115.pdf

MINUSTAH (2010) "MINUSTAH Facts and Figures", *United Nations Stabilization Mission in Haiti.* Available at http://www.un.org/Depts/dpko/missions/minustah/facts.html

United Nations (1996) *The United Nations Mission in Haiti,* September. Available at http://www.un.org/Depts/DPKO/Missions/unmih_b.htm

United Nations (2000) *Report of the Panel on United Nations Peace Operations,* 17 August. Available at http://www.un.org/peace/reports/peace_operations/

United Nations (2008) *Haiti Flash Appeal,* 10 September. Available at http://ochaonline.un.org/humanitarianappeal/webpage.asp?Page=1695

UNSC (2008a) "Resolution 1840: The Situation Concerning Haiti", United Nations Security Council, S/RES/1840, 14 October.

UNSC (2008b) *Report of the Secretary-General on the United Nations Stabilization Mission in Haiti.* United Nations Security Council, S/2008/586, 27 August.

UNSC (2009) "Security Council Welcomes Progress in Consolidating Stability, Stresses Need for Security Gains to be Accompanied by Social, Economic Development", Security Council 6101st Meeting, 6 April. Available at http://www.un.org/News/Press/docs/2009/sc9628.doc.htm

US Department of State (2009) "Remarks with Haitian President Rene Préval", 16 April. Available at http://www.state.gov/secretary/rm/2009a/04/121828.htm

Zoellick, Robert B. (2008) "Fragile States: Securing Development", The International Institute for Strategic Studies, Geneva, 12 September. Available at http://web.worldbank.org/WBSITE/EXTERNAL/NEWS/0,,contentMDK:21898896~pagePK:34370~piPK:42770~theSitePK:4607,00.html

# 7

# Peace operations: On the importance of perceiving versus just seeing

*Eduardo Aldunate*

## Introduction

From September 2005 to September 2006 I served as Deputy Force Commander and, temporarily, as Acting Force Commander of the United Nations Stabilization Mission in Haiti (MINUSTAH). During that year I was under the command of two brilliant Brazilian generals and responsible for a total of 7,500 soldiers from 11 countries. I strongly believe all can benefit from reflecting on the lessons learnt while serving with the United Nations. For some of us, delivering reports on performed activities is just part of our job. Sometimes our experience transcends the regular UN administrative conduit and can be shared with a wider audience. Volumes such as this allow for sharing and hopefully reinforcing and optimizing future peace missions.[1]

Some 100,000 blue helmets are currently deployed worldwide in 18 peace missions. These figures indicate the complexity of the new challenges the international community faces. The United Nations has a response system to crises. When needed, and following multilateral consultation, the Security Council issues its resolutions, which outline the needs of the country in conflict and how these needs are to be resolved in order to enforce peace and protect people. The first step for those responsible for a peace operation is to become fully acquainted with the UN mission's mandate, its reasons and the resources provided. Success depends on being knowledgeable about realities on the ground. This means going beyond learning only about a country's geography, history

*Fixing Haiti: MINUSTAH and beyond, Heine and Thompson (eds),*
*United Nations University Press, 2011, ISBN 978-92-808-1197-1*

and Wikipedia-like data on the territory, and acquiring a deep understanding of the society. Only by doing so does one stand a chance of formulating an appropriate strategy of engagement, and implementing it successfully.

## From great to grim

Haiti was the second country in the New World to become independent, immediately after the United States of America. At that time, ships came and went to distribute its coffee and sugar worldwide. This promising beginning of the Haitian nation did not go hand-in-hand with the development of a political structure and democratic behaviour. Quite the contrary: time after time, Haiti has been under the omen of the word "crisis". History did not make it easy for Haiti to continue thriving, and today Haiti's splendour derives from its culture and art, which are widely appreciated worldwide, and not from its riches.

Yet, those residing in this beautiful, potentially massive tourist attraction find themselves living well below the poverty line. There is a common feeling that Haiti is a "could-be paradise"; it is only a short flight away from the United States and Canada, potential markets booming with consumers eager to spend their time and money in a dream-like location. Haiti's beaches and tropical weather could be an excellent tourist resort for North America and other neighbouring countries. Similarly, given the low cost of labour, Haiti would be an ideal location for setting up industries. But MINUSTAH is not in Haiti for its immense potential and its incredible beauty. On the contrary, MINUSTAH is in Haiti because of its violence and political instability, which have been parts of Haitian reality for far too long.

In February 2004, chaos in Haiti led President Aristide to flee the country. Events seemed to indicate that there would be a humanitarian catastrophe and that an intervention was necessary. At the request of the interim authorities, the United Nations arranged for an intervention by the Multinational Interim Force in Haiti (MIFH), MINUSTAH's predecessor. The MIFH was created under Resolution 1529 of the UN Security Council. It included soldiers from the United States, Canada, France and Chile. Its mandate was to prevent chaos in Haiti. Specifically, it was instructed to protect the population against the attacks of armed gangs. The MIFH relieved tensions and prevented a massacre. However, UN authorities quickly realized that lowering the patient's fever would not cure the illness. A more effective treatment had to be found. This included providing Haiti with a duly legitimized government via a process new to Haiti: free and democratic elections.

Following the insurrection, an interim government was needed to allow the state to fulfil its function, to organize and manage the existing services and resources to support its population. Basic security rights of the population had to be preserved, especially against the threat posed by the armed gangs. These were the foundations for the creation of MINUSTAH, established by UN Security Council Resolution 1542. This resolution emphasized the need to continue supporting Haiti during its transition period, as well as the need to achieve two goals: protection of human rights and supporting the electoral process, in order for a democratic government to take charge.

## MINUSTAH and the long road to elections

MINUSTAH's mission was to enforce the UN mandate. Obstacles of all kinds abounded. They included initial local incomprehension, communication difficulties, differences in scenario appreciation, as well as political and financial problems. We – meaning those in command of the mission – realized that concepts such as the state and the rule of law were not part of Haitian life. The interim government was weak and lacking in basic capabilities. And not everyone understood we were there to enforce a UN mandate. We were aware that Haitians did not understand the reasons for our presence in their country. We knew that the contingents would have to make a great effort and commitment to be perceived as legitimate players, an essential requisite for accomplishing the mandate. To have our presence acknowledged as legitimate and to have the population join our efforts was an uphill struggle.

Being able to communicate with the people, meaning "to speak their language", was crucial to the success of the mission. In any mission, relations between the military and the local population go much farther than just providing security. Good relations require effective communications with locals. This is crucial to gain their trust. When international forces arrived, none of the foreign contingents spoke Creole, and only a few could speak English or French. Eventually, we ended up hiring Haitian translators and interpreters to help us.

Even more crucial is the ability to "read" the environment. To "read" a scenario, and not just "see" it, requires knowledge and sensitivity. Deep knowledge means being well acquainted with current developments. Sensitivity refers to the ability to appraise a scenario accurately. This entailed realizing that MINUSTAH efforts could not rely solely on the use of 5.56 calibre weapons. Insecurity and confusion are a product of Haiti's miserable poverty. Everything is tainted by the destructive effect of poverty, even military leadership. Yet, we knew that solutions would only emerge from working hand-in-hand with Haitian society and complying with the UN mandate.

Support for the interim government was tepid. Any solutions to Haiti's problems would only be possible with a legitimately elected president in office. But holding elections was by no means an easy enterprise. In 2006, when the electoral process began, 36 candidates ran for the presidency, a reflection of the absence of any consensus within the Haitian society at the time. It was also proof that local problems were deeply rooted.

There were also financial difficulties. Each presidential election can cost as much as US$12 million, and twice that amount should none of the candidates achieve a majority of votes and a second round of voting is required. For a society in which 70 per cent of the population lives on less than US$2 per day, and 60 per cent of their income depends on remittances from abroad, elections are a tremendously expensive activity.[2]

## Knowing where one stands

Usually, personnel participating in peace missions have a basic knowledge regarding the areas of responsibility (AORs) where they will deploy but learn gradually about locals. Our men's respect for locals grew quickly when they saw that Haitians, despite their painful poverty, never failed to pay their fare while boarding a "tap tap", a fragile-looking vehicle used as public transportation, or when they learned that the freely roaming goats that one could see everywhere had an owner and no would ever dare "take" one despite their need for food and protein.

It is standard practice that prior to their departure military contingents are fully trained by their countries on UN regulations concerning Rules of Engagement (ROE), and that all are provided with information on the history and culture of the country to which they are being deployed. This kind of information must be provided beforehand, because once the mission begins, the outgoing unit will transfer its AOR to the incoming unit, and from then on there will be no time for anything but active duty. Should any mistakes occur once deployed, the price to be paid is usually a high one. In military science, we are taught that generals are responsible for making strategic decisions and soldiers are assigned tactical missions. In peace missions, however, one mistake committed by a soldier can have serious consequences for the mission itself. Lieutenants and sergeants are thus strategically relevant as well. They are required to exert effective, permanent and proactive leadership. Contingents need to have comprehensive knowledge of their AOR in order to be able to team up and work with other players.

In situations where the state is virtually non-existent, as in the case of Haiti, blue helmets become the only reference available to locals. In such cases, command and leadership over the contingents becomes even more significant. We learned about local reluctance towards the Haitian National Police (HNP) and about difficulties in administering justice. Between November 2005 and February 2006 the number of kidnappings and deaths, of violence in general, exceeded all levels to be considered tolerable. From an average of 35 kidnappings per month, by December 2005 the number soared to 250. In Cité Soleil, the main hotspot, the Haitian police did not dare set foot. No employment, health or education programmes were available. People lived in excruciating poverty. The performance of the judiciary was no better. No detention orders against the gang leaders were being issued. No reliable information on the criminals was available. Only UN troops were present.

## Team work is a must

One of the greatest difficulties I encountered was to determine which international institutions and organizations to work with and which ones to trust; in other words, who to listen to. Straightforward and transparent relations between the military and the other international agencies are critical. This is particularly true for agencies working on political affairs, legal matters and human rights, and the press, given that any military decision will have an impact on the work of other entities. In an ideal world the UN military command would work closely together with the other players from all of the UN divisions – a situation far from the commonly imagined lonely military command. Granted, conflicts and disagreements among the members of a mission and other agents such as NGOs are not unusual. At times everyone is questioning everyone else's contribution. The local population is not aware of these disagreements, or of the different sensitivities felt by the different parties involved, and appraises the efficacy of the authorities and agencies on the actual help they receive. Thus, the mission command and agencies must seek ways to get everybody to contribute, as opposed to focusing on disagreements.

NGOs have a legitimate mission to accomplish. But I am convinced that it is highly desirable and possible to work closely and cooperatively to achieve the goal of the mission, which in our case is to help Haiti. All stakeholders should do their best to generate a climate of mutual cooperation which will then spread to the contingents. Despite the reluctance and misconceptions by some, I was able to get support from the Red Cross and Médecins sans Frontiéres (MSF) as a result of honest, straightforward communication with them. There were problems, and some accusations were made against our contingents. But in the end we were able to establish good relations with those NGOs and others. Transparency when dealing with civil society organizations and compliance with the ROE on the part of the military were key factors. I committed to conduct in-depth boards of inquiry any time one of our men was accused of human rights violations. Irregularities were not tolerated. One of the tangible results of this mutual trust and cooperation was that we were able to provide safe transport and deliver medical service in critical areas. Coordination of all the actors operating in Haiti proved to be a difficult task. The latter included: the military force, the UN police (UNPOL), various UN agencies, many NGOs, the local police, local authorities, religious groups, representatives of international organizations and a variety of armed gangs. Many of them did not grasp the causes of Haiti's problems, and were reluctant to be team players. It was tempting to work exclusively with foreign personnel, to impose our solutions and to use the military as mere enforcers of security. But we knew how sensitive Haitians are to undue foreign interventions. The key was to partner with the Haitian population. If something accounts for the success of our contingents during the time I participated in the mission, it was the fact that our men blended the locals into the solidarity work they performed and responded to their problems respectfully and effectively.

## When structure "destructures"

There was a duality in command between the two organizations focusing on security. One of my concerns was how information was disseminated and how to work in an environment in which intelligence gathering is lacking. Intelligence is vital to elaborate initiatives and strategies. Yet, no UN information or "intelligence" structure was considered when the mission was deployed. An organization to coordinate and analyse news coming from the local forces, the local police, local governmental agencies, embassies, NGOs, the militia and the mission itself was essential. With it, we could have had a clearer picture of who the enemies were, where they were and who the violent ones were. Without it, much of the information coming in from different sources could not be processed. This made it difficult for a newly arrived force to conduct a successful military or police operation, let alone fulfil the tasks of the mission. Multiple sources of information are common at the beginning of any peace operation and represent a challenge for the command, as it needs to move cautiously so as not to lose control of its mission. We obtained the best information we could from military personnel alone.

We had just been in Haiti for a few months when the international press began reporting on the activities of armed groups known as ex Fad'h (the Haitian Armed Forces). More than once we were pressured – sometimes even by members of the mission – to launch massive military operations against them. But we had learned that rumours are an important part of Haitian culture, and thus, most of what was being reported was just that – rumours. We realized that these supposed situations were aimed at triggering troop movements, and perhaps even at provoking possible mistakes in order to blemish MINUSTAH's image.

We ran into such a situation in September 2005. There was what appeared to be an unending escalation of violence in one neighbourhood of the capital. To some, the situation was indicative of an impending war. Following each violent act, a rather incomplete account was given of what had happened. Rarely were these incidents explained in the Haitian context. Usually, an ex-post analysis of an incident was performed. But what would have been useful would have been a broad analysis integrating all data provided by the agencies of the mission, state authorities and the press so as to provide a clear picture of the ongoing situation. We also quickly realized that the HNP lacked credibility with the citizenry.

In August 2005, the United Nations responded and created the Joint Military Analysis Center (JMAC), a structure which provided the UN Chief-of-Mission Special Representative of the Secretary-General (SRSG) with useful strategic information but which was insufficient for the operational needs of the mission. This led us to create a department of our own, but this was not the solution that was needed. At the beginning of missions such as the one in Haiti, a multidisciplinary unit with civilians and military personnel should be established to provide accurate, up-to-date intelligence to all personnel.

In terms of the military personnel (MP) and UNPOL contingents, who were both responsible for security, there was a difference in strength and capability. The military force was comprised of 7,500 soldiers from 11 countries and the UNPOL had approximately 1,500 men from five countries. The military force HQ was made up of more than a hundred officers from 21 countries; the UNPOL had a small advisory group of no more than 10 people. The military personnel were all active professionals; many members of UNPOL were former police officers hired for this mission, with previous experience ranging from traffic control to guerrilla warfare.

The two groups had to work in parallel, not under one command as any elementary manual on operations would suggest. Coordination between the MP and the UNPOL was based on the UNPOL police commander's goodwill. Luckily I always had his support and we had a good relationship. Still, in complex situations a unified command is best. I am not suggesting that the military force should take on administrative or training duties for the police. In an operational area, for security reasons, there should be one command and it should incorporate all parties in its planning. A unitary command was eventually achieved, but only after several months and several unnecessary failures which could have been prevented.

The international press reported that given the mission's efforts to support a transition government and to organize an election, MINUSTAH was not providing security. We were accused of failing in our mission, of allowing gangs to overpower the United Nations and of not protecting the population. This was also suggested by visiting authorities, some of the local press, the interim local government, the Haitian bourgeoisie and even some members of our forces whose personnel were attacked by gangs. There was pressure on us to use force more decisively, particularly at a time when kidnappings and killings were peaking. A simplistic reading of the situation could lead one to believe that by combating gangs we would be able to provide security for the local population. Yet, such a course would have led to the death of many civilians. It would also have distracted us from our mandate, which included the holding of elections and setting up a legitimate government.

A tactical success could have been a strategic disaster. Requests for using more force are easy to make when a contingent has lost men. Yet, success through the use of force is often difficult to achieve and even harder to explain. Those who demanded a heavier hand against the gangs wanted it to comply with standard ROE. What was the real situation? In a small part of Port-au-Prince the level of violence was unacceptable. It was no pleasure for me to have to attend the funerals of four blue helmets killed by the gangs. Fortunately, the rest of the country did not show any signs of violence. It all happened in Cité Soleil.

We knew that gangs used women and children as human shields, and an intervention could have resulted in their injury or death. This would not have helped the UN mission, whose mandate was to lead the country to an election process. When talking to government authorities I pointed out that you could not ask the military to use force when schools in Cité Soleil were not open, hospitals were not working and drinking water and power supplies were not available. Even the local police were absent and did not dare set foot in Cité Soleil. To make matters worse, the elections, initially to take place in December 2005, were repeatedly postponed; this affected security. So as not to affect the elections, the military command postponed enforcing more effective strategies in areas under gang control. We knew that the use of force would not solve the problem of insecurity.

But even in situations where the use of force is necessary, there are bureaucratic obstacles. The amount of red tape needed in order to deploy military helicopters and military engineers was huge. Mission regulations specified that all such military requests were to be addressed to the civilian administrator. The logical procedure would have been to have given military officials operational control of helicopters and military engineers, and leave administrative issues to be dealt with by the civilian authority in the mission. By February 2006 MINUSTAH had fulfilled its mandate to help the Haitian people hold free and fair elections.

After the elections, we moved from a General Control Zone Strategy in the capital to a Continuous Advance Strategy. This allowed us to consolidate our presence by breaking up the areas controlled by gangs, and to provide peace, security and protection to the civilian population in Haiti's capital. That Haiti's population, with the sole exception of Cité Soleil, was under UN control speaks volumes. That Haiti had a chance to have a legitimate election and a president-elect, Rene Préval, also speaks volumes. We thus accomplished the UN Security Council mandate. Extreme poverty, deficient political and administrative structures, and the lack of commitment of the Haitian society to social reforms still need to be dealt with in the future.

## Applying a suitable strategy

MINUSTAH designed a sensible strategy of military and police presence, which worked. As I remember the daily gang attacks against us and the faces of the soldiers as they saw their comrades leave in a coffin, I am convinced that the military command we exercised was vital for their morale. They behaved and conducted themselves as we expected. I suggested commanders share the risk with the soldiers, and be present in hard times, not as mere witnesses but to remind them how to act in difficult moments. I will always be grateful to our contingents and remember them with deepest appreciation for their work. A fluent relationship between the troops and mission commanders is essential.

In MINUSTAH, I must highlight the work of the two special representatives of the UN Secretary-General (SRSG) with whom I worked, Juan Gabriel Valdés and Edmund Mulet. They led the mission effectively, and established an excellent relationship with the military command. I also wish to underline the capable leadership exhibited by the two force commanders I worked for: the late General Urano Bacelar and General Elito, both of them exceptional Brazilian officers. Considering the challenges we faced, we designed a sensible strategy by isolating the area of conflict, and controlling it through our military presence. This allowed most of the population to register and be part of the elections. We chose to postpone a tactical goal for the sake of a strategic one.

During my courses on strategy at the Chilean Army War College, I always told my students that a commander must distance himself from the operations map and provide his people with a wider view of the situation. Commanders who are too close to tactical considerations lose sight of why they are there. While I was on duty, we resisted the temptation to confuse strategy and tactics. Yes, we had casualties and we were attacked by gangs, but we never forgot that we were not to interfere with the election. It was not easy to resist the natural instinct to use force when visiting the battalions who had suffered the losses. My suggestion to all commanders and authorities is to never get off track when making decisions. No matter how difficult the situation may be, military personnel must collect the essential data and not forget the purpose of the mission. A clear picture of the purpose of the mission helped us make decisions. This put more responsibility on our contingent but also prevented us from making mistakes. In peacekeeping missions, credibility comes down to whether locals perceive the contingents as a supportive rather than as an occupying force.

## MINUSTAH's success

We knew exactly the type of challenge we were taking on, and thus were able to give our troops a clear orientation. We understood that the mission's success would depend on how locals reacted to our troops. The blue helmets mingled with the population on a daily basis. Sometimes they would be soldiers in security-related situations. On another occasion, they would be riot police, social workers, builders or rescuers in natural disasters, and so on. In short, our men could play multiple roles, understand local idiosyncrasies and the demands and needs of Haitians. This type of soldiering helped us to gain the hearts and minds of the population, one of our main objectives.

MINUSTAH's performance was due to multiple "pro-people" activities, such as water delivery, road construction, street cleaning, medical care, training courses and so on. As our soldiers became police, social workers and providers of medical help, they showed they were able to provide the population with support. Ultimately, a blue helmet is much more than a combatant. They gained the people's trust and respect, and learned to have a better understanding of who they are.

Quick-impact projects also helped win the trust of the population. Small projects such as those conducted by the contingents using their own means proved to have a greater and faster impact than those carried out by some agencies. Small-scale initiatives should be developed, multiplied and provided with the necessary resources to succeed. For example, led by General Elito, the Brazilian force commander, the Brazilian contingent in conjunction with Chilean military engineers, cleaned and repaired a playground in Cité Soleil. They recovered public space in the most dangerous neighbourhood and at the most dangerous period of the mission. This was much appreciated by the population.

## Keeping the UN mandate in sight

As important as grasping the reality in which one is immersed, is the faithful interpretation of the UN mandate. This is more easily said than done, particularly with the daily pressures of the mission. These pressures affect all of those involved: military troops and command, as well as civilians. One of the first requirements for a commander is to understand and fulfil the UN mandate. This means adhering to the mandate, analysing the alternatives that have led to a military presence, considering daily events, making the right decisions and keeping all parties involved. Solid knowledge along with the implementation of suitable measures will avoid being influenced by the sheer volume of information that reaches the military command. This may be a symptom of something deeper. A good commander and his advisers should be able to interpret the situation properly and follow the best strategy.

I fear, however, that the international community itself has not understood the depth of the problem. Haiti's solution does not solely depend on the international community. Help and an international presence are not enough. It needs time, support and help to cover basic needs. What may have worked in other missions, will not necessarily be applicable in Haiti. Cookie-cutter solutions do not work. Our challenge was to provide security to Haiti at a very delicate moment. The initiatives that the military command developed in my time there were successful in getting people to trust and respect soldiers. To this day, MINUSTAH is consolidating its role in helping find the way to solutions.

The problem is not violence. The problem is a confluence of factors that lead to poverty and corruption, and it is the latter that leads to violence. In 2008 we witnessed violent acts and riots breaking out over the high price of rice. These confirmed my belief of the essence of the problem; that the international community has little understanding of the situation of Haiti. Long- and mid-term objectives derived from the UN mandate need to be established. These should focus on how we wish to see the country develop, what is important at each stage and how this relates to force organization. We all wish to have the military presence give way to strong and active civilian instances. We also hope to see a self-supporting country in terms of security.

# Notes

1. I have recently published *Backpacks Full of Hope: The UN Mission in* Haiti (Aldunate, 2010) about my experience – what we did and how we faced our mission – in MINUS-TAH as a Chilean military commander. This chapter is an abridged version of that book.
   The views expressed in this chapter are my own, and represent neither those of the government of Chile nor those of the institution to which I belong.
2. Expensive elections are not Haitians' only concerns: 90 per cent of its prisoners have never come to trial, 30 per cent of the national police are involved in corruption and 80 per cent of Haitians who have completed their higher education live abroad.

## REFERENCE

Aldunate, Eduardo (2010) *Backpacks Full of Hope: The UN Mission in Haiti.* Waterloo: Wilfrid Laurier University Press.

# 8

# Latin American peacekeeping: A new era of regional cooperation

*Johanna Mendelson Forman*

## Introduction

Latin American armies have been involved in United Nations peace-keeping from the outset of multilateral operations in 1948. Beginning with the United Nation's operations in Lebanon, Latin American officers participated in the UN Truce Supervision Organization (UNTSO) in 1948 and in the Indian–Pakistan observer mission in 1949 (UNMOGIP). In 1960 Argentine pilots helped support supply lines for the UN Mission in Congo (UNOC). In spite of continued troop contributions, Latin American military units did not view peacekeeping as part of their obligation to the United Nations. Not one of the region's armies embraced peacekeeping as part of their defence doctrine during the Cold War (see chart, Appendix A).

With the fall of the Berlin Wall and the end of the Cold War, the global security environment changed, and Latin American participation in peacekeeping increased exponentially. Beginning in 1990, many Latin American military units were deployed as part of the United Nations Observer Group in Central America (ONUCA). Before and after the 1992 peace accords in El Salvador, contingents from Argentina, Brazil, Chile, Colombia, Mexico and Venezuela served in the UN Observer Mission in El Salvador (ONUSAL). By 1994 there were 2,816 Latin American military personnel from 10 different countries serving in 13 UN operations throughout the world. These missions helped to transform the view of the region's armed forces from being obstacles to democracy and

*Fixing Haiti: MINUSTAH and beyond, Heine and Thompson (eds),*
*United Nations University Press, 2011, ISBN 978-92-808-1197-1*

good governance to being partners with civilian leaders. Latin American military units now were deployed around the world as part of UN peace operations whose missions were to enforce peace accords, to prevent state failure and to participate in post-conflict reconstruction and peace-building.

In 2008 there were 6,468 Latin American troops participating in peace operations around the globe (UN, 2008). Several factors account for this expansion. On the geopolitical level, the increased troop contributions to multilateral operations represented the region's re-emergence on the world stage as it reinserted itself into the international political system. The most specific manifestation of this situation was that many of the region's military units revised their doctrine to include peacekeeping and peace operations as important components of their military missions. In addition, peacekeeping training institutes began operations in the Southern Cone (Argentina and Uruguay), and others followed. A new centre has opened in Guatemala.

Financial incentives also account for this increased involvement in peace operations. The United Nations pays the salaries of participating soldiers, thus relieving the burden of national governments to finance the total operation and maintenance of their armies. Most important, however, is that as Latin American military units participate in peace operations, their presence in these missions reflects a maturing of civil–military relations in the Americas. Today the use of their armed forces in support of global commitments is considered a way for national governments to project their power both abroad and at multilateral forums.

The 2004 Brazilian-led UN Peace Operation in Haiti, MINUSTAH, put a regional face on an international mission. The military leadership of Brazil allowed the United Nations to bring in other states from the hemisphere to collectively provide security in Haiti after the departure of its president Jean-Bertrand Aristide. Not only did Brazil help to stabilize the on-the-ground situation in Haiti, but it also assumed a leadership role among troop-contributing states in order to provide better support for security in the region through their respective roles as partners in Haiti. MINUSTAH also catalysed a process of regional security meetings among defence ministers that ultimately led to the creation of a Brazilian-led regional security council. Thus, the Brazilians parlayed their work in Haiti into a larger and more vocal body of defence experts that brought order to the regional security situation in the absence of US participation or interest.

This chapter will review the role of peacekeeping in the Americas. It will discuss the Latin American contribution to date, followed by the specific case of Haiti, whose status as a post-Cold War mission has had a profound impact on a wide range of actors working in the field. Finally,

Table 8.1 Latin American troop contribution MINUSTAH, September 2008

| Country | Personnel | Number |
|---------|-----------|--------|
| Argentina | Military | 553 |
| | Police | 4 |
| Bolivia | Military | 217 |
| Brazil | Military | 1,212 |
| | Police | 4 |
| Chile | Military | 499 |
| | Police | 12 |
| Colombia | Police | 2 |
| Ecuador | Military | 67 |
| El Salvador | Police | 4 |
| Grenada | Police | 3 |
| Guatemala | Military | 118 |
| Paraguay | Military | 31 |
| Peru | Military | 205 |
| Uruguay | Military | 1,143 |
| | Police | 6 |
| | | Total Contribution: 4,080 |

*Source*: United Nations, 2008

we will explore how Latin American participation in overall peace missions has added to a growing awareness of regional security demands. It is precisely through the events in Haiti that the regional interest in peacekeeping has engendered a deeper interest in peacebuilding as a serious mission of the region's armed forces.

## After the Cold War: Transforming the armed forces

A new dynamic began as the United Nations expanded its peacekeeping agenda in the wake of the withdrawal of Soviet support in states around the globe. During the 1990s Africa, in particular, was a region of multiple peace operations. A concomitant set of events, including a decline in military funding and a concerted effort to change national and international opinion through a renewed effort in democratic governance, also spurred an interest in peace operations in the Americas. According to Antonio L. Pala (1995), "the spread of democracy, the control of the debt crisis, and an increased focus on economic integration appear[ed] to be at the apex of regional issues". Regional leaders turned their focus away from both financial and ideological authoritarian policies aimed at routing enemies and concentrated their energy and funds on democratic governance and economic self-sufficiency.

A significant downsizing of military personnel accompanied the democratization of the Southern Cone after decades of military rule. This waning military involvement in national security sparked a reduction in military spending, creating a shortage of funds to support military operations. This situation laid a foundation for wider participation in peacekeeping operations since these missions provided both an economic and a social safety net for the armed forces of many South American countries as funds to pay military personnel were guaranteed upon deployment. The continued dedication of Latin American troops to Peacekeeping Operations (PKO) in the midst of budget crises highlights the changing nature of the region's armed forces. In a statement made to the United Nations addressing late payment issues, Uruguayan delegate Santiago Wins (para phrased in UNGA, 2003) remarked that

> his country was strongly committed to the difficult task of keeping and reestablishing peace in regions in conflict ... As most developing countries contributing troops, participation of Uruguay depended on timely reimbursements, given its limited financial capacity.

Money, especially after the neo-liberal policies of the 1980s and 1990s, was an important factor in regional participation.

While finances often motivated regional participation, PKOs offered Latin American countries the opportunity to use their armed forces for the common good. The first post-Cold War peace operations in the Central American countries of El Salvador, Guatemala and Nicaragua created opportunities for other Latin American countries to express their new commitment to peace. The United Nations Observer Mission in El Salvador (ONUSAL), initiated in 1991, was a pivotal part of a rise in Latin American participation in peacekeeping. Claimed as a success by the United Nations, ONUSAL occurred at a crucial point in both the UN's peacekeeping agenda and Latin America's budding role in these processes. With a multidimensional base that centred on human rights, ONUSAL represented a mission, like the United Nations Stabilization Mission in Haiti (MINUSTAH) today, that not only focused on demilitarization but also incorporated goals of national reconciliation and infrastructure building (Montgomery, 1995: 140, 142, 146). Its success after the failures of missions in Bosnia, Somalia and Rwanda legitimized both PKOs and regional participation (ibid.: 139). Latin American troops were fundamental to the mission's success. Argentina, Brazil, Chile, Colombia, Mexico and Venezuela sent troops, and Uruguayan Police General Homero Vaz Bresque was pulled from his post in Western Sahara to head up the mission in light of his expertise (ibid.: 151). After the end of

ONUSAL a new mission that worked in consolidating peace accords, the United Nations Mission in El Salvador (MINUSAL) began under the direction of the last ONUSAL director, Venezuelan Enrique ter Horst, Special Representative to the Secretary-General (ibid.: 160).

The United Nation's success in Central America redefined Latin American armed forces and their commitment to PKOs. As Mexican security analyst Raúl Benítez Manaut (2008) noted, these regional UN operations in El Salvador, Nicaragua and Guatemala were as important as the democratization of the political systems that occurred after the conflicts in these countries ended.[1]

This twofold positive reinforcement began a process of transformation for Latin American armed forces. Now peacekeeping operations, according to Pala (1995), helped "form new images for these historically controversial armed forces". While the Southern Cone had recently emerged from the same internal warfare now plaguing Central America, countries such as Argentina and Brazil solidified their new position as regional democratic leaders by participating in PKOs.

## International recognition and improved morale

Regional leadership in peacekeeping operations gained international recognition as well. As Sir Brian Urquhart, former UN undersecretary, said of Argentina's commitment in the region, "Argentina has provided hospitals, troops, engineers, police, and electoral observers. I wish that all countries would participate at this level and diversity" (quoted in Pala, 1995). Favourable opinions were not kept to rhetoric and praise. During the presidency of Carlos Saúl Menem in Argentina, the United States agreed to sell the country upgraded fighter planes in view of their peacekeeping and regional arms-control participation. Similar transactions occurred in Uruguay and Chile (ibid.).

Opinion within the troops also changed. The deployment of troops to other parts of the world expanded the world view of soldiers who previously had not been exposed to other regions, not to mention other military units, outside the Americas. As Argentine army general and former UN sector commander in Croatia Carlos María Zabala (quoted in ibid.) notes:

> On a professional level, it is an occasion to operate in a complex operational environment. You have the opportunity to work with other armies and appreciate their capabilities as well as your own. It provides firsthand knowledge of the effects of war, allowing our troops to appreciate the importance of the UN and its peace operations. On a personal level, it lends opportunity for travel to

foreign locations and exposure to other cultures and customs. Additionally, it allows the troops to feel as representatives of their country in an important mission abroad.

Officers who previously had fought against their own countrymen were now asked to support and uphold conflict-resolution strategies in war-torn countries across the globe. Being abroad also added to troop training.

For many Latin American troops, this experience abroad marked their first exposure to different countries and expanded their view on international affairs and military operations. Troops interact socially with the population they work with. The cultural affinity that exists between Brazil and Haiti highlights this point. A soccer match in August 2004 between the two countries increased non-military relations. The majority of Haitians welcomed Brazil's involvement. According to Amélie Gauthier and Sarah John de Sousa (2006), "the acceptance of the Brazilian presence by Haitians is positive and this facilitates the social legitimacy of the stabilization and peacekeeping process" (see also Hirst, 2007). Additionally, morale within the armed forces has risen. PKOs provide an alternate mission for the armed forces, one that entails international governance, a commitment to regional democracy and a rejection of authoritarianism. Argentina's participation in PKOs is case in point. According to Monica Hirst (1995): "There is a clear contrast between the confidence derived from accumulated PKO experience and the manifest sensitivity caused by degradation suffered by the military as a consequence of both the defeat in the Malvinas-Falklands War and the record of human rights abuse during the authoritarian regime."

Through peacekeeping, troops can attempt to salvage their own views of their role in national and international security and move away from the past. This is reaffirmed by political scientist Juan Tokatlian (2008: 6):

> quite apart from the humanitarian sentiment behind the LA involvement in a Haitian contingent, many countries of the region assign a growing value to their armed forces in processes of pacification, stabilization, and reconstruction beyond their borders. The kinds of intra-military linkages that are being made in the hemisphere, the internal training that foreign military missions requires, and the impact in the medium term on civic-military relations and domestic democratic evolution are questions worth some careful reflection.

Peacekeeping was not seen as a "weak" alternative to past "harsh" military actions but rather as a democratic yet powerful alternative to past policies.

Peacekeeping participation also changed national attitudes towards the armed forces. With dictatorships targeting internal enemies and violently

Table 8.2  Peacekeeping training centres in Latin America

| Country | Name of the Centre | Date of Foundation |
|---|---|---|
| Argentina | Argentine Centre for Joint Training in Peacekeeping Operations (CAECOPAZ) | 27 June 1995 |
| Uruguay | Uruguayan Army Peacekeeping Operations School "Mayor Juan Sosa Machado" (EOPE) | 22 December 1998 |
| Paraguay | Joint Training Centre for Peacekeeping Operations (CECOPAZ) | 8 October 2001 |
| Chile | Joint Peacekeeping Operations Centre (CECOPAC) | 15 July 2002 |
| Ecuador | Peacekeeping Unit School "Ecuador" (UEMPE) | 10 November 2003 |
| Peru | Joint Training Centre for Peacekeeping Operations (CECOPAZ) | 11 November 2003 |
| Brazil | Centre for Peacekeeping Operations of the Brazilian Army (CI OP Paz) | 23 February 2005 |
| Guatemala (office) | Regional Training Centre for UN Peacekeeping Operations (CEOMPAZ) Guatemala, El Salvador, Honduras and Nicaragua | 8 June 2005 |
| Bolivia | Centre for Peacekeeping Operations of the Bolivian Army (COMPEBOL) | 23 January 2007 |

*Source*:  Courtesy of Resdal, http://www.resdal.org

crushing dissenting opinion, civilians fostered a large anti-military sentiment during the 1970s and 1980s. Mistrust, based on past human rights
violations and military involvement in civil democracy, was the overarching relationship between civil–military society. As Pala notes, the region's
newfound peace activism did not erase past atrocities, but it did lessen
the animosity between the two arenas (Pala, 1995).

## Peacekeeping training centres

Heightened Latin American involvement in the peacekeeping process
is also evident in the growth of peacekeeping training centres in the region. Table 8.2 illustrates the growth of these centres from 1995 to the
present.

The first training centres opened and operated in the Southern Cone.
Argentina, Uruguay, Paraguay and Chile all had centres by 2001, with
Ecuador, Peru and Venezuela not far behind. The Argentine Center for
Joint Training of Peacekeeping Operations (CAECOPAZ) is located at
Campo de Mayo, which, ironically, was the site of some of the most noto-
rious detention centres of Argentina's "Dirty War" in the 1970s. CAECO-

PAZ was founded in 1995, and it trains approximately a hundred students each year.

The Cobán training centre in Guatemala is a regional school for peacekeepers from Central America. Approximately a thousand students study in Cobán at any given time. In August 2008, there were 1,030 students from Honduras, El Salvador, Guatemala, Nicaragua and the Dominican Republic preparing for deployment with the United Nations.

The importance of regional training demonstrates the growing commitment to preparedness among the armed forces of Latin America. It also underscores the impact that MINUSTAH has had on the region's need to expand training to prepare troops for eventual deployment to Haiti. In August 2008 seven countries established ALCOPAZ, the Latin American Association of Peacekeeping Operations Training Centers. This group represents the regional commitment to this type of military mission as central to the global security role that so many states see themselves playing in the years to come.[2] What is also of interest are recent attempts by Russia to become an observer to this new organization. The request speaks to the broader geopolitical changes that are occurring in the Western Hemisphere as multipolarity replaces historically unipolar politics (Pala, 1995). Many of these peacekeeping centres also have received additional assistance from both the US and the Canadian governments, who maintain active programmes to complement regional training needs.

## The US and UN peace operations in Haiti, 1994–2008

From initial UN involvement in 1990 to facilitate a democratic election,[3] to the present UN and OAS engagement as intergovernmental organizations charged to restore order, security and economic development, Haiti remains a political challenge, and still verges on being categorized as a failed state. In spite of Haiti being a test case for post-Cold War peace operations, these UN-mandated interventions have done little to provide long-term improvements in the daily lives of the average Haitian, even though the costs to date have totalled US$1.8 billion. Eighty per cent of Haitians live in abject poverty; the literacy rate is only 53 per cent. Combining measures of income, life expectancy, school enrolment and literacy, Haiti ranks 177 out of 192 countries on the UN Development Programme's Human Development Report (UNDP, 2005). Haiti is also 98 per cent deforested, so that agriculture is precarious and many parts of the country can easily be destroyed by natural disasters such as floods and hurricanes.

US intervention in Haiti in 1994 through participation in a multilateral peace operation was significant, not only because of its international dimensions at the end of the Cold War but also because, of the four pre-vious US interventions in the Caribbean since 1965, this was the first that was done under a Security Council mandate (Dobbins et al., 2003: 84). It reflected the "assertive multilateralism" that former Secretary of State Madeleine Albright had called for at the beginning of the Clinton years.

Reports of the initial UN experiences in Haiti have provided many lessons for the international community in subsequent peace operations. For example, the United Nations learned about the importance of police forces and using civilian police in its operations. Some believe that the 1994 intervention in Haiti represents the first case of humanitarian inter-vention, a precursor to the concept of "responsibility to protect", even though restoration of a deposed elected leader was the basis for Security Council action.

The restoration of President Jean-Bertrand Aristide to his elected posi-tion as president of Haiti in October 1994 was carried out with UN and US forces standing side-by-side. Cooperation between the United States and other international actors represented a new era of nation-building that included a focus on security and a commitment to governance that focused on the creation of a new judiciary and other institutions that could move Haiti forward. But Haiti came in the wake of a failed UN mission in Somalia, and US forces were not willing to dedicate the time or resources to Haiti. The military mission was construed very narrowly so that "mission creep" would be avoided. By November 1994 US forces exited Haiti, leaving the policing to the United Nations. Today we know that no successful peace operation has ever been accomplished in less than five years. We also know that only half of post-conflict situations ac-tually stabilize in that same period of time. Thus, the return of the United Nations in 2004 was to be expected (Azam et al., 2001).

Since the forced resignation of President Jean-Bertrand Aristide in February 2004, Haiti has seen the deployment of its tenth international peace operation in a decade – six missions, two multinational forces and two regional missions (Mendelson-Forman, 2007). Both the Haitian-interim government and the United Nations requested the US-led Multi-lateral Interim Force. Comprised of troops from the United States, Canada, France, and Chile, the Force landed in the Haitian capital of Port-au-Prince to bring stability to the country until the United Nations could act. In April 2004, the United Nations Security Council approved Resolution 1542, which established the UN Stability Mission in Haiti (MINUSTAH). From then on, the mandate has been re-approved at six-month intervals by the Security Council. It is currently extended to 15 October 2011 with the intention of further renewal.[4] But Haiti is a diffi-cult case that raises questions about the timeframe of a reconstruction programme in a country where institutional capacity is weak, and the economic conditions so dire. Former UN Secretary-General Kofi Annan, in March 2004, asked the central question about cases such as Haiti:

> Should we have learned by now that outsiders cannot solve Haiti's problems? ... For a time in the early 20th century it was a US protectorate. Should it not now be left alone to sort itself out? The proposition is attractive only in the abstract. Haiti is clearly unable to sort itself out, and the effect of leaving it alone would be continued or worsening chaos. Our globalized world cannot afford a political vacuum, whether in the mountains of Afghanistan or on the very doorstep of the remaining superpower. (Annan, 2004)

These powerful words sum up the dilemma of peacekeeping in situations like Haiti not only for US policy but also for other parts of the globe that are affected by deep-rooted poverty, weak governance and a set of development problems that cannot be solved without long-term commitment to financial and technical support. It goes to the core of how the United States will manage cases like Haiti that require not only security for the long haul but also intensive investment in institutional capacity building and support to the private sector to promote trade and investment. The US government still remains unable to muster an adequate civilian response to the needs of societies like Haiti. The United Nations is by far more capable of making long-term commitments through its various development and humanitarian agencies which understand the culture, have international staff and the mandate to work in development over the course of the next decade.

One of the most distinctive aspects of this current UN intervention in Haiti has been the absence of the United States from MINUSTAH after the successful removal of President Aristide in February 2004. Once the UN Peacekeeping Office was able to mobilize sufficient international forces to take over the Haiti mission, the US military left and turned military operations over to the Brazilians. It demonstrated that for the United States, the United Nations was a tool of US foreign policy to be used when needed but ignored or circumvented when core American values were threatened elsewhere.

Another feature of this ongoing UN mission in Haiti has been the leadership of regional powers, and especially Brazil. Timing of events in Haiti clearly had an effect on the level of US government interest. Aristide's departure and the consolidation of the MINUSTAH forces occurred at the same time as the US-led Coalition Provisional Authority was ending in Iraq. The United States did not have the military capacity or the patience to deal with Haiti. When Brazil stepped up to a leadership role, the United States gladly accepted the offer.

Resolution 1542 marked the first UN mission headed by Latin Americans (Manuat, 2008:17). Southern Cone countries have taken the lead in the MINUSTAH operation, especially after the pullout of the United States and Canada. Brazil, Chile, Argentina and Uruguay are supporting what is termed "diplomacy of security" in an effort to reposition themselves as geopolitical actors in the international security system (Manuat, op cit: 10). Participation in MINUSTAH has provided the political space to create a more cohesive regional peacekeeping force among Latin American military units. The ongoing commitment to support the UN operation has also led to the establishment of consultative processes in the hemisphere that have served not only as confidence-building exercises but also as genuine attempts to increase the independence of decision-making about peacebuilding in the Americas.[5]

## Collaboration: The evolution of "the 2 × 4 process"

Starting in May 2005 with a meeting in Buenos Aires, the vice ministers of foreign affairs and defence of Argentina, Brazil, Chile and Uruguay met to discuss ways to strengthen the regional contribution to MINUS-TAH. This meeting, known as the 2 × 4 process, expanded in August 2005 to a 2 × 7 group, when Ecuador, Guatemala and Peru joined. This cohort reaffirmed its commitment to a democratic Haiti and to continued support of MINUSTAH. In a meeting in Lima in February 2007 the group expanded to nine countries (2 × 9), adding Bolivia and Paraguay to the mix. All countries were also troop contributors. The absence of the United States from these consultations is significant, suggesting a new age of regional security. New leaders are defining what can only be called the new civil–military relations of this century.

The timing of the Haiti crisis was actually a politically propitious moment for Brazil. As a regional leader in the Americas, Brazil has had a long history of support for the United Nations. Events in Haiti coincided with the emergence of a more aggressive regional policy on security where Brazil, using its leadership in MINUSTAH, was able to convene defence ministers of other Latin American nations to begin a process of collaboration and coordination for the Haiti mission. The 2 × 4 process described above led to improved regional coordination among the region's nine troop-contributing defence ministers. Out of this process came the roots of what is now being proposed by Brazil, a regional defence council for the Americas.

Although regional military integration had been discussed in the past, the topic was recharged by Brazilian President Luiz Inacio "Lula" da Silva during the diplomatic crisis sparked by Colombian military incursions into Ecuadorian territory in March 2008. Brazilian Defence Minister Nelson Jobim officially reintroduced the idea of creating a regional defence organization, to be known as the South American Defense Council (CDS), and member states of the Union of South American Nations (UNASUR) signed a pact on 23 May 2008 in Brasília to establish judicial and political components for the limited yet emerging union (Council on Hemispheric Affairs, 2008a).

The Council is intended as a forum for the increasingly divided South American continent to cooperate in security matters and as a response to the waning US influence in the region. The United States has expressed an interest in participating in the Council but has been rebuffed. The CDS is meant to be distinct from the OAS – excluding the United States or Canada while including Cuba (Council on Hemispheric Affairs, 2008b).

## Regional debate

Another important outcome of the Latin American participation in MINUSTAH is that it integrates many facets of a national security organization in a democratic framework. The decision to send troops to UN missions supports civilian control of defence policy. It also encourages defence efficiency through the requirement that budgets for troops participating in UN missions must be debated by Defence Committees in the legislatures of each nation. The impact of the Haiti mission has gone far beyond the ranks of the armed forces. Based on press reports from Chile, Brazil and Bolivia, it has stimulated important and open discussion among civilian leaders about the role of the military in Latin America and the costs associated with peacekeeping.

Participation in PKOs, and especially MINUSTAH, has not been without debate. Regionally, opposition has occurred in response to MINUSTAH. The Caribbean Community (CARICOM) initially opposed the operation. As MINUSTAH's positive presence grew, however, especially in the wake of natural disasters, CARICOM supported reconstruction plans and efforts (Hirst, 2007).

Internal debates in the ABC countries (Argentina, Brazil and Chile), as well as Uruguay, have been centred on the individual country's quest for greater presence in the international arena. At the same time, unique domestic concerns shaped the debate from one country to the next. These concerns are expressed by political scientist Monica Hirst:

> During the 1990s, participation was motivated in large part by the need to redefine the role of the Armed Forces in the context of local re-democratization processes. In Argentina, due to the importance of civil-military subordination; in Uruguay, mainly as a [sic] economic source for the maintenance of the military; in Brazil, as a source for a renewed and prestigious engagement in international affairs (ibid.).[6]

Hirst also suggested that despite domestic differences, regional discussions centred around four issues: (1) the pro-coup origin of the mission; (2) its "de facto" subordination to US interests; (3) the costs and benefits for the presence in Haiti; and (4) the mission's chances of success (Hirst, ibid.). Debates in each country were shaped by different visions of international policy, domestic priorities and past actions of the armed forces; nevertheless, they reflect regional similarities.

In Chile, popular opinion, influenced by foreign policy interests, supports Chilean support for local and regional peacekeeping missions to ensure stability in the hemisphere (Mora, 2000). This debate argues for the need to stabilize global interest areas and contribute to the growth of strategic national policy in the international setting. Interestingly enough, Chile expressed the most support for MINUSTAH, shown in its participation in the US-led multinational force (Hirst, 2007). Argentina, however, was the least willing to participate in the mission. In large part, hesitation reflected popular opinion which linked PKOs to the Menem administration. It was under the now unpopular Menem that Argentina participated in 22 PKOs in the 1990s. Yet after these initial doubts, opinion shifted as Argentina's cooperation with neighbouring armed forces changed opinion of past defence policy (ibid.). Uruguay has seen debate with respect to international peacekeeping operations. The country seeks to prove its worth in foreign policy talk and establish itself as a greater international actor while staying true to Multinational Force and Observers (MFO) commitments and its desire to further democracy. One primary argument is that Uruguay, and any country for that matter, can further their own economic goals by way of peacekeeping, which gives them greater "positive exposure" to foreign actors (Ulery, 2005).

Due to its leadership role in MINUSTAH, Brazil has seen the most debate surrounding PKO participation, which is discussed in Chapter 11 in this volume. In fact, the Lula administration faced opposition from the beginning of its involvement in MINUSTAH. Opposition leaders, including legislators, intellectuals and union leaders focused on two key issues: the imperialistic nature of an occupying force and the economic cost of the operation. Even members of Lula's Workers' Party, the PT, opposed deployment. As Amélie Gauthier and Sarah John de Sousa write: "According to opponents, the fact that Haiti suffered a *coup d'état* supported by American armed forces, which, along with French and Chilean forces, installed the transition government, made any foreign military mission in the country an occupation force" (Gauthier and de Sousa, 2006).

After Lula encouraged legislators to visit Haiti, however, key opponents changed their minds. The result was increased support for troop deployment. These visits also identified the need for cultural and educational programmes between Haiti and Brazil. Nevertheless, opponents continued to complain that money spent on MINUSTAH would be better spent at home where social projects combating urban violence were needed (Gratius, 2007; Gauthier and de Sousa, 2006). Brazilian elites counteracted this position, citing that the training the armed forces received in Haiti was crucial to more efficient domestic policies that battled organized crime (Hirst, 2007). Brazil's executive branch faces restrictions put forth by the legislature, and only the foreign ministry and the armed forces may be deployed abroad. Gaining the support of the legislature was a crucial step in resolving internal debate (Hirst, *op cit*).

## Conclusions

The history of Latin American participation in UN peacekeeping has evolved over the last 60 years from individual nations' troop contributions to UN missions to a cohesive regional phenomenon. MINUSTAH has served as a springboard for the hemisphere's security forces to discuss issues that go beyond the operation in Haiti. Thus, the role of Latin American armed forces in peacekeeping has benefited from this effort while bringing into public debate the importance of peace and stability in Latin America.

The growth of peacekeeping training centres since the end of the Cold War has served the region's armed forces well. While all centres have provided important courses to prepare military units for UN operations, they also have reflected a shift in military doctrine around the region. Peacekeeping is now a central component of the region's military objectives. The most recent centre in Guatemala is working to create a Central American peace contingent, something that would have been unheard of 20 years ago when those nations were in the throes of their own internal conflicts. These centres also benefit from external support in the form of training and technical assistance from the US, Canadian and European governments.

MINUSTAH also has created a genuine Latin American-dominated peace operation in the Western Hemisphere under UN auspices. This is significant since the leadership of Brazil has shown a new dedication to peace operations while, at the same time, acknowledging the profound challenges to regional peace and stability that remain. This attitude has united governments around the tragic conditions of poverty and deprivation that characterize the situation in Haiti. MINUSTAH also has spurred a regional security consultation process comprised of defence and foreign ministers. This summit has built upon the situation in Haiti by using the forum to discuss a broader regional security agenda. The recent creation of the Defense Council and the emergence of UNASUR reflect a deepening role by Latin American states in a regional geopolitical system that is independent of US influence. Since efforts are in their formative phase, it is unclear how they will coordinate with US, Canadian and European governments. There is evidence, however, that US involvement in other parts of the world, especially in Iraq and Afghanistan, has provided an opening for regional actors to move into the space once dominated by the United States.

Judging from the discussions in the region about troop commitment and financial support of MINUSTAH, a healthy public debate exists around the appropriate role of the armed forces in peace operations. On the one hand, the transitions to democratic governance in the late 1980s and early 1990s were successful in part due to the reintegration of the armed forces into peacekeeping missions. This not only provided the military with a new mission but also fit into the popular notion of civilian control of the armed forces. The increased use of the armed forces in UN operations provided an important outlet for soldiers at a time when there was pressure to downsize forces while also paying for the increased costs of maintaining security in a democratic society.

If MINUSTAH has been the driver of a wider agenda for peace and security in Latin America, it still remains unknown whether it will continue to serve that purpose as the mission comes to a close (at present, it is scheduled to leave in 2011). Haiti's problems will continue as the nation's ability to govern itself and provide security for its population will require external security presence for some time. Recent natural disasters have devastated the island, undermining much of the economic progress that had taken root. Great challenges remain in the wake of these humanitarian crises. The UN presence, however, will facilitate recovery, though it might create a longer timeline for MINUSTAH.

What is important to take from this experience in Haiti is the capacity regional leaders hold to unite around a problem and to support a solution that works multilaterally with the United Nations. Whether this multilateralism will translate into the creation of a regional peacekeeping force to provide stability after the UN operation ends is unresolved. What is clear, however, is that collective security in the Americas will never be the same after MINUSTAH.

## Notes

1. As Manaut writes, "Los procesos de paz en Centroamérica revaloraron la geopolítica de las operaciones de paz en el hemisferio, y se dieron a la par de la democratización de los sistemas políticos. Tanto los países donde se implementaron dichos procesos (principalmente El Salvador y Guatemala), como los países que participaron, evaluaron muy positivamente la forma de lograr el desarme y la pacificación."
2. "Siete países latinoamericanos crearon este lunes 'ALCOPAZ'", *Diario crítico* Ecuador, 8 August 2008. Available at http://www.diariocritico.com/ecuador/2008/Agosto/noticias/90701/latinoamerica.html The countries included Argentina, Brazil, Chile, Ecuador, Guatemala, Peru and Uruguay.

3. United Nations General Assembly Resolution 45/2, 10 October 1990, asked the secretary-general to provide the broadest possible electoral support to Haiti. It created ONUVEH to meet this mandate. The OAS was also asked to participate in this effort.
4. Please see UNSC resolution 1892 (2009). Available at http://www.unhcr.org/refworld/category,LEGAL,,,HTI,4ad886272,0.html
5. As of 29 February 2008, the United States provided a total of 313 forces, or 0.3 per cent, to all UN peacekeeping missions. Of this number, 11 were military troops, 284 were police troops and 18 were military observers. In Haiti, the United States provides 4 police personnel and 45 military troops for a total of 49, or 0.5 per cent of total troop strength. There currently are no US participants in UN peacebuilding operations.
6. Like Uruguay, Peru's debate focuses on monetary conditions (see Obando, 2005).

## REFERENCES

Annan, Kofi (2004) "Helping Hand: Why We Had to Go into Haiti", *Wall Street Journal*, 15 March, p. A12.

Azam, Jean-Paul, Paul Collier and Anke Hoeffler (2001) "International Policies on Civil Conflict: An Economic Perspective", Unpublished Working Paper, 14 December. Available at http://users.ox.ac.uk/~ball0144/research.htm

Council on Hemispheric Affairs (2008a) "The Brazilian Military is Back as it Fleshes Out its Weaponry and Strategies", 9 September. Available at http://www.coha.org/2008/09/the-brazilian-military-is-back-as-it-fleshes-out-its-weaponry-and-strategies/

Council on Hemispheric Affairs (2008b) "Brazil Spearheads UNASUR Defense Council, but in Surprise Move, Colombia Withdraws", 28 May. Available at http://www.coha.org/2008/05/brazil-spearheads-unasur-defense-council-but-in-a-surprise-move-colombia-withdraws/

Dobbins, James, John G. McGinn, Keith Crane, Seth G. Jones, Rollie Lal, Andrew Rathmell, Rachel Swanger and Anga Timilsina (2003) *America's Role in Nation-Building: From Germany to Iraq*. Washington, DC: Rand Corporation.

Gauthier, Amélie and Sarah John de Sousa (2006) "Brazil in Haiti: Debate over the Peacekeeping Mission", *FRIDE Comment*, September. Available at http://www.fride.org/publication/430/brazil-in-haiti-debate-over-the-peacekeeping-mission

Gratius, Susanne (2007) *Brasil en las Américas: Una potencia regional pacificadora?* Madrid: Fride.

Hirst, Monica (2007) "South American Intervention in Haiti", *FRIDE Comment*, 20 April. Available at http://www.fride.org/publication/192/south-american-intervention-in-haiti

Manuat, Raúl Benítez (2008) "América Latina y la seguridad internacional: El Caso de Haití y las misiones de paz", *Revista Enfoques*, 6(8): 7–22.

Mendelson Forman, Johanna (2007) "Special Section on Haiti", in RESDAL, *Atlas Regional de Defensa de America Latina 2007*. Buenos Aires: RESDAL. Available at www.resdal.org

Montgomery, Tommie Sue (1995) "Getting to Peace in El Salvador: The Roles of the United Nations Secretariat and ONUSAL", *Journal of Interamerican Studies and World Affairs*, 37(4): 139–172.

Mora, Oscar Aranda (2000) "Operaciones multinacionales: Mantención o imposición de la paz?" *Revista de marinas*, 1: 30–36.

Obando, Enrique (2005) "Operaciones de mantenimiento de la Paz en Haití: La Participación Peruana", *Security and Defense Studies Review*, 5(1): 179–195.

Pala, Antonio L. (1995) "The Increased Role of Latin American Armed Forces in UN Peacekeeping: Opportunities and Challenges", *Airpower Journal*, Special Edition. Available at http://www.airpower.maxwell.af.mil/airchronicles/apj/apj95/spe-ed95_files/pala.htm

Tokatlian, Juan Gabriel (2008) "A New Doctrine of Insecurity: US Military Deployment in South America", *NACLA Report on the Americas*, 41(5): 6–10.

Ulery, Eduardo (2005) "The Uruguayan Armed Forces and the Challenge of 21st Century Peacekeeping." Master's Thesis, December. Monterrey, CA: Naval Postgraduate School.

UNDP (2005) *UNDP Human Development Report*. New York: Oxford University Press.

UNGA (2003) "Budget Committee Continues Review of Peacekeeping Financing, Addressing Need for Timely Reimbursement of Troop Contributors", United Nations General Assembly, Press Release GA/AB/3561. Available at http://www.un.org/News/Press/docs/2003/gaab3561.doc.htm

United Nations (2008) *United Nations Missions Summary*. 30 September. Available at, http://www.un.org/Depts/dpko/dpko/contributors/2008/sep08_3.pdf

## Appendix

Table 8.A1  Latin American participation in UN peace operations, 1948–2008

| Mission | Original Contributors | Dates |
| --- | --- | --- |
| UNTSO: UN Truce Supervision Organization, Middle East | Argentina, Chile | 1948– |
| UNMOGIP: UN Military Observer Group in India and Pakistan | Argentina | January 1949– |
| UNEF I: UN Emergency Force Gaza | Brazil, Colombia | November 1956–June 1967 |
| UNOGIL: UN Observation Group in Lebanon | Argentina, Chile, Ecuador, Peru | June–December 1958 |
| UNOC: UN Operation in the Congo | Argentina, Brazil | July 1960–June 1964 |
| UNIPOM: UN India–Pakistan Observer Mission | Initial Stages: Chile Full mission: Brazil, Venezuela | September 1965–March 1956 |
| UNEF II: UN Emergency Force, Suez Canal and Sinai Peninsula | Peru | October 1973–July 1979 |
| UNGOMAP: UN Good Offices Mission in Afghanistan and Pakistan | Representative of Secretary-General: Diego Cordovez, Ecuador | May 1988–March 1990 |

Table 8.A1 (cont.)

| Mission | Original Contributors | Dates |
| --- | --- | --- |
| UNIIMOG: UN Iran–Iraq Military Observer Group | Argentina, Peru, Uruguay | August 1988– February 1991 |
| UNAVEM I: UN Angola Verification Mission I | Argentina, Brazil | January 1989–June 1991 |
| UNTAG: UN Transition Assistance Group in Namibia | Barbados, Costa Rica, Guyana, Jamaica, Panama, Peru, Trinidad and Tobago | April 1989–March 1990 |
| ONUCA: UN Observer Group in Central America | Argentina, Brazil, Colombia, Ecuador, Venezuela | November 1989– January 1992 |
| UNIKOM: UN Iraq– Kuwait Observation Mission | Argentina, Chile, Uruguay, Venezuela | April 1991– October 2003 |
| UNAVEM II: UN Angola Verification Mission II | Argentina, Brazil, Colombia | June 1991– February 1995 |
| ONUSAL: UN Observer Mission in El Salvador | Argentina, Brazil, Chile, Colombia, Ecuador, Guyana, Mexico, Venezuela | July 1991–April 1995 |
| UNAMIC: UN Advance Mission in Cambodia | Argentina, Uruguay | October 1991– March 1992 |
| UNPROFOR: UN Protection Force Former Yugoslavia | Argentina, Brazil, Colombia, Venezuela | February 1992– March 1995 |
| UNTAC: UN Transitional Authority in Cambodia | Argentina, Chile, Colombia, Uruguay | March 1992– September 1993 |
| ONUMOZ UN Operation in Mozambique | Argentina, Brazil, Guyana, Uruguay | December 1992– December 1994 |
| UNOMUR: UN Observer Mission in Uganda-Rwanda | Brazil | June 1993– September 1994 |
| UNOMIL: UN Observer Mission in Liberia | Brazil, Uruguay | September 1993– September 1997 |
| UNMIH: UN Mission in Haiti | Antigua and Barbuda, Argentina, Bahamas, Barbados, Belize, Guatemala, Guyana, Honduras, Jamaica, Saint Kitts and Nevis, Saint Lucia, Surinam, Trinidad and Tobago | September 1993– June 1996 |
| UNAMIR: UN Assistance Mission for Rwanda | Argentina, Brazil, Guyana, Uruguay | October 1993– March 1996 |
| UNASOG: UN Aousou Strip Observer Group | Honduras | May–June 1994 |
| UNMOT: UN Mission of Observers in Tajikistan | Uruguay (January 1995–May 2000) | December 1994– May 2000 |

Table 8.A1 (cont.)

| Mission | Original Contributors | Dates |
|---|---|---|
| UNAVEM III: UN Angola Verification Mission III | Brazil, Uruguay | February 1995– June 1997 |
| UNPREDEP: UN Preventive Deployment Force Macedonia | Argentina, Brazil | March 1995– February 1999 |
| UNMIBH: UN Mission in Bosnia and Herzegovina | Argentina, Chile | December 1995– December 2002 |
| UNTAES: UN Transitional Administration for Eastern Slovenia, Baranja and Western Sirumium | Argentina, Brazil | January 1996– January 1998 |
| UNMOP: UN Mission of Observers in Prevlaka | Argentina, Brazil | January 1996– December 2002 |
| UNSMIH: UN Support Mission in Haiti | Trinidad and Tobago | July 1996–July 1997 |
| MINUGUA: UN Verification Mission in Guatemala | Argentina, Brazil, Ecuador, Uruguay, Venezuela | January 1997–May 1997 |
| MONUA: UN Observer Mission in Angola | Argentina, Brazil, Uruguay | June 1997– February 1999 |
| UNTMIH: UN Transition Mission in Haiti | Argentina | August–November 1997 |
| MINOPU: UN Civilian Police Mission in Haiti | Argentina | December 1997– March 2000 |
| UNPSG: UN Civilian Police Support Group in Croatia | Argentina | January–October 1998 |
| UNOMSIL: UN Observer Mission in Sierra Leone | Bolivia, Uruguay | July 1998–October 1999 |
| UNAMSIL: UN Mission in Sierra Leone | Bolivia, Uruguay | October 1999– December 2005 |
| UNTAET: UN Transitional Administration in East Timor | Argentina, Bolivia, Brazil, Chile, Uruguay | October 1999–May 2002 |
| UNMEE: UN Mission in Ethiopia and Eritrea | Bolivia, Brazil, Guatemala, Paraguay, Peru, Uruguay | July 2000–July 2008 |
| UNMISET: UN Mission of Support in East Timor | Argentina, Bolivia, Brazil, Chile, Peru, Uruguay | May 2002–May 2005 |
| ONUB: UN Operation in Burundi | Bolivia, Guatemala, Paraguay, Peru, Uruguay | June 2004– December 2006 |

*Source:* Compiled by Cassia Paigen Roth from UN sources

# 9

# UNPKO and the Latin American forces

*Juan Emilio Cheyre*

## Introduction[1]

Peacekeeping operations (PKO) arise from a mandate of the United Nations, which, through the Security Council, adopts collective measures to maintain international peace and security. Although this has been a key goal of the United Nations since its inception, the term "peace operation" itself is not found in the text of the UN Charter. The framework in which PKOs are initiated, developed and activated is found in Chapters VI, VII and VIII of the UN Charter. Chapter VI refers to peaceful conflict resolution; chapter VII to actions undertaken in response to threats to peace, the interruption of peace or acts of aggression; and Chapter VIII is tied to regional agreements, stating specifically that the United Nations is not opposed to these alliances if they are geared toward peacekeeping and regional security, and only if their actions are compatible with the principles and goals of the United Nations (2010).

Currently, close to 100,000 troops carry out peacekeeping missions throughout the world, including in Africa, the Americas, Asia, Europe and the Middle East. This peacekeeping force, drawn from some 120 countries, is handled by the UN's Department of Peacekeeping Operations (DPKO), which was first headed by Kofi Annan before his election as secretary-general, and whose director reports directly to the UN secretary-general.

The evolution of peacekeeping has been closely tied to the development of the international system: the application of multilateral policies

*Fixing Haiti: MINUSTAH and beyond, Heine and Thompson (eds),*
*United Nations University Press, 2011, ISBN 978-92-808-1197-1*

that seek to resolve problems that are beyond the capacity of individual states and threaten the principles of global peace and stability. Many changes have occurred since the first peacekeeping mission. In 1948, the UN Security Council authorized the deployment of the organization's military observers to the Middle East, charged with the mission to oversee the ceasefire between Israel and its Arab neighbours. Since then, PKOs have evolved in terms of the willingness of states to participate in them, the types of roles which missions undertake, the way in which they are met, the effects produced in the areas where they are carried out and in the type of objectives they must assume. A review of deployments to date reveals 63 UN peacekeeping operations, of which 20 are active as of this writing.

The changing nature of peacekeeping is directly tied to global dynamics, and specifically to the end of the Cold War and the imperatives of globalization. From there sprung the early 1990s programme "An Agenda for Peace" (1992), led by then UN Secretary-General Boutros-Ghali, which laid the foundations for preventive diplomacy, peacemaking, peacekeeping and post-conflict peacebuilding. These concepts were placed in a regulatory framework that defined state actions under the mandates of the United Nations Charter.[2]

Initially somewhat limited in their participation, Latin American countries (LACs) have increased their commitment to PKOs. This is not an accident. With more and more countries in the region becoming active participants in the global order, involvement in PKOs has increased considerably – albeit unevenly, in large part because of the differing world views and perceptions of the international system held by various LACs. Why? A view of PKOs, based on the model of complex interdependence (Keohane and Nye, 1987; Kauppi, 1999: 309), removes LACs from the idealist framework of international relations theory. Rather, the origin, characteristics and the willingness of states to participate in these operations can be explained through realist theory, which allows us to understand Latin America's participation in PKOs, and specifically their high levels of participation in the United Nations Stabilization Mission in Haiti (MINUSTAH).

This chapter discusses the role of LACs in UN peacekeeping operations and their growing involvement in them. With specific reference to MINUSTAH and its predecessors, it examines the underlying causes as to why the Chilean government has been involved in these operations. It then looks outwards to the rest of Latin America to assess how and why other LACs are opening up to these operations as a means to becoming part of the multilateral world order, as well as helping to create a regional security agenda. It concludes with a discussion of what the growing role of LACs in UN PKOs in the region means for their involvement in operations elsewhere.

## MINUSTAH and the regional scenario

Latin American countries hold different perceptions of the necessity and benefits of interdependence and active participation in international organizations. Differences also exist in terms of the involvement of each state in the support of UN resolutions, especially if they are tied to the use of military force for the promotion of peace (Chapter VII of the UN Charter).

In this respect, MINUSTAH has marked a milestone. This is partly the product of the evolution of the international system and the perceptions of the benefits of being part of multilateral operations. The consolidation of democratic systems, as well as the resolution of internal and external conflicts, has also led to greater participation in PKOs. This shift has favoured an integrationist view in support of international cooperation.

It is curious that the poorest country of Latin America, located on the western half of the small island of Hispaniola, marks a regional turning point in terms of commitment to PKOs. The importance of MINUSTAH lies in its origin and in the manner in which it has tried to reach its objectives. The decision of the Chilean government to participate in it provides evidence about emerging regional trends.

Table 9.1 shows the percentage of the contributions to MINUSTAH by Southern Cone countries in relation to their contributions to PKOs around the world. Table 9.2 shows the contribution of troops and police by each region of the world to MINUSTAH (Marcondes de Souza, 2009). Both demonstrate the significant regional commitment of Latin America to the mission in Haiti. Why?

Table 9.1 Percentage of Southern Cone's contributions to MINUSTAH in relation to Southern Cone's general contributions to UNPKO (including troops and police officers)

| Country | MINUSTAH | Total | Percentage |
|---------|----------|-------|------------|
| Argentina | 562 | 893 | 62.9 |
| Brazil | 1,283 | 1,352 | 94.89 |
| Chile | 519 | 525 | 98.85 |
| Uruguay | 1,143 | 2,538 | 45.03 |

*Source:* UNDPKO, December 2008

Table 9.2 MINUSTAH troop and police contribution by region

| Region | Troops | Police | Percentage |
|--------|--------|--------|------------|
| Asia, Africa, Europe, Oceania and Americas | 7,036 | 2,053 | 100 |
| Latin America | 4,102 | 38 | 45.54 (of the total contribution) |
| South America | 3,985 | 34 | 97.07 (of Latin American contributors) |
| Southern Cone (including Paraguay with 31 troops) | 3,504 | 27 | 87.85 (of South American contributors) |

*Source:* UNDPKO, December 2008

In 1993 chronic instability in Haiti led to UN Resolution 1940 which authorized the first PKO in Haiti, known as the United Nations Mission in Haiti (UNMIH). The mission's purpose was to re-establish democracy, create a secure environment and reinstate the power of the police force. In July 1994, 20,000 soldiers were deployed to back up the multinational force. Despite its size, UNMIH failed to reach its objectives.

The series of subsequent international missions reflect the complexity and uniqueness of the Haitian predicament. Between 1994 and 2001 we had: the UN Support Mission in Haiti (UNSMIH); the UN Transition Mission in Haiti (UNTMIH); the UN Civilian Police Mission (MIPONUH); and finally the International Civilian Support Mission (MICAH) in 2001; as well as an Organization of American States (OAS) initiative that deployed a limited civilian human rights mission, MICIVIH. In these missions, Latin American countries were not significantly represented, nor did they bring together a collective willingness to become part of the solution. The problems of a regional neighbour simply did not generate sufficient interest.

Yet, the geographic position of Haiti is key. The country shares an island with the Dominican Republic along a virtually open border. Haiti is located a short distance from both Miami and Caracas, and it has a privileged position in the Caribbean Sea, which surrounds its north, south and west coasts. It is a central hub for the drug trade. This is particularly heightened by its position in a region where this threat has become a key issue, directly related to narco-terrorism, crime and political instability.

None of the above-mentioned missions achieved their goals, thus leaving the country in the hands of successive governments that failed to generate stability, progress or peace. This culminated on 29 February 2004 when President Bertrand Aristide – elected in 2000 – was forced to leave the country following a bloody armed insurrection against him. Subsequently, the president of the Supreme Court, Boniface Alexandre, was sworn in as interim president after announcing Aristide's resignation (see Aldunate, 2010).

The same day, the new Haitian authority requested international assistance from the United Nations and authorized troops to enter the country. The United Nations had already sent a representative to the country and responded to the country's request by approving Resolution 1529, which authorized the deployment of the Multinational Interim Force for Haiti (MIFH). The mandate also called for the establishment of a follow-up UN stabilization force to maintain peace and permit a constitutional process aimed at stabilizing the tumultuous country. The MIFH had a three-month mandate which ended on 29 May 2004. On 29 February, Chile, located 8,000 km away and in a groundbreaking decision, committed itself to Haiti.

## Chile and the mission in Haiti

That same day, Chile received the first news on the subject from then president Ricardo Lagos and then minister of defence Michelle Bachelet. Chile sought to both manage the flow of information on the island's situation and follow the United Nation's decisions closely. Chile's willingness to integrate a multinational force, alongside France, Canada and the United States, was met with interest. The United Nations also made it very clear that it desired to rely on regional powers, in part because previous military missions, missions that were very large but foreign to the Haitian reality, had failed. This was a vital step that opened a space for other countries in the region to participate. It represented a new solution to an old problem that had been impossible to resolve.

In Chile, government opinion was divided as to whether the United Nations would decide to use force. For the army, Sunday, 29 February 2004, became a day to gather background information and create a preparatory order, as is done in these situations. The General Staff for planning was activated; a link was established with Chile's attachés in the United States and the United Nations; and a plan to enlist a unit ready to act from a distance, with a force trained to fulfil whatever type of mission was to be authorized, was assembled. Few armies in the world are capable of mobilizing in such a short time. Indeed, on 3 March, I had the honour of introducing then president Lagos to the commanders of the unit; in the afternoon, then Defence Minister Bachelet oversaw the troops and gave a farewell to the battalion.

There are currently over 5,500 men and women who make up the Chilean XI Battalion. In the first months many of them became part of the MIFH, and following UN Security Council Resolution 1542, on 30 April

2004 they joined MINUSTAH. The transition from MIFH to MINUS-TAH saw the US, Canadian and French forces withdraw and replaced by a contingent that was led on the military side by Brazilian General Augusto Heleno. Leading the mission was Special Representative of the UN Secretary General in Haiti, Chilean Ambassador Juan Gabriel Valdés.

Below are excerpts of the speech I delivered to the military force prior to their departure. They outline the understanding of the mission and orientation of the military responsibilities, which differ considerably from previous missions. They are fully in sync with our objectives of re-establishing peace, avoiding conflicts and laying the foundations for the Haitian people to take charge of their own destiny. These are the guiding principles which lead our conduct in Haiti.

> As I have already reiterated, we do not have enemies, we are not an occupational force, nor are we at war. Our mission was given by the Chilean State, with the authorization of the Senate to cross our borders, by mandate of the United Nations, to work with the Haitian people so that they may once again find peace and civic harmony ... It is with them, and not only among soldiers, but with the people of Haiti, that we must pacify altered spirits and attitudes, leading to a logic of understanding and giving up of arms ... As soldiers, from the moment we embrace this career and prepare ourselves for the missions we must accomplish, we know that the cost may be our lives. And that – because we are fully aware of it – leads us to undertake exhaustive planning. It is a plan that has considered all scenarios, where the goal is zero losses of our own soldiers, and zero losses of the counterpart ... The Coordinator in Haiti is in contact with the delegate from the United Nations that has already arrived on the scene, because every day we must have more coordination, not only among military actors, but also between the actors who are offering sanitary support, health support, and political support, because our effort is to bring peace, and that must be constructed with the many organisms with which we are in contact. No one is alone or conducts himself with individualism. (Cheyre, 2004)

It was thus that Chile, through its army and as a product of a presidential decision, supported by the senate, became the only Latin American country to join the MIFH. This was the first time that the country took on such a task. It moved Chile from a position where it had previously participated only with limited forces – originally as military observers and later with forces of no more than 50 troops – to one in which it plays an active role in UN initiatives involving Chapter VII initiatives. Furthermore, as illustrated in Tables 9.1 and 9.2, the assertive use of Chilean forces led other countries in the region to evaluate and to commit to participate with forces.

Therefore, Haiti marks a critical turning point in relation to the commitment of Latin American countries to PKOs. In the following sections of this chapter, we will analyse the variables that are believed to play a role in this process, as well as the considerations that may prevent other countries from joining in this emerging trend.

## Variables influencing a greater commitment of Latin American countries with PKOs

### *The case of Chile*

The deployment of Chilean forces first in MIFH and later in MINUS-TAH marks a change in Chile towards greater commitment with PKOs. This shift is then projected to other countries in the region.

Figure 9.1 depicts the Chilean army's participation in PKOs. Between 1935 and 1960, 20 members of the army participated in these operations, while between 1990 and 2000, the number jumped to 186. In turn, between 2001 and 2006, the number reached 2,057 troops. The numbers speak for themselves – they reflect the change from timid participation to an assertive commitment. This change can be attributed to a number of factors:

### *The fall of the Berlin Wall*

This event marked a paradigmatic shift in which the Cold War logic dissipated, bipolarity ended, and through UN Secretary-General Boutros-

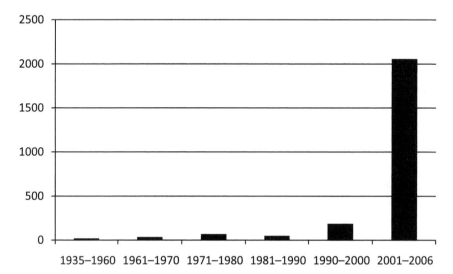

Figure 9.1 Participation of the Chilean Army in peace operations
*Source*: Appendices and data from Varas (2006)

Ghali's aforementioned "Agenda for Peace", the United Nations began to undertake preventive diplomacy and a new type of PKO, in places such as Angola, Cambodia, the former Yugoslavia and Somalia. According to Thomas Weiss:

> these operations were qualitatively and quantitatively different from UN operations during the Cold War. The formal consent of the parties simply could not be assumed to mean much on the ground. Also, the military effectiveness required from, and the dangers faced by, UN military forces went far beyond the parameters of traditional lightly armed peacekeepers. Moreover, these operations suggest the magnitude of the new demands on the UN for services that threaten to overwhelm troop contributors and "break the bank," so to speak. (Weiss, 2001: 60)

Threats thus do not exist only between states, but within borders, changing the nature of conflict and the way in which the United Nations intervenes.

*Chilean commitment to PKOs*

In Chile, the executive, Parliament and armed forces responded to this new trend in 1996 by defining a policy for Chilean participation in PKOs, termed the "National Policy for Participation of the State in Peacekeeping Operations". In 1999, it was supplemented by legislation that assigned the ministers of foreign relations and national defence with the task of assessing and informing decisions by the Government of Chile relating to participation in peacekeeping operations. This presidential directive limited the support of the armed forces to missions established under Chapter VI of the UN Charter (Le Dantec, 2006: 118). Then in December 2008, Parliament further codified Chile's commitment to international peacekeeping by passing the Law on Peacekeeping Missions, which allows for the creation of an Inter-Ministerial Commission for Peacekeeping Operations. This Commission is charged with permanently advising the ministers of foreign relations and national defence on issues relating to participation of national troops in PKOs. This same legislation also states that the president should request the approval of the senate for the dispatch of troops by means of an official document and with the signatures of the ministers of foreign relations and national defence. Chile has thus embraced the new international sensibilities of the post-Cold War era. When a state takes on such commitments, the government and the armed forces need to be in agreement regarding the standing of those from neighbouring countries over border disputes. Decisions about involvement in international PKOs must also be made in a democratic context that allows the armed forces full dedication to these duties, meaning they cannot be involved with domestic activities such as those that occurred in Chile and elsewhere in the hemisphere during the military regimes of the 1970s and 1980s.

In Chile, the successful resolution of 22 border disputes with Argentina in 2000 created an atmosphere of confidence that allowed the armed forces to lower their involvement in the defence of national territory, thus opening a space for PKOs. Mutual confidence with Argentina led to the groundbreaking creation of a joint unit that, in 2003, sent a military force to the UN PK mission in Cyprus. In 2006, the unit became the basis of what is now known as the bi-national "Southern Cross Force", with integrated commands and general staff, a groundbreaking initiative.

At the time of military rule in Chile and other countries of the region, there was a lack of confidence in these bodies, specifically the United Nations but also the OAS.[3] Regarding participation in PKOs, this persisted even after President Patricio Aylwin came to power with the return to democracy on 11 March 1990. This was due in part to the fact that General Augusto Pinochet remained as army chief. Pinochet did not believe in PKOs. His position in this regard was reflected in a statement made in 1997: "the Army, being consequent with national policy, sustains the doctrine that, regarding peace operations, these are exclusively humanitarian, therefore the use of coercive force to impose peace is considered inappropriate" (quoted in Le Dantec, 2006: 119). With his departure, a different view emerged.

*A shift in Chilean foreign policy towards multilateralism and international integration*

The third factor that plays a role in the paradigm shift in Chile is the large number of Free Trade Agreements it has signed. These agreements brought the country into close ties with important regions such as the United States, the European Union and Asia. Table 9.3 depicts the large network of agreements that have multiplied by several levels of magnitude the scope of Chile's foreign trade.

This engagement with the international community influenced the way in which the government, the opposition and society viewed the world. Chile linked up with remote nations and benefitted from it. The conclusion was reached that stable countries with the means to do so should contribute to pacifying countries experiencing instability and conflict.

*A shift in the military and its mentality*

Participation in a PKO requires that armed forces have a doctrine, with planning, organization, equipment, instruction, training and personnel with a sufficient level of expertise to confront the challenges this entails. Chile transformed and modernized its armed forces in general and the army in particular. The changes began in 1999, and were consolidated in

Table 9.3 Chile–Asia trade (US$ millions)

| | 1998 | 1999 | 2000 | 2001 | 2002 | 2003 | 2004 | 2005 | 2006 | 2007 | 2008 |
|---|---|---|---|---|---|---|---|---|---|---|---|
| South Korea | 974 | 1,098 | 1,343.80 | 1,116.90 | 1,152.80 | 1,554.50 | 2,500.70 | 3,283.20 | 5,046.60 | 6,933.2 | 7,044.7 |
| China | 1,338.20 | 1,207.30 | 1,908.50 | 2,128.30 | 2,441 | 3,294.5 | 5,263 | 6,927.35 | 8,633.00 | 14,864 | 16,655.5 |
| India | 120.7 | 156 | 194.6 | 192.9 | 291.6 | 298.8 | 526.7 | 627 | 1,653.40 | 2,420.1 | 2,221.7 |
| Japan | 3,066.92 | 2,912.30 | 3,250.00 | 2,715.80 | 2,426.40 | 2,871.30 | 4,494.40 | 5,544.70 | 7,184.70 | 8,705.2 | 9,896 |
| Total Asia | 5,499.82 | 5,374 | 6,696.90 | 6,153.90 | 6,312.10 | 8,019.10 | 12,784.80 | 16,382.25 | 22,517.70 | 32,923 | 35,817.9 |

*Source:* Created by the author based on data from Customs

2002–2006, and are scheduled to be completed by 2010. The army transitioned from being a territorial, vertically and hierarchically organized force, employing materials, equipment and weapons from the 1950s, towards an institution that is functional, inter-operative and equipped to NATO standards. A new strategic and operational doctrine with emphasis on the challenges associated with PKOs was also developed.

*Cases in the region*

Considering the four variables mentioned above, we can examine in the experiences of other Latin American countries, which have also resulted in a greater commitment to the needs of the United Nations, especially regarding the PKO in Haiti.

The countries in Table 9.4 – particularly the Latin American ones – have experienced changes with respect to their attitudes towards PKOs that are not dissimilar to those of Chile. The result has been a more active commitment to PKOs. Those countries where the factors have been stronger have contributed more prominently (Brazil, Chile, Argentina and Uruguay). Those countries where the variables have been weaker have contributed in a more limited fashion (Bolivia, Ecuador, Guatemala, Paraguay and Peru).

Table 9.4 Breakdown of MINUSTAH forces

| No. | Country | Officials | Troops | Total by Country |
|-----|---------|-----------|--------|------------------|
| 1 | Argentina | 9 | 549 | 558 |
| 2 | Bolivia | 3 | 205 | 208 |
| 3 | Brazil | 15 | 1267 | 1282 |
| 4 | Canada | 4 | – | 4 |
| 5 | Chile | 6 | 497 | 503 |
| 6 | Croatia | 3 | – | 3 |
| 7 | Ecuador | 1 | 66 | 67 |
| 8 | France | 2 | – | 2 |
| 9 | Guatemala | 4 | 113 | 117 |
| 10 | Jordan | 10 | 718 | 728 |
| 11 | Nepal | 10 | 1067 | 1077 |
| 12 | Paraguay | – | 31 | 31 |
| 13 | Peru | 4 | 204 | 208 |
| 14 | Phillipines | 2 | 155 | 157 |
| 15 | Sri Lanka | 11 | 949 | 960 |
| 16 | Uruguay | 14 | 1123 | 1137 |
| 17 | United States | 4 | – | 4 |
| | Total | 102 | 6,944 | 7,046 |

*Source:* CECOPAC data. See www.cecopac.cl

The numbers above refer to the mission in Haiti. This suggests an understanding that conflicts in one country can be a threat to the region as a whole. Governments of different political persuasions now have similar views regarding PKOs in a multilateral context. PKOs also provide the forces with a means of interaction and cooperation that builds trust, even between countries with a history of border differences, such as Peru with Ecuador and Chile with Argentina.

The aforementioned countries make up 48 per cent of the total troop contributions to MINUSTAH (UN, 2009). There are, however, important countries that are absent, such as Mexico, Venezuela and Colombia. Also, Central America and the Caribbean are only represented by Guatemala. In these countries, the factors cited above have either not been present, or are still developing. Domestic problems or government positions towards foreign involvement may also prevent them from contributing to PKOs.

## Missing in action? Neighbours' reasons for not being involved in Haiti

### Mexico

In the case of Mexico, its legislation prevents the deployment of military forces beyond its borders. Mexico is also currently fighting drug traffickers at home. This has meant the deployment of the armed forces for internal security purposes.

Nonetheless, there have been important indications of a greater willingness on the part of President Calderón's administration to take a more active role regarding Mexico's integration into PKOs and, particularly, in its closest area of influence, Central America and the Caribbean. A possible scenario in the medium term may be the evolution of military ideology and a shift in political will, altering Mexico's traditional absence from these initiatives. While Mexico is contributing development assistance to Haiti, an invitation from international organizations and from countries like Chile and Brazil to join these military initiatives would be of help. It would certainly benefit a regional policy on the subject, where the presence of Mexico would be a great asset.

### Colombia

In the case of Colombia, which contributes a smaller number of police forces to MINUSTAH, the reason for their minimal involvement lies in the country's more than 40-year battle against narco-terrorism. This confirms the proposition that a state does not participate in PKOs when problems of this nature exist within its territory.

## Venezuela

Venezuela is certainly a different case, in that its unique form of managing its foreign policy is directly tied to the ideology of twenty-first-century socialism. This translates into constant denunciations from President Hugo Chávez that international organizations like the United Nations serve as a disguise for the political interests of the United States. This position implies a rejection of UN actions. This indifference to international cooperation through the United Nations has stood in the way of a Venezuelan contribution to the missions. While Venezuela does give considerable amounts of aid to Haiti, initial cooperation by Venezuela has been selective. It is only undertaken in situations where unilateral leadership can be exercised and is focused on those countries with an ideological affinity.

## Central America

In Central America, only Guatemala has some degree of involvement in Haiti. As in the cases of Mexico and Colombia, the reason for this subregional absence, even considering that these are the countries most affected by Haitian instability, results from governments and armed forces that have a high degree of involvement in the battle against so-called emerging threats within their borders, which have reached a worrying level in the subregion (OAS, 2009: 8). Levels of violence, crime and drug trafficking are high in Central America. For example, in Figure 9.2 and Table 9.5 we see that the levels of homicide in Latin America are higher than in many other regions of the world, and have increased in recent years. These figures relate directly to the high levels of violence and drug trade that plague the region and monopolize the concerns and use of its armed forces and police.

# Conclusion

In Latin America, the last decade has marked a PKO paradigm shift, implying greater support for multilateralism, trust in international organizations and a willingness to use armed forces beyond domestic borders. It shows that the participating countries have been capable of resolving

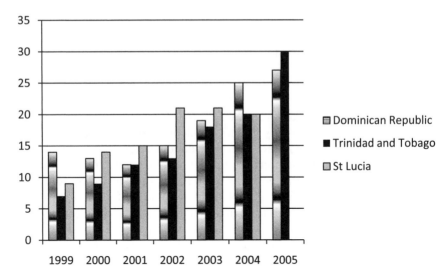

Figure 9.2  Homicide rates in the Dominican Republic, St Lucia, and Trinidad and Tobago, 1999–2005
*Source*:  UNOD/LAC World Bank, 2007: 13

Table 9.5  Number of homicides in world regions (per 100,000 people)

| | |
|---|---|
| Caribbean | 30 |
| South/West Africa | 29 |
| South America | 26 |
| East/SE Asia | 22 |
| Central America | 22 |
| East Europe | 17 |
| Central Asia | 9 |
| East Africa | 8 |
| North America | 7 |
| South Asia | 4 |
| Southeast Europe | 3 |
| Oceania | 3 |
| West/Central Europe | 2 |
| North Africa | 1 |
| Middle East/SW Asia | 1 |

*Source:*  OAS, 2009

their internal problems, strengthening their armed forces, developing national policies on the issue, and in doing so, taking on missions that until recently had been quite alien to them.

The mission in Haiti constitutes the best proof of this. The fact that this is the first PKO mission formed by contingents of Latin American troops is telling. The region has finally taken on a commitment in its own geopolitical space. However, this does not translate into Latin American support for PKOs in other regions of the world. In 2009 there were 19 missions controlled by the DPKO, with 93,530 deployed troops from 118 contributing countries. Only 13.5 per cent of these countries are Latin American, and in terms of deployed forces they only contribute 7 per cent of the total operating in the world.[4]

Comparing this contribution to that of MINUSTAH, one notes an important difference. In the case of MINUSTAH, the region's contribution is 48 per cent of the troops, much greater than the 7 per cent on a worldwide level. Additionally, analysing the data of the 20 countries that contribute the most to PKOs, Uruguay is the only one from the region that appears on the list, coming in at number 15. Paradoxically, higher on the list are states of less influence than many in the region that are located in distant territories and distanced from the effects of international conflict, such as Bangladesh, Nigeria, Nepal, Rwanda and Ghana (UN, 2009).

Even so, looking forward, one can envisage the possibility of greater involvement in operations of this nature. On the regional level, Mexico's commitment is desirable, as it would carry an explicit example to Central American countries. For states that are not currently contributing to PKOs, the resolution of their internal problems, the consolidation of democracy, a greater professionalization of their armed forces for this type of operation and the political will to assume a multilateral commitment are required.

Finally, the world's current conflicts, of which a majority are in Africa, raises the question of whether Latin American countries should go to distant places, separate from their historical and cultural identity, and with levels of complexity greater than those that result from operating in closer and more familiar places. With current data, we cannot answer whether Latin American troops will join missions in foreign regions. The decision to participate in these new scenarios will depend on the importance that states give to the character of and commitment to multilateral action. This will involve a debate on foreign policy that has not yet taken place.

## Notes

1. This chapter was written with contributions from Mariana Perry, candidate for Master of International Studies, University of Chile; Licentiate in History, Catholic University of Chile and Analyst of the Center for International Studies, UC.
2. It is vital to highlight that the creation of the Peacebuilding Commission originated in Resolutions A/RES/60/180 and S/RES/1645(2005) of 20 December 2005, of the General Assembly and the Security Council, respectively, with the objective of joining forces for peace in post-conflict countries. This highlights the commitment of PKOs, not only to

controlling a conflict situation but also in setting the institutional foundations for the future that allow the state in question to sustain the stability that permits growth and development.

3. In this regard, Paulina Le Dantec (2006:50) establishes that "Chile, for the first time in the history of the 20<sup>th</sup> Century, breaks with its multilateral tradition of international work framed in the context of the United Nations, and with this it also distances itself politically from regional organizations like the OAS".

4. Calculated based on an analysis of force deployment in UN 2009 Report and MINUS-TAH Force Report corresponding to March 2009.

## REFERENCES

Aldunate, Eduardo (2010) *Backpacks Full of Hope: The UN Mission in Haiti.* Waterloo: Wilfrid Laurier University Press.

Cheyre, Juan Emilio (2004) "Discurso del comandante en Jefe del Ejército al despedir al segundo contingente del batallón Chile", Speech delivered in Santiago, 9 March.

Kauppi, Mark (1999) *International Relations Theory: Realism, Globalism and Beyond.* Boston: Allyn and Bacon.

Keohane, Robert and Joseph Nye (1987) "Realism and Complex Interdependence" in Frank J. Lechner and John Boli (eds), *The Globalization Reader Second Edition.* Oxford: Blackwell Publishing, pp. 77–83.

Le Dantec, Paulina (2006) *Chile y las operaciones de paz: estudio comparado de la política exterior de los tres gobiernos concertacionistas: de la reinserción internacional a la participación en Haití.* Santiago: ANEPE.

Marcondes de Souza, Danilo (2009) "Challenges for Latin American Peacekeeping in Haiti". Presentation prepared for the Congress of the Latin American Studies Association, Rio de Janeiro, Brazil, 11–14 June.

OAS (2009) *Declaration on Security in the Americas.* Commemoration of the Fifth Anniversary of the Declaration on Security in the Americas, Department of Policy and Program Coordination, Secretariat of Multidimensional Security, Washington, DC: Organization of American States, 19 February.

United Nations (2009) "Report of the Secretary-General on the United Nations Stabilization Mission in Haiti", 1 September, S/2009/439. Available at http://www.cecopac.cl

United Nations (2010) *Charter of the United Nations.* New York: United Nations. Available at http://www.un.org/en/documents/charter/

UNOD/LAC World Bank (2007) *Crime, Violence and Development: Trends, Costs and Policy Options in the Caribbean.* A Joint Report by the United Nations Office on Drugs and Crime and the Latin America and the Caribbean Region of the World Bank, Report No. 37820, March. Available at http://www.unodc.org/pdf/world%20bank%20C&V%20Report.pdf

Varas, Antonio (2006) *Visión histórica de la participación en Operaciones de paz del Ejército de Chile 1935–2006.* Santiago: The Chilean Army and the Geographic Military Institute.

Weiss, Thomas, David Forsythe and Roger Coate (2001) *The United Nations and Changing World Politics.* Boulder, CO: Westview Press.

# Part III
# The hemispheric players

# 10

# Haiti and the regional dynamics of international cooperation

*José Raúl Perales*

## Introduction

The myriad problems in Haiti are too daunting for the fragile state to address on its own. Recognizing this, the international community has directed a large amount of support towards this Caribbean country. In the aftermath of the January 2010 earthquake, this support was dramatically increased; a March 2010 United Nations donor conference saw more than a dozen donors pledge nearly US$10 billion, twice the amount that the country had requested (quoted in Carroll, 2010). This group of international donors includes countries that have been traditionally active players in Haiti's stabilization, such as "The Big Three" of the United States, Canada and France, as well as a group of rising Latin American and Caribbean (LAC) actors who are becoming increasingly involved in their regional neighbour's security and future (Loredo, 2009) – most noticeably the ABC countries of Argentina, Brazil and Chile.

Much of Latin America's newly found activism and self-confidence in global politics, especially on the diplomatic, humanitarian, political and peacekeeping fronts, can trace its origins in collaborative efforts to stabilize Haiti since 2004. As an initiative undertaken by Latin American countries within the context of multilaterally sanctioned mandates, stemming from shared principles of global responsibility in matters of abject poverty and political instability, Latin American cooperation in Haiti is an exemplary case for understanding the evolution of the region's foreign policy choices and behaviour.

*Fixing Haiti: MINUSTAH and beyond, Heine and Thompson (eds),*
*United Nations University Press, 2011, ISBN 978-92-808-1197-1*

Haiti has become an important test case for examining the ways in which multiple foreign actors of various juridical and institutional characteristics work with one another. Efforts in Haiti illustrate the successes and failures of: new developments in inter-regional cooperation; the role of international institutions in mediating domestic crises and building democratic governance; and the role of international factors and variables in legitimizing – or hindering – changes in the institutions of countries involved in (and subject to) sustained humanitarian cooperation efforts.

The aim of this chapter is to focus on this interaction, to examine regional cooperation in Haiti through the lens of international relations theory and to provide a critical assessment of certain aspects of international cooperation and international institutional behaviour as applied to the case of Haiti. In this sense, and contrary to other chapters in this volume, Haiti appears as a sole variable for analysis, though its treatment as a case study is in no way meant to diminish the enormity of the task for which international cooperation is sorely needed. Yet it is hoped that this exercise may ultimately offer possible avenues for further research on understanding the interplay between theory and praxis of international cooperation among developing countries.

## Situating Haiti in the international system

Much of what analysts and observers of international politics or international relations discuss about Haiti stems from treatment of the country as a failed or quasi-failed state. In principle such statements seem appropriate given the circumstances affecting Haitian politics, the economy and society. Indeed, there is a large amount of literature on "failed states" that touches upon many of the most prescient questions and circumstances at play in Haiti (see Kaplan, 1994; Rotberg, 2002). Studies on the international politics of such countries focus on aspects of regional stability or instability resulting from state failure or breakdown; foreign military interventions in cases where failed states are zones of military conflict (especially civil wars); questions of transnational actors (terrorists, NGOs) and their work in these countries given inorganic, weak or non-present state institutions; and other thematic considerations such as environmental decay, public health problems, migration or other problems spilling over national borders (see Chesterman, et al., 2005; Rotberg 2003; Miliken, 2003).

However, analysts disagree on the treatment of Haiti as a case of state failure. An example of this is when distinguishing between state failure and state collapse: the first being the case of a government losing its ability to provide public goods such as security and the right to participate in politics given the persistence of intense conflict; the second, a geographic expression of a territory where centralized political authority has all but disappeared. Rotberg characterizes Haiti as an endemically weak but not failed state. Haiti has no ethnic, religious or other communal cleavages that are typically found in failing states. Although violence and crime are a major concern, there is no insurgency in Haiti, nor is there any rapid deflation or economic collapse. In this respect, Haiti may be better regarded as a "fragile state" (see Shamsie and Thompson, 2006).

While useful, many of these approaches confine Haiti to a rather narrow place in terms of our understanding and appreciation of the features of normalcy in the country and as a member of the international system. This focus distracts from the tools available in Haiti to effect long-lasting change, which is the objective of international involvement in the country in the first place. In addition, it could deprive us of empirical material and analytical lessons that may be learned from circumstances at play in Haiti for theoretical development in fields of inquiry such as international institutions, theories of international cooperation, state behaviour and other such areas.[1]

In order to discuss the regional dynamics at play in Haiti, it is necessary to understand the factors and circumstances influencing Latin American and other actors involved in the various operations in Haiti as well as the way in which the country relates to the broader international system through which it seeks trade, investment, cooperation, security and other state goals.

## Situating Haiti in Latin American international relations

International assistance efforts in Haiti, from peacekeeping to stabilization, have been deemed so daunting that even before the January 2010 earthquake a few calls had been made for an "international trusteeship" (Ward, 2006), despite the presence of MINUSTAH.[2] The idea for a trusteeship is rather controversial in Haitian politics, as it runs counter to deeply rooted sentiments of sovereignty and national independence that have characterized Haiti's complicated relations with foreign powers.[3] Yet this is where Latin American and Caribbean cooperation in MINUSTAH brings important new elements to the table. Assistance to Haiti has traditionally come from actors such as Canada, the United States and France, the latter two important foreign powers whose past role in Haitian politics often makes their involvement a politically charged affair, more so in the climate of public unrest and volatility in post-Aristide Haiti. In contrast, Latin American and Caribbean involvement carries no such political undertones, and thus lends itself to a different type of relationship with the population and the relevant political actors through which peace and stability must be achieved and institutionalized.[4]

To be sure, Latin American involvement in Haiti did not start with MINUSTAH, just as this is not the United Nations' first mission in the country, although it can be considered a turning point in Latin America's involvement in peacekeeping affairs.[5] Latin American participation in peacekeeping missions had been relatively rare; even in the case of Haiti, in which four missions had preceded the current MINSUTAH effort, participation by neighbouring countries was strongest in the first effort (UNMIH) and much diminished at their end. Their relatively weak participation in UN missions can be attributed to a variety of factors, including political susceptibilities regarding foreign intervention in another Latin American or Caribbean country (as will be explained below); the ambiguous relationship between fragile democracies and the armed forces in many Latin American countries during the earlier part of the 1990s; and the absence of an obvious political "anchor" to domestic interests.[6]

From a foreign policy standpoint, participation in multilateral military expeditions, even for peacekeeping purposes, conflicted with an historical apprehension most Latin American and Caribbean governments have felt regarding foreign military units in national territories. The concern lies not so much in nationalistic posturing but rather in the complicated history of foreign interventions (military, political, economic) that these countries have endured throughout much of their independent lives.[7] This apprehension finds in Haiti an acute case, to the extent that its occupation by the United States (and the blockade imposed by the French after independence) still plays an important role in the historical memory and political repertoire of politicians and other leaders, not just in Haiti but elsewhere in the Caribbean.

Yet some of these perceptions and attitudes have been changing since the mid-1990s, especially in cases of egregious human rights violations or instances of dire need and potential humanitarian disasters.[8] The consolidation of democratic rule and the rule of law throughout much of Latin America have also reduced the seeming conflict between peacekeeping work, the establishment of democratic rule and domestic politics, especially in the Southern Cone and Central America. This may help explain why it is only in 2004 that a UN peacekeeping mission has consisted of a majority of Latin American troops.

Indeed, Latin American cooperation in Haiti builds on regional precedents stemming from the Contadora process of the 1980s that subsequently led to the Rio Group, as well as unilateral or bilateral mediating efforts launched by Brazil and Argentina in cases of crisis and regional instability, such as their responses to the Peru–Ecuador war of 1995 and Paraguay's attempted coup in 1996. The ideological principle underlying the evolution of this cooperation is the search for regional solutions to regional problems – a practice more recently witnessed in several African (Zimbabwe, Congo) and Asian (East Timor) cases – that has become entrenched in Latin America and the Caribbean.

The MINUSTAH mission in Haiti also builds on the expertise that the ABC countries (Argentina, Brazil, and Chile) have developed in peacekeeping since the return of democracy to the region, as explained above. This is also why regional intervention in Haiti has originated from Southern Cone countries rather than from Haiti's more immediate neighbors (and potentially those with a larger vested interest in a stable and successful Haiti), such as Mexico, Venezuela, Cuba and the Dominican Republic.

ABC countries also possess a particular trajectory in human rights, links to democracy and governance, and other humanitarian affairs, together forming the backbone of a principled policy that finds in Haiti a moral case for action. This is all the more relevant because a unifying and consistent feature of most Latin American foreign policies has been the strict observance of the principle of non-intervention in the domestic affairs of other countries. Countries in the region have altered their perceptions regarding sovereignty to allow for international intervention for humanitarian purposes (see Farer, 1996). As demonstrated in the case of Kosovo in 1999, the ABC countries did not reject NATO's intervention even if it did not have a stated mandate or approval from the UN Security Council but was based on a principled position that national sovereignty should be related to respect for human rights (Serrano, 2000).

As in most cases of international cooperation, absolute and relative gains, as well as multiple levels and intersections of national interests, were at play in the decision of the ABC countries to intervene in Haiti – the maintenance of the military and technical presence, and the necessary collaboration and coordination with other actors (state, intergovernmental and non-governmental) at work in Haiti.

## MINUSTAH and beyond: The ABCs

Intervention in Haiti following President Aristide's departure from power in 2004 was a controversial matter for the ABC countries. It was debated in the Argentine congress and was an issue of much internal discussion in the Brazilian executive, on account of the nature of the mission: namely, whether it would be an occupation force (because Aristide left power through violent means) or a peacekeeping one. Given the recent history of these countries, especially the lessons from democratic breakdowns, this was no small consideration. It bears some parallel to the case of CARICOM, whose initial sanctioning of Haiti began on account of a break in the democratic order of the country.

Other matters were also an issue of debate. The expenditure of financial and military resources in foreign operations in the face of citizen insecurity at home in Brazil and the collapse of Argentina's economy, as recently as 2002, and the problem of resources for military missions, were also considered.

The mission in Haiti entailed different considerations for the respective foreign policies and international interests of the ABC countries. Brazil's leadership role in MINUSTAH fits with its aspirations to play a larger global role in security and governance affairs, thus supporting its bid for a permanent seat in the United Nations Security Council.[9] In spite of its economic travails, Argentina had a serious interest in participating in the mission in Haiti, not only because of its long trajectory in UN peacekeeping operations (of the more than 50 peacekeeping operations created since 1948, Argentina has participated in 35) but also because of concerns over not being left out of what was becoming a "regional mission". Additionally, Argentina, for whom MERCOSUR occupies a key role in the formulation of its foreign policy, saw in regional collaboration in MINUSTAH a chance to give MERCOSUR a security and common foreign policy component. In Chile, as in the other countries, participation in MINUSTAH played an important role in the transformation of the identity and missions of the country's armed forces, a process that has also included Chilean participation in peacekeeping operations elsewhere.

## Argentina

In spite of its trajectory in peacekeeping operations and its previous involvement in such activities in Haiti, Argentina's decision to participate in MINUSTAH was a divisive and controversial affair in government and civil society. Considering the circumstances surrounding the removal of President Aristide from power, it was not entirely clear that MINUSTAH would be a peacekeeping operation in the strict sense of the term (as opposed to a "peace-imposition" mission). Were it to be the latter, it would run counter to longstanding principles of Argentine foreign policy, specifically on matters of non-intervention but also on the possible use of the country's armed forces in policing and repressive actions (Lengyel, 2006). Yet Brazil's and Chile's relatively quick joining of MINUSTAH, without consulting Argentina, introduced strategic concerns in the Kirchner government about both countries' interests in increasing regional influence and international projection at the expense of a financially weakened Argentina. This convinced the Argentine foreign policy establishment about the importance of participating in MINUSTAH: a line of thought had evolved from neighbourly suspicion to a new thinking about confidence-building measures and strategic cooperation among the ABC countries in matters of collective security and other foreign policy goals.

Argentine participation in MINUSTAH thus was originally conceived (and authorized by Congress) as a short-term mission to control violence and allow the safe provision of international humanitarian assistance to meet basic social needs. The early success of MINUSTAH and the assessment of the dramatic political and economic situation and needs in Haiti, however, shifted Argentina's perception of its role in the multinational force from a short-term commitment to a broader, more comprehensive notion of development and democracy involving functioning institutions, sustainable growth and social justice. This shift translated into a new legitimacy for Argentine participation, including a renewed and extended mandate from Congress (which must authorize all uses of Argentine armed forces abroad) and a greater involvement by civil society and other actors.

Yet one should be careful about reading too much into such interest and policy transformation. In spite of long-term efforts and substantive participation in policy debates concerning its democratic and economic development, Haiti remains a distant land for Argentine political audiences and an isolated "topic" in Argentine foreign policy, a political realm that itself has suffered important transformations in recent governments.[10] Argentina's involvement in Haiti remains a symbol of principles guiding Argentine foreign affairs, from multilateralism to strategic cooperation, but is also a reminder of limits to the type of sustained engagement in Haiti that can be expected when a middle income country's attention to international affairs and its capability to deliver much needed public goods are compromised over domestic and other regional, equally pressing concerns.

## Brazil

Brazilian involvement in Haiti also proved controversial in domestic politics, in light of debates regarding fiscal spending and foreign policy strategies in the newly inaugurated Lula government. After the return of democratic rule in 1985, international cooperation, especially South–South forms of technical and diplomatic cooperation focused on the regional context, assumed a pivotal role in Brazilian foreign policy. Successive governments supported initiatives such as the Rio Group, the Buenos Aires Act and other attempts to build cooperative forums with regional partners, in the process helping to build trust in Brazil as a regional leader and partner. As in the case of Chile, these efforts also provided an important vehicle for recasting the armed forces away from old doctrines of national security and perceptions of threats associated with domestic politics and national developments. Thus the groundwork was laid for an increasing role of Brazil in regional and global affairs as we see today.

Involvement in Haiti seemed like a natural progression in the evolution of these multiple facets and identities of Brazilian foreign policy and the country's armed forces. It came in the context of an evolution of Brazilian thinking about the role of international organizations and their role in peacekeeping – the difference between keeping the peace and peace imposition, and the degree to which institutions are called to exert a bigger role in deeply conflicted zones (see Valler Filho, 2007), while also recognizing and strengthening the centrality of sovereignty and non-intervention as principles of Brazilian foreign policy. It became a testing ground for Brazilian leadership and international projection in the context of renewed aspirations for a permanent seat in the Security Council of the United Nations. The effort to lead a multilateral peacekeeping mission with a UN mandate acquired a deep significance and place in Brazil's foreign policy agenda, especially if the mission was to take place in a Latin American or Caribbean country, an area commonly regarded in Brazil's foreign policy establishment as its traditional sphere of action.

Principles of solidarity, cooperation and democratic consolidation notwithstanding, Brazilian participation in MINUSTAH was at first the subject of much domestic debate in the legislative and executive branches of government. Because some Brazilian politicians perceived the mission as peace imposition and not peacekeeping, as had also been the case in Argentina, the possibility of Brazilian involvement (not to mention leadership) in the multinational force became the subject of attacks from the opposition through media and other public channels. As the Lula government implemented ambitious programmes to curtail increasing fiscal deficits and contain urban violence, some politicians speculated about the appropriateness of sending the largest contingent of Brazilian troops since World War II to a mission that was considered to be a legitimization of American imperialism and of the violent removal of democratically elected President Aristide (see Diniz, 2005).

## Chile

In keeping with its trajectory of participation in UN peacekeeping missions to Haiti, Chile's role proved critical at the onset of the governability crisis following the departure of President Aristide, and later as the mission morphed into the MINUSTAH stabilization mission. While President Lagos's decision to send troops to Haiti (at the request of UN Secretary-General Kofi Annan as well as the US and French governments) was quick and made without consultation with the Chilean senate (a politically risky and controversial move), important political interests brought about this course of action. Chile had been criticized for its relative indifference to regional problems, its excessive reliance on commercial diplomacy and its relative isolationism (see Llenderozas, 2006). The fact that MINUSTAH elicited a regional response from Brazil and later Argentina reaffirmed for the Chilean foreign policy establishment the political significance of the mission for Chilean hemispheric relations. Chilean politicians also perceived that the country's unwillingness to support a UN Security Council resolution authorizing the invasion of Iraq a year earlier, followed by the ratification of a free trade agreement with Chile in the US Congress, required sending a strong signal to the United States about Chile's commitment to strengthening bilateral links.

In this sense, it is very important to note the regional identity of MINUSTAH (in spite of the individual motivations of its participants) and the ways in which the ABC countries have come to develop a sense of community in their work on Haiti. This is no small feat considering that until very recently these countries had considered each other as security threats and maintained the possibility of armed conflict in strategic scenarios. MINUSTAH became a catalyst for a strategic security dialogue, especially between Chile and Argentina (all the more important after the gas crisis of 2003). But more generally, cooperation on Haiti and MINUSTAH galvanized a vision of the ABC countries as mature democracies operating in a region of peace and stability, built on certain governance principles.

The challenge confronting the ABC countries and others currently involved in Haiti is how to move this cooperation beyond matters of stability (still a daunting and delicate task) towards institution-building. Regional cooperation in Haiti has been a sort of learning process for the Latin Americans as much as the first intervention in peacekeeping was a lesson for their militaries and foreign policy/security doctrines. ABC countries ought to be considered as mature democracies which can therefore bring a variety of resources and instruments to bear upon the institutional construction that needs to develop in Haiti. The question now is from the perspective of the ABC countries: how does their involvement in Haiti evolve into building governance and the basis for political and administrative sustainability of Haiti, especially given the level of commitment, coordination and resources required to carry through this uncertain task? This is a more pressing matter following the January 2010 earthquake that has raised the notion of "refounding" Haiti as the way forward.

## The Caribbean context of Haiti

At this point it is also instructive to discuss the role of international institutions and the regional dynamics at play in Haiti. Following the analytical logic proposed in the introduction to this chapter, the discussion of international institutions here will not highlight the work of bodies such as the United Nations, the Organization of American States (OAS) or the World Bank, though coordination among these bodies and national governments itself offers an interesting scenario for developing hypotheses and propositions about the interrelationships between layers of governance in the international system and specific policy scenarios.[11] Instead, the focus in this chapter is on organizations to which Haiti belongs, particularly ones with more stringent terms of member commitments and rules of behavior. Most salient among these is the Caribbean Community (CARICOM), to which Haiti acceded in 1995 as one of the only two non-English speaking members of the Community.

A note should be made regarding the capacity of states like Haiti to effectively participate in international bodies and rule-based institutions. Given its particular domestic circumstances, Haitian participation in international organizations and other interstate forums has been constrained and determined by its dire governance and economically strained circumstances, not to mention domestic political vetoes that hinder Haiti's ability to strike bargains and maintain policy consistency. Nevertheless, Haiti belongs to several relevant international institutions in the Caribbean region whose policies and activities are, or ought to be, a very important component of the regional dynamics at play in any effort to build effective governance in Haiti. Because Haiti is not a failed state, in the sense described by the literature and highlighted earlier in this chapter, it is still possible to speak about the domestic role of international institutions, particularly the import of rules and the supply of a variety of public goods that can influence state behaviour.

International institutions are important in this sense because they would seem to be ideal providers of the long-term, stable and predictable environment for international cooperation in Haiti. While the story of international institutional involvement in Haiti is well known (especially OAS, UN and economic agencies such as the World Bank and the Inter-American Development Bank), the potentially powerful role that rule-based institutions (clubs) with sanctioning mechanisms can play in the domestic behaviour of states, even anomic ones like Haiti, ought to be examined.

A growing body of literature highlights two features of international institutions and the ways in which they play into the domestic politics of member countries (rather than other approaches to the study of international institutions, which look the other way round at how international institutions are determined by the national – even rational – interests of its members; see, for instance, Pevehouse and Russett, 2006). One is the relationship between democracy and international institutions. Countries undergoing democratization processes have a strong incentive to join international institutions (especially those with democratic charters or other such political requirements) because the rules of these organizations help leaders maintain political reforms over a long period of time, given the sanctioning capacity of the international body in case of defections from the rule. The credible presence of the sanctioning mechanism would facilitate the consolidation of democracy. Haiti's accession to CARICOM in the 1990s can be examined in this light.

A second feature is that of state socialization in international organizations (IOs): changing the behaviour of states through the iterated interaction of different policy networks involved in IO membership. This is an important feature because it does not mean that IOs work simply or solely through sanctioning mechanisms (like democratic charters – again, in the case of CARICOM and Haiti in 2004) but also work "from below" – through the dense policy network that international institutions ought to be building in order to strengthen their functioning and enhance their capabilities. In CARICOM one could cite the University of the West Indies as an example of such a network but also the longstanding democratic tradition of individual CARICOM members throughout their history, and how this became a constitutive principle for CARICOM membership for almost as long as the institution has existed. In other words, the concept ought to apply both to formal and informal rules and policy networks within the international organization.

CARICOM's inability to impose its institutional network (both formal and informal institutions) on Haiti speaks not only about that group's inattention to the concerns of one of its members (thus calling into question many of the supposed advantages of belonging to the club in the first place) but also questions the essence of CARICOM itself as an international institution and its ability to create precisely such policy networks that allow for a different socialization of its member states. In this sense, as has often been pointed out for the ABC countries in terms of Haiti's relevance for the principles of human rights and personal freedoms in their foreign policies, a failure or collapse of Haiti ought to be considered as a failure of the international institution – CARICOM – itself, to become more than a club of like-minded countries or even to provide more than just a sanctioning mechanism. While Haiti's membership in the organization has been limited by the administrative and economic constraints facing the Caribbean's poorest country, acceptance of Haiti as a member of CARICOM could have proven an important moment for institutional strengthening and consolidation of the Community as an engine for growth, development and political stability in the region.

Like almost everything else after the January 2010 earthquake, CARICOM's role in the reconstruction of Haiti, especially the political and institutional one, can be regarded both as a challenge and an opportunity. CARICOM has designated former Jamaican prime minister P.J. Patterson as its special envoy to Haiti and coordinator of the Community's efforts toward rebuilding Haiti. Patterson has made repeated statements about the need to integrate Haiti into the Caribbean Single Market and Economy, as this offers the best possibilities for the Community to remain engaged in Haiti through a long-term project that should be beneficial to both Haiti and the region in general. Legislative elections in Haiti should have taken place in March 2010, but the level of destruction, voter displacements and sheer magnitude of the human emergency after the earthquake made these impossible. Yet as plans for elections and other political processes get underway, it remains to be seen whether much of this seeming level of CARICOM involvement can be sustained and targeted over a long period of time. Indeed, how can the Caribbean Community articulate a contribution that sets the bases for fully integrating Haiti into the Community in a way that fosters a more fluid socialization and active participation of the grouping's poorest member?

Finally, the role of Haiti's most immediate neighbour, in this case the Dominican Republic, cannot be overlooked. Haiti raises a variety of questions about the foreign policy responsibilities and capabilities of countries such as the Dominican Republic, which are at more advanced stages of development and thus possess certain capabilities that can impact upon the travails of their poorer, more troubled neighbours. Indeed, while not usually addressed in this fashion, one can think of the relationships between the two neighbours occupying the island of Hispaniola in light of comparable cases like South Korea and North Korea, South Africa and Zimbabwe, or Ethiopia and Somalia. Yet Dominican policy towards Haiti has not been sufficiently taken to task and brought up to appropriate scrutiny in light of this seeming responsibility as a neighbouring, more developed country. The fact that they are both members of most organizations involving important principles of international behaviour (including the OAS, the WTO and possibly CARICOM if the Dominican Republic's request for admission is sanctioned favourably) further highlights the importance of examining the interplay between international institutions and the policy behaviour of neighbouring countries.

Again, the earthquake drama has been changing some of these oversights and is perhaps beginning to move matters in the direction of a closer involvement and leadership role for the Dominican Republic in efforts to help its ailing neighbour. In the aftermath of the January 2010 catastrophe, the Dominican Republic became an important conduit for rescue and other humanitarian operations moving into Haiti, and since has become a meeting point for international discussions and planning sessions regarding Haiti's reconstruction. Dominican leaders have made important efforts and financial commitment toward the reconstruction of Haiti, a move that serves both international aspirations of the Dominican Republic as a "mediator" of sorts in regional crises (as evidenced in President Leonel Fernandez's role in the Honduran crisis, and in the dispute between presidents Uribe of Colombia and Chávez of Venezuela) and the immediate interest of the Dominican Republic in having a stable and prosperous neighbour, besides the critical position of the Dominican Republic as a conduit for relief to Haiti.

## Conclusion

Haiti's prolonged history of unstable governance and weak institutions have made the country seem like it is perpetually dependent upon foreign assistance. The nature and character of this assistance has been changing since MINUSTAH was first launched in 2004, when for the first time Latin American countries have been the leaders of the effort to help Haiti become a stable country. The magnitude of the January 2010 earthquake, both in terms of the disaster and the strong international response, may yet open a new chapter for understanding the complex interplay between international cooperation and state building, especially the new ways of crafting such cooperation and how different kinds of actors (international institutions, states and non-governmental organizations) can act cohesively and constructively.

The urgency of Haiti's plight and the sheer scale of the reconstruction work – both physical and political – highlight the fact that institutionalized cooperation does not only work through the explicit mechanisms of foreign assistance like military and technical aid, capital and funding, and the supply of services but also through other, less obvious channels, especially when foreign assistance and cooperation take place over a prolonged period of time. In the same way that the rules of international institutions help make stable predictions about the international choices of states (and socialize states into patterns of behaviour), this "assistance from below", in the sense that it is less tangible than direct assistance, can carry an important weight into the creation of stable and predictable institutions in countries that belong to such organizations. Yet this effect is proportional to the level of interaction through the mechanisms afforded by the international institution, a feature for which some of the region's bodies, like CARICOM, should be taken to task.

# Notes

1. A very important and useful exception to this literature, as related to our understanding of political developments in Haiti, is Robert Bates (2008). By problematizing public order rather than treating it as an independent variable, Bates applies social choice and game analysis to build a political economy of public disorder and state failure. His analysis of African conflicts captures the complex relationship between agents and structures, and opens the possibility of multiple scenarios of state "success" and "failure" coexisting under the same political system.
2. United Nations Stabilization Mission in Haiti, based on the French name of the mission.
3. The idea has even been proposed by senior US politicians such as Senator Christopher Dodd (D-CT) in March 2010.
4. An important exception to the absence of political undertones, of course, is the Dominican Republic, whose relationship with Haiti has been a tense one for many decades. The case of the Dominican Republic and the current Haitian juncture is a separate matter in this chapter.
5. Of the current Latin American participants in MINUSTAH, only Argentina had participated in previous UN missions to Haiti: specifically, in the earlier United Nations Mission in Haiti (UNMIH) in 1992, and subsequently in the United Nations Transition Mission in Haiti (UNTMIH) and the United Nations Civilian Police Mission in Haiti (MIPONUH). Other Latin American and Caribbean countries, including Honduras, Antigua and Barbuda, Bahamas, Barbados, Belize, Guyana, Jamaica, St Kitts and Nevis, St Lucia, Suriname and Trinidad and Tobago have participated in UNMIH; one Caribbean country (Trinidad and Tobago) had participated in the United Nations Support Mission in Haiti (UNSMIH).
6. On the need for domestic "anchors" for foreign intervention in states under severe crisis (or "failure", depending on assessments), see Ignatieff (2005).
7. An important exception to the nationalist posturing in this argument has been, of course, Cuba, whose 1959 revolution and subsequent foreign policy have been based on strong nationalist roots.
8. On the relationship between national sovereignty and doctrines of international humanitarian intervention such as responsibility to protect, see Farer (1996).
9. For more on Brazil's involvement in Haiti and the connection with global governance more generally, see Chapter 11 in this volume.
10. On the recent evolution and shifts in Argentine foreign policy philosophy and priorities, see Corgliano (2008).
11. On the coordination of multiple international actors in Haiti, see Bryan, et al. (2007).

## REFERENCES

Bates, Robert (2008) *When Things Fell Apart: State Failure in Late-Century Africa.* New York: Cambridge University Press.

Bryan, Elizabeth with Cynthia J. Arnson, José Raúl Perales and Johanna Mendelson Forman (2007) *Governance and Security in Haiti: Can the International Community Make a Difference?*, Creating Community in the Americas No. 27, Washington, DC: Woodrow Wilson International Center for Scholars.

Carroll, Rory (2010) "Haiti promised $10bn in Aid – Double what it Asked For", *Guardian*, 1 April. Available at http://www.guardian.co.uk/world/2010/apr/01/haiti-earthquake-10-billion-aid

Chesterman, Simon, Michael Ignatieff and Ramesh Thakur (eds) (2005) *Making States Work: State Failure and the Crisis of Governance.* Tokyo: United Nations University Press.

Corgliano, Francisco (2008) "Política exterior argentina 1973–2008: debates teóricos", *Criterio*, 2336: 175–179.

Diniz, Eugenio (2005) "O Brasil e a MINUSTAH", *Security and Defense Studies Review*, 5(1): 90–108.

Dodd, Chris (2010) "Place Haiti under 'trusteeship'", *Miami Herald*, 29 March. Available at http://www.miamiherald.com/2010/03/29/1552739/place-haiti-under-trusteeship.html

Farer, Tom (ed.) (1996) *Beyond Sovereignty: Collectively Defending Democracy in the Americas.* Baltimore: John Hopkins University Press.

Foweraker, Joe, Todd Landman and Neil Harvey (2003) *Governing Latin America.* Cambridge: Polity.

Gros, Jean-Germain (1996) "Towards a Taxonomy of Failed States in the New World Order: Decaying Somalia, Liberia, Rwanda and Haiti", *Third World Quarterly*, 17(3): 455–472.

Ignatieff, Michael (2005) "Human rights, power and the state" in Simon Chesterman, Michael Ignatieff and Ramesh Thakur (eds), *Making States Work: State Failure and the Crisis of Governance.* Tokyo: United Nations University Press, pp. 59–76.

Lengyel, Miguel F. (2006) "Argentina's participation in Haiti: Trends and prospects". Paper prepared for the IDRC-sponsored meeting, "Haiti: Desafíos para el Desarrollo", 4–5 December.

Llenderozas, Elsa (2006) "Argentina, Brasil y Chile en la reconstrucción de Haití: intereses y motivaciones de la participación conjunta". Paper presented at the XXVI Congress of the Latin American Studies Association, San Juan, Puerto Rico, 15–18 March.

Loredo, María Luisa (2009) "Latin American Leadership in the Process to Bring Stability to Haiti", *Sistema: Revista de ciencias sociales*, 208–209 and 211–224.

Miliken, Jennifer (ed.) (2003) *State Failure, Collapse, and Reconstruction.* Malden, MA: Blackwell Publishing.

Pevehouse, Jon and Bruce Russett (2006) "Democratic International Governmental Organizations Promote Peace", *International Organization*, 60(4): 969–1000.

Rotberg, Robert I. (2002) "The New Nature of Nation-State Failure", *Washington Quarterly*, 25(3): 85–96.

Rotberg, Robert I. (ed.) (2003) *State Failure and State Weakness in a Time of Terror*. Washington, DC: Brookings Institution Press.

Serrano, Mónica (2000) "Latin America: The dilemmas of intervention" in Albrecht Schnabel and Ramesh Thakur (eds), *Kosovo and the Challenge of Humanitarian Intervention: Selective Indignation, Collective Action, and International Citizenship*. Tokyo: United Nations University, pp. 223–244.

Schelhase, Mark (2010) "The Successes, Failures and Future of the Mercosur" in Gordon Mace, Andrew F. Cooper and Timothy M. Shaw (eds), *Inter-American Cooperation at a Crossroads*. Basingstoke: Palgrave Macmillan, pp. 171–186.

Shamsie, Yasmine and Andrew S. Thompson (eds) (2006) *Haiti: Hope for a Fragile State*. Waterloo: Wilfrid Laurier University Press.

Valler Filho, Wladimir (2007) *O Brasil e a crise haitiana: a cooperação técnica como instrumento de solidaridade e de ação diplomatic*. Brasilia: Fundação Alexandre de Gusmão.

Ward, Major Michael T. (2006) "The Case for International Trusteeship in Haiti", *Canadian Military Journal*, 7(3): 25–34.

# 11

# Brazil's mission in Haiti

*Marcel Biato*

## Brazil steps up to the plate

The history of Haiti is an example of the long-lasting, pernicious effects of colonization and slavery. Since independence, Haiti has been plagued by the legacy of colonial rule. The inability of the Haitian state to overcome these challenges is due to myriad factors – both internal and external – which have contributed to a seemingly perpetual fragile state. In early 2004, the Haitian crises led to a debate as to whether the country could ever become a self-sustaining state. After only a decade since last being occupied by foreign troops, life in Haiti was deteriorating again.

In many ways, Brazil's history is similar to Haiti's. Both countries were born under the same conditions: a collision of cultures, the forced intermingling of ethnic groups and a long journey towards political adulthood and economic self-reliance. Partly because of this, Brazil came to Haiti in 2004 with both a mission and a vision. It led the United Nation Security Council's (UNSC) peacekeeping mission to Haiti to help the Haitian people back on the road to political reconciliation and economic recovery. If Haiti were to move from its precarious economic position, and not become a proto-failed state threatening regional security, a new paradigm for peacekeeping was required.

Brazil believes that lasting stability in Haiti is possible only if there is a social safety net that is built upon economic prosperity and social justice. In the last six years, with assistance from the United Nations Stabilization Mission in Haiti (MINUSTAH), Haiti has been making encouraging

*Fixing Haiti: MINUSTAH and beyond, Heine and Thompson (eds),*
*United Nations University Press, 2011, ISBN 978-92-808-1197-1*

strides. The country's security has been improving, the government has been gradually increasing activities and improving its standing and signs of economic improvement have been appearing, even though un- and underemployment remained a persistent problem.

In this context the earthquake that hit outside of Port-au-Prince on 12 January 2010 was a major setback. Much of the city's infrastructure was destroyed and the country experienced the loss of some 230,000 lives. The full force of the earthquake was quickly brought home to Brazilians. Over 20 of Brazil's civilians and military troops died in the earthquake, including a well-known aid worker, Zilda Arns, and the UN's Deputy Head of Mission, Luiz Carlos da Costa. Will the ensuing economic and human crises put the modest progress that Haiti experienced during MINUSTAH's operations at risk?

The destruction caused by the earthquake underscores the nature of the challenge in Haiti. MINUSTAH's engagement with the country is not based on bringing peace to the country by creating a security blanket that allows foreign forces to leave quickly. Instead, MINUSTAH is focused on helping to facilitate a stable and sustainable Haiti. As the international community helps the Haitian people recover from the earthquake, few Brazilians question the role that their country is taking, a role that had previously been considered beyond the scope of Brazil's foreign policy traditions. In 2004, opponents of Brazil's involvement with MINUSTAH argued that the country's traditional respect for the principle of non-intervention was being compromised. There were accusations that joining the mission amounted to doing the "dirty work" of former colonial powers, despite the Brazilian government's belief that leading the mission would improve that country's chances of gaining a permanent seat on the UN Security Council. A group from the Brazilian Congress even flew to Port-of-Prince to highlight their opposition, only to return convinced that the country did have a role to play in Haiti.

Brazil's reaction to the earthquake was swift. The country's defence minister, Nelson Jobin, flew to Port-au-Prince the next day to supervise Brazil's relief support. The Brazilian military took emergency aid to Port-au-Prince on a daily basis. The Brazilian navy provided medical personnel, food and equipment. Congress earmarked US$210 million to double Brazil's present aid effort to Haiti. Brazil's troop levels in MINUSTAH doubled to 2,600. Brazil is also offering scholarships for 500 Haitian university and secondary school students to complete their academic training in Brazil.[1]

Brazil's decision to take an active role in Haiti's recovery is consistent with key tenets of Brazilian foreign policy. Non-intervention does not mean indifference or inaction. In the post-Cold War world of multiplying intra-state conflicts – where civilians are more often than not the major victims – strict adherence to traditional notions of absolute non-intervention is no longer tenable. Brazil could not stand by as Haiti remained fragile. The country's national sovereignty was threatened but not in terms of the Haitian state, which was largely non-existent. Rather, what was at stake was the right of the Haitian people to have a better future.

This belief is underpinned by a growing sense among Latin American countries that the region must begin to take on greater responsibility for its own future (see Chapter 9, this volume). This is the true meaning of the notion of sovereignty. In 2003, Chile and Mexico demonstrated the region's newly assertive position by refusing to support the US invasion of Iraq in the UN Security Council. Many in the region believe that outside military intervention is hardly the best solution; it is rather a symptom of the international community's failure to effectively engage with crisis situations. Haiti's ongoing situation is a striking example of this. Despite its limited geopolitical and economic stature, the mission in Haiti is a litmus test. Believing that Haiti is an opportunity to test the newly found resolve of Latin America, Brazil decided to head the military wing of the UN mission.[2]

The Brazilian government's encouragement of regional responsibility has a strong social and political basis. This has coincided with the election of governments committed to addressing the concerns and expectations of the popular sectors in the region (for more, see Cooper and Heine, 2009). Throughout Latin America, groups that had been traditionally marginalized from mainstream economic and political life are now demanding access to the benefits of sustained growth and globalization. National sovereignty becomes a question of how to enable people to create policy spaces, ensure public debate and facilitate democratic decision-making for the common good. The growing concern for social equity is critical to understanding why Latin America has collectively taken up the task of assisting Haiti.

At a time when the debate over the "Responsibility to Protect" gained new impetus, Brazil believed that preventive engagement is the answer to large-scale threats to basic human rights. The international community needs to become involved before the only option is a highly intrusive intervention. With Haiti, Latin America has a chance to test this new paradigm for international involvement in crisis management. Refusals to allow outside intervention, due to an absolutist sense of national sovereignty, have been rejected. From the new perspective, the global community – and especially nearby neighbours – have a duty to act to prevent situations from deteriorating. Haiti's historical experience provides a cautionary tale of how a wrong-headed understanding of the principle of non-intervention can be a recipe for disaster. MINUSTAH offers the opportunity to show how things can be different.

## MINUSTAH: liberators or occupation force?

A new path for Haiti meant reversing the long-standing pattern of establishing peace and then pulling out before the same was done with stability. Brazil agreed that it is unrealistic to imagine that military security by itself will foster long-term economic and political recovery. It was clear from the beginning that social reconciliation and political re-engineering could not be achieved through force alone. This belief was later expressed in UN Secretary-General Kofi Annan's (2005) report *In Larger Freedom*, where a direct linkage between development and security was stated.[3] By accepting command of MINUSTAH Brazil sought to avoid the mistakes of previous missions. Contrary to past practices, operations against criminal elements and the political insurgency would be as unobtrusive as possible. Tangible progress in Haiti would be more likely if international forces focused on improving the lives of average Haitians and on reinstating a sense of individual agency and collective dignity.

Yet, the first months of the mission seemed proof that this was unsustainable. Fanmi Lavalas,[4] Aristide loyalists, exploited the unrest in Haiti in the hope of forcing the former president's return. Lavalas were encouraged by the modest size of the MINUSTAH contingent – initially only 3,000 troops – that had replaced the 20,000-strong United States force that first landed on the island. Flairups in Port-au-Prince, most notably in Cité Soleil, threatened to engulf the capital. This meant that the populace's initial open-armed support for the UN troops was affected by the lack of improving conditions. Many of MINUSTAH's initial supporters were threatening to turn against it. Even Prime Minister Gérard Latortue, head of the interim government, suggested that if the troops could not contain the violence, they might as well leave. As the invasion of Iraq had shown, in the eyes of the local population a liberating army can quickly become an occupation force.

There was little hope that MINUSTAH would bring about lasting change without local support. Political leadership was necessary to restore faith in government. Yet this could not be achieved without progress on the issues that concern voters everywhere: basic public services, such as sanitation, energy, transportation and law and order. Progress was frustratingly slow in the first months. The interim government soon proved incapable of meeting the task. Many of the cabinet members had been pressured by gangs to accept public office, while others lacked the necessary managerial skills. This government was essentially a government in waiting – waiting for elections to be called so that its members could return to anonymity.

The challenge before the international community was clear. Plagued by looting gangs and disillusioned by MINUSTAH's apparent ineffectiveness, the populace had little hope in the success of the mission. MINUSTAH was being criticized on many fronts. Voices in US and European security services began to question the command's unwillingness to act more forcefully. Lack of decisiveness, it was alleged, risked the success of the mission and the safety of the troops. Given the modest pace at which basic services were being restored, the whole rationale behind MINUSTAH's strategy for recovering popular support seemed untenable.

## From dialogue to elections

In order for MINUSTAH to succeed a new elected government was needed, but the political climate in Haiti was a mix of precarious groupings and shifting allegiances operating in an atmosphere of mutual suspicion and intimidation. This made political dialogue and accommodation between opposing factions seemingly impossible. Rumours of Aristide's return loomed over any attempt at crafting a post-Aristide path to political stability.[5]

This was the situation that Marco Aurélio Garcia, President Lula's foreign policy adviser, encountered upon his arrival in Port-au-Prince in October 2004. Heading a Brazilian mission, Garcia was there to find a way to restore the political process and increase the pace of reconstruction. It was decided that the first step was to establish the logistical and political conditions necessary for the scheduled 2005 election to go ahead. Only an elected government would have the credibility necessary to mobilize citizens around an agenda of national renewal. This meant a national dialogue between all democratic and non-violent groups. Over five days of negotiations, progress was made towards setting up a political coalition that would agree upon ground rules for scheduling the elections. Aristide would not be allowed to return to power.

Organizing fair elections meant more than providing secure voting booths. The logistical nightmare began with the lack of organized and effective oversight of the balloting process. The legitimacy of the outcome also required guaranteeing credible voter turnout despite potentially adverse conditions. For the most part, Haiti lacked the roads and transport infrastructure to get voters to polling stations. Brazil joined other countries in providing the financial and material support needed for this.

Technical hurdles made it impossible to hold electronic voting – seen to be faster and more secure than traditional paper ballots – as the Brazilian government had initially proposed.

Despite these obstacles, the elections took place on 7 February 2006, only a few months behind the initial schedule, with a turnout of approximately 4.6 million voters. The frontrunner, René Préval, was unable to win an outright victory in the first ballot, having failed by a fraction of a percentage point to achieve a clear 50 per cent majority. The risks of prolonging the electoral process led almost all contenders to agree to acclaim Préval the winner. To avoid the uncertainties of having a second ballot, Brazil urged the United Nations Security Council to issue a presidential declaration highlighting the urgency of achieving a constitutionally sound electoral outcome. This encouraged other presidential hopefuls not to challenge the outcome and speeded up recognition of Préval's victory.[6]

## Getting the international community onboard

Holding fair and transparent elections was the first hurdle to establish an effective government in Haiti. The dysfunctional nature of the post-Aristide political system made international donors reluctant to disburse large-scale support for the Haitian government. There were concerns over Haiti's history of government ineptness and corruption. Thus, much of the international aid that had been pledged was slow to come. Foreign governments and agencies instead funnelled resources through non-governmental organizations (NGOs), mostly foreign, perceived to be more trustworthy. This means that aid is often slow to reach needy communities. This has also fed a cycle where the Haitian government and people have little say in how foreign aid is allocated, fostering a sense of ineffectual leadership and loss of confidence in both the government and the international community.

The need for immediate action to rebuild basic infrastructure and for the local government to take effective charge was compounded by the 2010 earthquake. Yet this was already the case in 2004, when flooding wreaked havoc in Gonaïves, an outlying city that was isolated and its dwellers stranded without access to relief. MINUSTAH responded by redirecting some of its activities to road clearing so that emergency supplies could get through. Following this, military engineers joined the Brazilian troops to provide the skills needed for rebuilding. Plans were drawn up to put the economy on a sustainable path of development. Haitian authorities took part in this process by providing a list of structural reforms that were required, demonstrating the availability and enthusiasm of local expertise.

Keeping political reconciliation and economic recovery going was further challenged in September 2007, when MINUSTAH's mandate came up for renewal. President Préval had made the case for a continued UN presence in Haiti during his trip to Brasilia soon after taking office in March 2006. Addressing the Foreign Affairs Committee of the Brazilian senate, he argued that Brazil's continued commitment and leadership were critical to the Mission's success and to the stability of the country. It therefore came as a shock when China threatened to veto the Security Council resolution renewing MINUSTAH's mandate. Haiti had become a major battleline in Taiwan's diplomatic row with the People's Republic of China over the island's international status. Beijing had become increasingly incensed at Taipei's cosy relationship with Port-au-Prince. Only after strenuous negotiations – involving the UN secretary-general, the Brazilian Embassy in Port-au-Prince and its military advisers, as well as other Latin American nations – did Beijing relent.

The parallels with the East Timor independence process are clear. This was a cautionary tale of the consequences of premature withdrawal of peacekeeping forces in a country still trying to gain its political balance. Timor's fragile institutions were not up to the challenge of shepherding the country through political pressures and economic imbalances. In Haiti, it was no different, given the ongoing feuding between the different branches of government. In the balance was the international community's willingness to contribute to the island's future. This was critical to retaining the confidence of foreign donors and prospective investors. The willingness of the Haitian diaspora to commit resources is of particular importance, as remittances annually average an estimated US$1.5 billion. Remittances are four times the combined yearly overseas development aid and multilateral support that Haiti receives. They play a key role in mitigating the impact of social and economic dislocation.

## Solidarity Brazilian style

President Lula has visited the island twice to encourage the international community to commit to Haiti as well as to instil confidence in the Haitian people. His trips to the country and other Brazilian initiatives underscore Brazil's commitment to assisting in Haiti's recovery. During Lula's initial visit, in August 2004, the Brazilian and Haitian national soccer teams played each other as a way of demonstrating Brazil's solidarity. On his second trip, in March 2010, Lula checked on post-earthquake recovery efforts. Despite well-placed security concerns, these visits have helped open the way for other leaders to follow suit. In the same vein, Brazil took the lead in encouraging the CARICOM countries to overcome their fears about the new Préval government.[7]

Brazil's commitment is not limited to symbolic gestures. Measures are being taken to help improve living conditions. Even before the 2010 earthquake, three-quarters of Brazil's technical cooperation budget for the Caribbean was earmarked for Haiti. This support helps to strengthen core institutions, such as the national police, the electoral oversight office and the human rights protection agency. Equally critical are projects addressing the economic frailties that hold the country back. Through technology transfer and financial support, Brazil helps to provide food security and energy self-sufficiency. Other priorities are improving basic sanitation[8] and providing affordable housing. During his most recent visit, President Lula announced what could be the most important Brazilian-financed initiative to date: the building of a hydroelectric dam[9] near Port-au-Prince, to upgrade local access to services requiring energy and water.

MINUSTAH has played a critical role in bringing services to local communities. Security has improved since 2007. Brazilian military engineers are active in road building. Technical and financial support for training and enlargement of the Haitian National Police has enabled MINUSTAH to reduce its own policing duties, allowing it to focus on medical and engineering activities, well drilling, border patrol and humanitarian relief. The mission has also been at the centre of major political events, such as organizing and supporting elections and monitoring and controlling street protests. There are signs that the mission has captured the global imagination: 46 countries are represented in MINUSTAH, though Latin Americans make up the majority of the contingent.

Brazil is also involved in triangular initiatives that maximize synergies among donor countries. These include an AIDS treatment project with Canada to make use of Brazil's experience in making affordable medicine available to poor communities through low-cost drugs. With Spain, work is underway to recover some of the roughly 96 per cent of vegetation cover lost to deforestation. This will help reclaim the country's agricultural potential and avoid the massive flooding that regularly affects rural communities. In cooperation with Argentina, Chile and the Inter-American Institute for Agriculture (IICA), Brazil is introducing modern practices to boost food production and productivity. The challenge of greater food self-sufficiency is critical to national security, given the low income of most of the population as well as the lack of foreign currency reserves to pay for imports.

Using Haiti to access the US market offers opportunities to local entrepreneurs. Brazilian-sponsored ethanol production in Haiti can be exported to the United States under a 2007 Brazil–United States Memorandum of Understanding on renewable energy cooperation that provides for tariff-free imports from the Caribbean Basin. This will allow

Haiti to replicate Brazil's biofuels programme, based on sugarcane-derived ethanol. A biomass-run electricity plant[10] to be built under Brazilian technical supervision will help reduce the country's dependence on imported fossil fuels. While generating employment and income opportunities for poor rural communities, this will cut the costs of imported oil as well as $CO_2$ emissions. Similarly, a Brazilian company is considering setting up garment production in Haiti with a view to tariff-free access to the US market under the HOPE Act.[11]

Brazil is also an active ally in lobbying donors to contribute to supporting the reconstruction process in Haiti. Brazil has regularly called on countries to fulfil their pledges to provide financial and technical support for Haiti. Brasília has stated it will remain engaged in Haiti as long as it takes to ensure that the country is on the mend.

## Taking stock

By late 2009, Haiti had won over many cynics by overcoming major hurdles on the road to recovery. Yet, well into MINUSTAH's sixth year, the task remained far from complete. Even before the earthquake of January 2010, it was evident that continued long-term commitment was critical if Haiti was to have a brighter future. Despite improvements in security, thanks in large degree to MINUSTAH, living standards remained very modest. The country has largely been living on borrowed time and resources. According to World Bank (2008) statistics, 80 per cent of all Haitians were living at subsistence level, with 54 per cent in abject poverty. Inflation had increased to 16 per cent, cutting into consumer purchasing power. Over many years average economic expansion has only marginally outstripped a demographic growth rate that hovers around 2 per cent. Per capita income remained at US$1,180 (the lowest in the Americas) and the unemployment rate was 60 per cent.

The massive scale of the damage done to Port-au-Prince's infrastructure by the 2010 earthquake and the humanitarian crisis that immediately followed have underscored the fragility of the progress achieved so far and the risk of "back-sliding", given the persistence of institutional and structural vulnerabilities. A dysfunctional political system reflects a society without self-confidence as a result of many interventions that reinforced squabbling within the governing elite. The resulting lack of governmental continuity – Prime Minister Jean-Max Bellerive is heading the fifth cabinet in as many years – helps keep Haiti a very poor country. Not surprisingly, in 2008 popular displeasure led to the senate failing to elect the necessary two-thirds of its members, hampering legislative work. Blame has often been laid at the feet of the 1987 constitution that allocates too much power to the president (see Chapter 3 this volume). However, attempts at constitutional reform face stiff opposition from many Haitians, many of whom fear that any changes are likely to further entrench vested interests. This distrust was demonstrated by the low turnout (roughly 11 per cent) for the 2009 senate race, and has been reinforced by the legal manoeuvres employed to keep Fanmi Lavalas from taking part in the election. As a result the vote was widely contested and boycotted by Lavalas (Al Jazeera, 2009). The mounting frustration reinforces mistrust and resentment, hampering attempts at meaningful compromise.

The failed expectations that Aristide embodied underscore this dark reality. Overcoming this cycle of failure will not be possible without the business community. Their reaction to the destruction wrought by the earthquake will be crucial. It will be a test of whether the opportunities for business loom larger than the uncertainties and perils associated with reconstruction. The diaspora's support is indispensable but far from sufficient. The challenge of modernizing the economy must include breaking up the control of a few powerful families[12] who dominate banking, sugar production, the footwear, plastics, beer and textile industries, as well as – and this is key for its relations with the United States – the manufacture of baseballs. These clan-run conglomerates fear change and reject outside competition. Their destabilizing impact on political institutions was highlighted in May 2009 when the local business guild – the Association des Industries d'Haïti (ADIH) – pressured the government to go back on legislation already approved in both houses of Parliament that raised the minimum wage to 200 gourds (US$5). It was argued that this hike would jeopardize the 20,000 jobs that the garment industry was expected to create as part of the Hope II Act. Growing pressure on then prime minister Michèle Pierre-Louis, mainly from student organizations and "rented crowds", to enact the new minimum wage weakened the government. Further destabilized by her refusal to give in to public service pay demands, she lost the support of the senate and of President Préval, both unwilling to face down her opponents in and out of Congress.

As a result, the country has not been able to carve out for itself an effective model of economic development and foster a competitive production environment. The radical rebuilding required after the earthquake offers an opportunity to begin anew. Yet the difficulties in attracting the investments and financing required to bring down unemployment remain daunting. This is compounded by the country's continued vulnerability to other natural and man-made external shocks (see Chapter 1, this volume). In 2008 food riots broke out in reaction to rising global food and oil prices requiring MINUSTAH to restore order. The country's dependency on large-scale food imports was aggravated by a series of major hurricanes that hit the island that same year and levelled most crops (see Chapter 2, this volume).

## Looking ahead

There are, however, signs that civil society in Haiti is on the mend. One example has been the recent deputation from Cité Soleil – previously under gang control – organized to voice demands before the government. This was the first time that public officials received such a delegation. Furthermore, the relatively smooth change over to the new prime minister, Joseph Jean-Max Bellerive (a savvy technocrat), has raised expectations that Haiti might avoid a new constitutional crisis, raising hopes for consolidating what was achieved by the Pierre-Louis administration. It is encouraging that in the aftermath of the 2010 earthquake, fears of total economic collapse and social unrest proved overdone. Despite enormous dislocation and a mounting death toll, order was quickly restored, with minimal outbreaks of violence.

Will the international aid be able, as in the first months of MINUS-TAH, to deal with mounting frustration over the slow pace of improvements? Will people begin to resent an overwhelming outside presence that begins to look more like foreign occupation than solidarity?

Some progress was made at the Haiti Donors Conference, held in April 2009, in Washington, under the auspices of the Inter-American Development Bank. It was titled: "Towards a New Paradigm in Cooperation for Growth and Opportunity". On that occasion, a total of US$324 million was pledged (Landler, 2009), largely for critical infrastructure projects, over a two-year period, bringing the total of outside aid to the US$3 billion mark originally promised. As for Brazil, its support for Haiti's is illustrated, as mentioned above, by the decision to finance a viability study for the construction of the US$55 million artibonite 4C hydroelectric dam. This will provide the much needed power and water required to generate economic activity and is the first priority in the post-earthquake recovery effort.

Once the immediate effects of the earthquake have passed and a semblance of normality – albeit a drastically altered one – returns, the challenges facing the Haitian people will be to build the productive capacity necessary to sustain growth. If Haiti is to identify a coherent development model, centred on identifiable economic variables, it must avoid the proliferation of stand-alone projects developed by some of the roughly 10,000 NGOs active in the country. These do not provide an integrated vision or coherent scheme for recovery but rather "balkanize" economic policy and reinforce popular disenchantment with a government relegated to the sidelines. Long-term policy proposals that have Haitian "ownership" are required to ensure legitimacy, effectiveness and long-term consistency.

Haiti's success and stability hinge on its ability to achieve self-government. Foreigners must continue to engage with the Haitian government, even as it struggles with inefficiency and corruption. Local authorities must be given the opportunity and resources to prove themselves worthy of the people's trust. Préval has been at pains to make this point in recent meetings to coordinate post-earthquake international assistance. Bellevue has made the same point more tellingly. As one of the international community's most vocal critics, he took office in 2009 by roundly denouncing lack of aid coordination, donors' broken promises and the hundreds of millions of dollars that pass through private organizations without Haitian government input. The international community must take his message to heart. Part of the answer could lay in setting up a unified trust fund under UN control to ensure that the Haitian people are directly involved in managing foreign aid.

## Overcoming a legacy of despair

The ongoing support of the international community is indispensable, yet the consent and participation of Haitians in identifying the way forward is crucial. Foreign models and criteria are ill-suited to this idiosyncratic Caribbean country. One must grasp Haiti's singularity of culture, ethnicity, religious background and social and political makeup (see Chapter 7 this volume). The international community can best help Haiti by putting its faith in the Haitian people and helping them renew their sense of pride and purpose.

The silver lining to be found among the ruins and chaos in the aftermath of the 2010 earthquake is the hope that the magnitude of the situation will awaken the international community to the nature of the challenge ahead. This was the undertone to several Brazilian authorities' comments that the earthquake would have been less destructive had the international community not dragged its feet over the years in helping Haiti. The earthquake has made clear the failure to ensure that the country was minimally prepared for such a catastrophe. The very lack of basic human resources and services, as well as institutional infrastructure, hindered initial efforts to provide emergency relief.

Our sense of urgency must be the same as that of the earthquake survivors who immediately turned to the task of unearthing fellow citizens from under the rubble, working for days on end without losing hope. That was the central message Brazil took to the March 2010 Donors Conference in New York. Brazil will remain engaged in encouraging and challenging the international community to use this second chance, as it were, to get things right. To this end, Brazil will contribute substantially to the US$300 million fund being set up by Union of South American Nations (UNASUR) for reconstruction work in Haiti. Brazil will call for Haiti's foreign debts to be forgiven and the opening up of developed country markets to Haitian produce. Building on the temporary suspension of bilateral restrictions in the name of speeding up the arrival of relief to Haiti, the United States and Cuba should grasp the collective recovery effort to overcome a half century of mutual mistrust.

The Brazilian government wants Haiti to become a nation that inspires generations and sparks acts of heroism. In the aftermath of the earthquake, Haiti is taking a stand in defence of its future. Its people and government have made it clear they will not bow to powerlessness and fatalism. The international community has the opportunity as well as the moral obligation to help make this happen.

Latin America and the Caribbean have taken these words to heart by seizing the opportunity to begin taking the region's destiny into its own hands and to bring an end to a history of frustrations and lost opportunities. Hopefully Haiti will serve as a model of what is possible as the region comes together.

# Notes

1. Besides the US$210 million to be appropriated by Congress, Brazil made has made or is in the process of making available the following resources for emergency relief:
   - US$15 million for humanitarian aid through the UN Office for Coordination of Humanitarian Affairs;
   - US$130 million in voluntary contributions to the World Food Programme for humanitarian aid;
   - US$50,000 for local acquisition and distribution of food;
   - US$100,000 for voluntary contributions to the UN Population Fund;
   - US$250,000 for the Brazilian Humanitarian Fund in association with the FAO;
   - US$200,000 for the UN Central Emergency Response Fund (CERF);
   - 100 tons of rice; 165 tons of food parcels; 50 tons of flour; 27 tons of milk; 11 tons of cereals and 40 tons of tinned food from government food stocks;
   - 144 tons of government medicine stocks and 32 tons of temporary shelters;
   - A field hospital and 26 medical personnel seconded for 6 months;
   - 65 tons of tinned meat; 13 tons of sugar; 39 tons of evaporated milk; 13 tons of orange juice and 400 thousand litres of water donated by private companies;
   - US$1 million collected by OCHA and the WFP;
   - 80 tons of foodstuffs; 100 tons of medicine and 16 tons of water delivered by a Brazilian naval vessel;
   - 63 military and 11 civilian doctors, as well as two helicopters made available through a joint Brazil–Italy navel operation;

- US$135,000 for school lunches; and
- US$400,000 earmarked for a UNESCO teacher-training course benefiting 110,000 secondary school students.

2. More recently, specific forums have been set up within the Union of South American Nations (UNASUR). The aim is to foster greater regional cooperation and coordination of defence and drug-trafficking issues.

3. The Report's preamble states "development is the indispensable foundation for collective security". The setting up of the UN Peacebuilding Commission is perhaps the most concrete outcome of the report. It seeks to ensure that the UN system provides the kind of timely engagement in support of sustainable development through conflict prevention. The goal is to act preventively rather than intervene intrusively when things are already out of hand and all options bad.

4. Meaning, quite appropriately, "family avalanche" in Creole.

5. Aristides' incendiary rhetoric, strongarm tactics and powerful grassroots support while in office helped unhinge the traditional party system and encouraged a motley of political interlopers and would-be usurpers.

6. René Préval was only the second president in Haitian history to take office after free and fair elections.

7. The CARICOM countries were slow to accept the 2004 intervention in Haiti, clinging to their long-standing position against foreign intervention. In this they were most certainly influenced by concerns that Haiti might provide a dangerous precedent and pretext for future outside interference in the Caribbean.

8. A Brazilian garbage-recycling project in Haiti was a finalist in the BBC 2009 World Challenge.

9. At a cost of US$55 million, the Artibonite 4C dam will be located near Port-au-Prince. Brazil is financing a technical viability study.

10. At a cost of US$27.3 million.

11. Haitian Hemispheric Opportunity Partnership Encouragement (HOPE) Act, passed in December 2006, has boosted clothing exports and investment by providing tariff-free access to the US market.

12. The similarities with Honduras, where the deposed president had sought to wrest some economic control from the local elite, is suggestive.

## REFERENCES

Al Jazeera (2009) "Haitians Shun Senate Elections", *Al Jazeera News*, 20 April. Available at http://english.aljazeera.net/news/americas/2009/04/2009419224231220542.html

Annan, Kofi (2005) *In Larger Freedom: Towards Development, Security and Human Rights for All*. Report of the Secretary General, 21 March. Available at http://daccess-dds-ny.un.org/doc/UNDOC/GEN/N05/270/78/PDF/N0527078.pdf?OpenElement

Landler, Mark (2009) "Clinton, in Visit to Haiti, Brings Aid and Promises Support", *New York Times*, 16 April. Available at http://www.nytimes.com/2009/04/17/world/americas/17diplo.html

World Bank (2008) "Statistics" in *Human Development Reports*. Available at http://hdr.undp.org/en/statistics/

# 12

# Canada and the travail of partnership in Haiti

*Stephen Baranyi*

Since the departure of President Aristide in February 2004, Canada has played an important role in international efforts to re-establish security and stability in Haiti and to assist longer-term development and reconstruction efforts. Today, Haiti is the highest beneficiary of Canadian development assistance in the Americas and the second largest in the world. (DFAIT, 2009a)

This passage, taken from the Canadian Department of Foreign Affairs and International Trade (DFAIT) website in 2009, reflects the common perception among Canadian officials that Canada has been an active, generous partner in the stabilization and development of Haiti since 2004. There is considerable evidence to support this view. Indeed, since the US-Franco-Canadian military intervention that removed President Aristide in February 2004, Canada has:

• Co-sponsored key UN Security Council resolutions including Resolution 1542, which provided the first mandate for the UN Stabilization Mission in Haiti (MINUSTAH).
• Promoted the active engagement of Latin American middle powers such as Argentina, Brazil and Chile in MINUSTAH and in broader reconstruction efforts.
• Made large, multi-year development assistance commitments to Haiti averaging around CA$100 million/year, and usually exceeded those allocations in its disbursements. This record made Canada the second-largest bilateral donor to Haiti after the United States until 2010.[1]
• Promoted greater investment and coordination by large multilateral and bilateral donors.

*Fixing Haiti: MINUSTAH and beyond*, Heine and Thompson (eds),
United Nations University Press, 2011, ISBN 978-92-808-1197-1

- Invested funds in key central agencies of the Haitian state to enhance its capacity to understand, track and lead development processes in the country.
- Made major contributions to humanitarian and reconstruction efforts in the aftermath of the January 2010 earthquake.

Yet there are other perspectives on Canada's role in Haiti. In 2008, Haiti's Minister of Planning and External Cooperation at the time, Jean-Max Bellerive, publically questioned Canada's and other Western donors' self-image by suggesting that they had not adapted their cooperation to Haiti's real situation. Speaking to important audiences in Ottawa, Minister Bellerive (2008) argued that despite his government's efforts to improve the management of its own and the international community's resources, and despite the principles enshrined in international instruments such as the Paris Declaration on Aid Effectiveness, traditional donors were not investing enough to reinforce the Haitian state. This tendency, he argued, put in peril the end-goal of sustainability, since national and state ownership were keys to durable development.[2]

Bellerive's concerns converge with certain academic analyses. Robert Muggah has observed that historically Canada's governance programming in Haiti has "oscillated between reinforcing public institutions and ... efforts that bypass the state altogether in order to strengthen 'civil society'" (Muggah, 2007: 168). For that analyst, Ottawa's declared shift back towards strengthening the state, after the military intervention in 2004, masks a continued mistrust of Haitian public institutions and a habit of channelling funds largely through international and civil society organizations.

Drawing on the academic literature pertaining to local ownership in conflict-affected societies, Timothy Donais offers a deeper analysis of the challenges of working with the Haitian state. He suggests that the international community's partnership-building efforts have been aided by the election of a moderate, legitimate president in 2006. Nonetheless, he argues that the Préval government and the international community have not been able to move from "regime ownership" to "national ownership" in the democratic sense of that concept. A key reason for this, aside from the weakness of Haiti's public institutions and the particularities of its political culture, lies in the realm of policy. Indeed, Donais (2009) argues that a major obstacle to democratic support for the post-intervention model is that its liberal economic policies have failed Haiti before, and are not seen by the majority of Haitians as offering them a better deal for the future.

Yasmine Shamsie (2006) brings this line of analysis back to Canada, arguing that despite Ottawa's considerable investments, its engagement tends to focus on institutional and market-oriented reforms that do not address the social bases of democracy or the real needs of the poor. Canada's support for democratic development in Haiti has privileged support for procedural mechanisms like elections and parliamentary institutions at the expense of popular participation in policy change. Its support for economic development has focused on debt forgiveness, private sector development and export-oriented manufacturing rather than on reactivating agriculture for the benefit of Haiti's extremely poor rural dwellers – who still account for over half of the country's population.

A network of solidarity and peace organizations grouped under the Canada Haitian Action Network (CHAN) has gone much further in its criticisms. CHAN accuses Canada of complicity in the 2004 "coup" and in the "reign of terror" since (Sanders, 2007). It suggests that Canadian NGOs active in Haiti unwittingly participated in Canadian International Development Agency (CIDA)-sponsored plans to destabilize the Aristide government from 2000 to 2004 (Sanders, 2008). Canada's intervention in 2004, according to Richard Sanders, has been part of a long-standing strategy to undermine the pro-poor reforms of President Aristide, and install friendly regimes that would make Haiti safe for business interests. In other words, Canada's current role in Haiti reflects its sub-imperial role in a larger system of capitalist globalization.

Some might dismiss CHAN's views as politically marginal or lacking in scholarly rigour. Yet this chapter treats them as contributions to an understanding of Canadian actions in Haiti. It does so out of respect for diverse perspectives, and because elements of CHAN's analysis converge with those of respected academics and of Haitian leaders like Prime Minister Bellerive. The methodological challenge is to identify the elements that stand up to empirically based scrutiny and weave them into a more nuanced view of Canada's role as a "good partner" in Haiti.

Before turning to the historical record, it bears explaining that our assessment is normatively and analytically rooted in two international instruments. The first is the Paris Declaration (PD), to which 55 Northern and Southern states (including Haiti), as well as numerous international agencies, adhered in 2005. The PD codifies the mutual responsibilities of donors and recipients to practise cooperation differently. It sets clear standards for donor alignment on national priorities and institutions, harmonization among donors, joint monitoring and accountability for results. The Declaration contains a chapter on fragile states that lowers standards on both sides of the cooperation relationship. Yet multilateral monitoring exercises coordinated by the OECD have held donors and fragile state governments to core PD standards even in such contexts (see OECD, 2005; 2009).

One reason for upholding core standards is that the PD has been "amplified" by the OECD DAC (Development Assistance Committee)

Principles for Good International Engagement in Fragile States and Situations, a document that influenced the PD and was formally adopted by OECD governments in 2007. The DAC Fragile States (FS) Principles codify 10 guidelines for engagement in fragile states. The key one, for our purposes in this chapter, is the commitment to "focus on state building as the central objective" (OECD, 2007). Though Southern countries have not formally adhered to this OECD instrument, in 2008 Haiti and six other self-designated fragile states agreed to jointly monitor its implementation in their countries. Several of the Latin American states most engaged in Haiti have agreed to join this process in Haiti. This is one reason why Prime Minister Bellerive regularly uses the PD and the DAC FS Principles as normative referents to analyse his government's and external actors' engagement in Haiti.

The chapter examines Canada's engagement based on these norms. In the next section we discuss the big picture of how Canada's approach crystallized during the transitional period from 2004 to the elections in 2006. In the following section we examine Canada's role during the initial years of the Préval administration, from 2006 to mid-2009. In the conclusions we extend the analysis to Canada's role in Haiti since the earthquake in January 2010.[3] Throughout the chapter, we focus on the core governance issues of strengthening the Haitian state and nurturing national ownership.

## Canada and the transitional government from 2004 to 2006

Before looking at the period since 2004, it is important to recall that Canada has been active in Haiti for several decades. Canadian missionaries have been on the ground since the late nineteenth century. Diplomatic relations were established in 1954, Haiti became an important recipient of Canadian development assistance in the late 1960s and Canada (mostly Quebec) has accepted tens of thousands of refugees and economic migrants from Haiti. Ottawa supported the democratic process that began in the mid-1980s, and opposed the 1991 coup against President Aristide. During the 1990s the Canadian government supported all UN and OAS missions, it was active bilaterally and it funded the field activities of many Canadian NGOs and church groups.[4] Like most other Western countries and international organizations, after the highly contested elections in 2000 Canada reduced its direct engagement with the state and channelled most of its assistance through civil society organizations (CSOs).[5]

Ottawa re-engaged in early 2004, first to support renewed CARICOM–OAS attempts to forge a peaceful solution to the political crisis. A few days before President Aristide's departure, Ottawa lined up behind the

US-French strategy of ousting Aristide through a combination of social pressure and armed rebellion, as well as external military and political intervention (Hallward, 2007). In the early morning of Aristide's departure, Ottawa deployed Special Forces to Haiti to protect Canadian assets and secure the international airport. Later on 29 February, Ottawa put those troops under the command of the Multinational Interim Force (MIF) established by the UN Security Council on the same day. Canada then increased its military presence to over 500 troops.

That intervention remains controversial under international law, in Haiti and in Canada. It is a key piece of evidence used by CHAN to support its view that Canada conspired to replace President Aristide with a government more attuned to Western interests. It is difficult, without conducting detailed historical research, to come to a definitive judgement on those events. It remains unclear whether Canadian officials truly discussed possibilities of sponsoring "regime change" in Haiti with their US and French counterparts in early 2003. What seems clear to this author is that Ottawa sided with Washington and Paris when they decided to move against Aristide in February 2004. This is presumably one of the issues that the Canadian parliamentary Standing Committee on Foreign Affairs and International Development was alluding to when it noted that "the Committee acknowledges past mistakes of international intervention in recent years, including the controversy over Canada's own role" (House of Commons, 2006: 2).

What is also clear is that since then Ottawa has played an active, multi-dimensional role in Haiti. The first axis of its actions has been a "whole-of-government" approach at the domestic level, involving the close coordination of diplomatic, security and development efforts. The second axis has been a multilateral approach at the international level, where Canada has championed a broad approach to stabilization in Haiti, mostly through the United Nations and with significant Latin American involvement. Let us touch on the second axis before examining the first in more depth.

While planning to remove President Aristide, Washington and its allies explored ways of avoiding the uncomfortable result of ending up as three Western occupying powers. By 29 February, they had persuaded Chile to join the MIF (see Chapter 9 in this volume). Although Brazil was open to playing a security role in Haiti, it indicated that this would have to take place under the aegis of a more legitimate UN mission, with Brazilian and other Latin American officials in lead posts (Brigagao and Fernandes, 2007: 25). Negotiations eventually led to the mandating of MINUSTAH on 30 April 2004, the appointment of a Brazilian to command its military component and officials from other Latin American countries to lead other pillars, and the official transfer of powers to that mission on

Table 12.1   Canadian ODA* disbursements to Haiti, April 2004 to March 2006

|  | FY 2004–2005, in CAN$ million | FY 2005–2006, in CAN$ million |
|---|---|---|
| CIDA | 104.62 | 96.13 |
| OGD* | 0 | 2.29 |
| Total | 104.62 | 98.42 |

*Source*: CIDA, 2006a: 33; CIDA, 2008a: 40
*Other Government Departments

1 June 2004. Canada actively promoted this evolution, on the understanding that a UN mission which represented a wide diversity of countries in the hemisphere would have more legitimacy in Haiti and internationally.[6]

The other axis of Canada's strategy after February 2004 has been the attempt to coordinate its own and others' approaches to security and political renewal, as well as economic and social development. Ottawa sent high-level representatives to Port-au-Prince, including Prime Minister Martin in November 2004, and invited Haitian officials to visit Canada. It was active in the Group of Friends formed to support the Haitian process in various capitals and in New York. Once MINUSTAH was deployed, Canada withdrew most of its military forces, replaced them with a contingent of police officers and took the command of the United Nations Police (UNPOL) element for two years.

Canada also championed and assisted the joint formulation of the Interim Cooperation Framework (ICF) by donors and the transitional government. It then invested a growing portion of its development assistance to support the implementation of the ICF. In mid-2004, Ottawa pledged CA$160 million over two years for Haiti. Table 12.1 shows that from April 2004 to the end of March 2006, Ottawa's disbursements actually exceeded its pledges to Haiti.

The distribution of Canada's assistance to Haiti is also noteworthy. As shown in Table 12.2, Canadian Official Development Assistance (ODA) seems to have been fairly evenly spread over all the pillars of the ICF – from democratic development and security to humanitarian assistance and longer-term socio-economic development – with the traditional areas of Canadian International Development Agency (CIDA) support receiving the greatest funding.

It is also important to note who "executed" those funds, in CIDA parlance. Canada is one of the few donors that invested ODA funds to help the Haitian Office of the President and Ministry of Planning participate in the elaboration of the ICF and in its follow-up processes. Yet during this period the lion's share of Canadian aid was channelled through international institutions like the United Nations, the World Bank and the

Table 12.2 Estimated distribution of Canadian ODA disbursements to Haiti, 2004–2006

| Theme | Percentage of disbursements |
|---|---|
| Democratic development | 18% |
| Security and justice | 19.5% |
| Economic development | 31.5% |
| Social development and humanitarian aid | 31% |

*Note*: CIDA does not report the thematic breakdown of its disbursements in its annual statistical reports. These estimates were calculated on the basis of disbursements that CIDA reported to the Canadian Parliament in ACDI (CIDA, 2006b). For a more detailed breakdown of these funds and of their executing agencies, see Baranyi, 2007.

Inter-American Development Bank, as well as Canadian NGOs, firms, crown corporations and universities (see Baranyi, 2007).

Of course, what matters most is the outcome of these investments, not only where the money was spent. The Canadian government's initial reports on results provide indications of key outcomes during the 2004–2006 years. The most notable result is perhaps in the realm of democratic governance, where the free and relatively fair conduct of three rounds of elections in 2006 is held up as a major positive outcome.[7] CIDA reported that its assistance contributed directly to the registration of 3.5 million voters, the broad participation of women as voters and candidates, training for several thousand Haitian election monitors, training of 250 journalists in responsible media coverage, etc. Canadian assistance also contributed to strengthening the foundations for a modern civil registry and a permanent electoral council, both of which are crucial to the sustainability of legitimate electoral processes in the country (CIDA, 2006b). This falls short of Shamsie's call for substantive democratization, yet there is no doubt that Canada contributed significantly to procedural democratization during the transitional period.

While the elections received much domestic and international attention in 2006, insecurity was also a concern during this period. Canada was active in the area of security and justice through three main channels. Its main involvement, by far, was through political support to MINUSTAH and the contribution of a commander as well as about 75 officers to its UNPOL element. The second was to support attempts to reform key institutions such as the Haitian National Police (HNP) and the judiciary. The third channel was to support civil society organizations and their attempts to promote the same reforms or human rights more broadly.

In its mid-2006 report to Parliament, CIDA claimed that these investments were producing significant results. It suggested that MINUSTAH had reinforced the HNP's security operations and that a reform plan had been approved by Haitian authorities. It noted that a plan to strengthen the administration of the penitentiary system had also been elaborated, and that both the HNP headquarters and the prison in Jacmel had been renovated with Canadian assistance. It also suggested that civil society campaigns had increased the quantity and quality of citizen engagement in debates on judicial reform.

Yet as noted in an April 2007 whole-of-government response to Parliament, the "security situation, while still fragile, is stabilizing thanks to a better integration of efforts between Haitian authorities and MINUS-TAH" though "progress has been slow and there are still many challenges that must be overcome to reverse the downward spiral in which Haiti has been caught" (Government of Canada, 2007: 2). The government's response also acknowledged that the reform plan formulated by HNP officers with Canadian assistance had been sidelined by the UN-drafted plan, while noting that the latter had incorporated elements of the first plan and was ultimately approved by the Haitian government. Finally, the government noted that Canada was having difficulties fulfilling its pledge to deploy the full contingent of a hundred police officers to MINUSTAH but was taking measures to boost its capacity for police deployments in this area.

In retrospect, the 2006 CIDA report probably downplayed the extent of the security crisis and exaggerated Canadian contributions during this period. Even if one does not accept all of CHAN's claims, there is no doubt that grave human rights violations were committed both by MI-NUSTAH forces and by the HNP during the grim years of 2004–2005. From mid-2005 to late 2006, the Brazilian approach of exercising restraint in the use of force (and investing in community service) became the guiding doctrine in MINUSTAH and the HNP, but by then both institutions had been tarnished by their initial abuses. Moreover, the United Nation's attempt to impose its HNP reform plan on the outgoing Haitian government in early 2006 undermined Canada's painstaking efforts to assist the formulation of a more home-grown plan by the HNP. It took the United Nations and others three months of negotiations with the Préval government to get its nominal agreement to a revised version of the so-called UN plan (see Fortin and Pierre, 2008). Finally, despite civil society efforts, judicial reform remained blocked during this period. Both the problem of national ownership and the missing link with justice reform would come back to haunt HNP reform.

With regard to economic and social development, the Canadian government argues that by paying CA$15 million of Haiti's arrears to the World Bank and CA$18 million of interest on Haiti's debt with the Inter-American Development Bank, Canada facilitated the country's inclusion in the Heavily Indebted Poor Countries (HIPC) Initiative, which will greatly reduce Haiti's debt burden over the coming years, thus freeing up scarce national resources for real poverty reduction in the country. Meanwhile, in mid-2006 CIDA reported that its more modest investments in local development projects had already generated results, such as strengthening a network of 64 savings and credit cooperatives, enhancing the provision of electricity services in Jacmel, creating 5,000 jobs in poor areas of the country, etc. It also reported that its social assistance had helped increase the quality of schooling in departments such as Artibonite and Nippes, and ensured the vaccination of thousands of children against diseases like rubella (CIDA, 2006a; Government of Canada, 2007).

So Canada contributed to macroeconomic stabilization, to local development in some regions and to the provision of essential social services during the 2004–2006 years. Canada supported a hybrid rather than an orthodox market-oriented approach to economic reactivation. Though agriculture was not a CIDA priority during this period, some of CIDA's investments in local development fostered natural resource management and production in rural areas.

Nonetheless, Shamsie's question about whether even this softer market-based approach is adequate for Haiti's conditions remains relevant. The ICF and the Interim Poverty Reduction Strategy Paper (I-PRSP) elaborated in 2006 were incomplete plans based on limited consultation. As we shall see in the next section, the neglect of agriculture for domestic consumption was one factor that detonated the governance crisis in 2008. Moreover, the extremely modest amount of Canadian (and other international) funds channelled through Haitian state institutions perpetuated the state's inability to take on a more active role in the economy.

In sum, Canada followed up on its problematic military intervention by contributing greatly to stabilization in Haiti. It championed a multilateral approach in diplomatic forums and coordinated a multidimensional, whole-of-government Canadian approach. Ottawa exceeded its considerable aid pledges through a balanced portfolio of democratic, security, economic, social and humanitarian assistance. Many initiatives supported by Canada yielded early results, from the relative success of the 2006 elections to the reduction of Haiti's debt service payments.

Yet a number of worrisome trends appeared during this initial period. These included Canada's inability to make a major difference in critical areas like security and justice reform, given the inherited situation on the ground and the problematic approaches of international actors such as MINUSTAH. It also included the tendency to channel the lion's share of Canadian funds through international or Canadian institutions, despite the declaratory commitment to "focus on state building as a central priority", in the language of the DAC fragile states principles.

Neither of these tendencies can be attributed solely to Canadian or broader international approaches. The lack of political legitimacy and the inherited administrative weakness of the Haitian state under the transitional government made it very difficult for international actors to respect its orientations and even more challenging to trust it to administer international funds. Let us see if these tendencies changed under the elected government of President Préval.

## Canada and the Préval government from 2006 to 2009

Shortly after taking office in mid-2006, President Préval and his officials began asserting their sovereign right to lead development cooperation processes in their country. They wanted the ICF and Interim Poverty Reduction Strategy Paper (PRSP) to be extended to the end of 2007, and they signalled their intent to lead the preparation of a full PRSP by the end of that year. During Canadian-sponsored expert consultations on the draft DAC Fragile States Principles, Haitian officials indicated their desire to move from these principles to the concepts of national ownership and full partnership codified in the Paris Declaration (see OECD, 2006). It was during this period that the Préval government insisted on some revisions to the HNP reform plan and appointed a more activist National Commission for Disarmament, Demobilization and Reintegration (CNDDR) to coordinate disarmament efforts. This was also when the government took steps to increase the solvency, transparency and accountability of public finances.

By late 2006, these attempts to strengthen state leadership ran into major problems on the ground. CNDDR's attempt to negotiate with the leaders of armed gangs generated little disarmament. Violent crime and citizens' demands for action continued to grow. After months of debate, in December 2006 MINUSTAH initiated aggressive security operations in the most crime-affected neighbourhoods of Port-au-Prince and in major drugs trans-shipment points like Les Cayes. These operations apparently disarticulated several gangs and decreased the incidence of violent crimes by early 2007, but the government's nationalistic discourse was dented by this reassertion of MINUSTAH's prominent security role (International Crisis Group, 2008).

The process of formulating the full PRSP, finally approved as the National Strategy Document for Growth and Poverty Reduction (DSN-CRP) in November 2007, also complicated the government's bid to reassert national ownership. As a positive move, with international assistance the government managed to consult some local officials, private-sector leaders and national experts, and draft a multipronged strategy to foster growth, human development and better governance. On the downside, many civil society organizations (CSOs) felt excluded from the consultations while key international actors felt that the DSNCRP lacked clear (and clearly budgeted) priorities. Even the president's commitment to the document was questioned, both nationally and internationally.

The economic downturn which began in Haiti in late 2007, and the resulting governance crisis in 2008, greatly weakened the attempt to reassert national ownership. The riots against the high cost of food and other essentials prompted President Préval to relieve Prime Minister Alexis of his duties in March 2008, and Haiti found itself without a functioning government for almost six months. This caused the postponement of the conference with donors which had been scheduled for April 2008. It put the rivalries within Haiti's political elite on public display. It also caused the financing and implementation of the DSNCRP to be postponed for a year.

By the time Prime Minister Michele Pierre-Louis truly took office in September 2008, the global economic crisis and four devastating hurricanes compelled her government and the international community to revisit the DSNCRP. It was only at the conference with donors in April 2009 that the Haitian state gained international confidence in its plans to implement an updated DSNCRP over the following years.[8] The introduction of external audits of government finances, competitive public procurement procedures and strengthened tax and customs administration, also helped generate international confidence in the state. Those changes continued when Jean-Max Bellerive became prime minister in late 2009. That is the backdrop against which Canadian engagement in Haiti must be assessed, particularly on the issue of national ownership.

Canada remained diplomatically active on Haiti during this period. At the highest levels, Governor-General Michaëlle Jean visited in 2006 and again in 2008, while Prime Minister Harper visited the country as part of his Americas tour in July 2007. Those visits were reciprocated by high-level missions from Haiti. The two governments established a Mixed Commission of senior officials for annual strategic consultations. At the second meeting of the Mixed Commission in March 2009, the Haitian side tabled a Mutual Accountability Pact to reinforce both sides' commitments to the principles of partnership. In Ottawa, the Haiti Taskforce was established in 2008 to strengthen whole-of-government coordination.

Canada remained very engaged in Groups of Friends of Haiti in New York and Geneva, as well as in numerous working-level committee-stables in Haiti. It broadened dialogue on Haiti with Latin American partners such as Argentina, Brazil and Chile. The key message of Canadian diplomats during this period was that the international community needed to "stay the course" in Haiti.

Table 12.3  Canadian international assistance to Haiti, April 2006 to March 2008

|  | FY 2006–2007, in CAN$ million | FY 2007–2008, in CAN$ million |
|---|---|---|
| CIDA | 92.57 | 103.7 |
| OGD | 30.08 | 30.08 |
| Total | 122.65 | 133.78 |

*Note*: The figures for FY 2006–2007 disbursements are reported in CIDA, 2009: 33. Those for FY 2007–2008 are based on CIDA's August 2008 mini-report on results. Since that report did not include data on OGD disbursements in FY 2007–2008, we used the figure for FY 2006–2007 as a proxy.

Canada also increased its financial engagement under the Préval government. At the first conference between donors and the new government in July 2006, Prime Minister Harper announced a five-year commitment of CA$520 million. In 2007, Ottawa increased that allocation to CA$555 million. Those were clear votes of confidence in the newly elected government and important signals to other major donors about Canada's engagement over the medium term. Table 12.3 suggests that Canada is on track to meet or exceed those allocations.

A preliminary analysis of CIDA reports on its and other government department OGD disbursements from 2006 to 2008 suggests that while Canada has maintained a balance of investments in the main areas of development cooperation, it seems to be spending more in the area of security and less in the area of democratic governance (CIDA, 2008a; 2009). This may reflect the winding down of electoral assistance after 2006 and the ramping up of DFAIT/START (Stabilization and Reconstruction Taskforce) and Royal Canadian Mounted Police (RCMP) programming on security. A closer examination of Canada's expenditures, by area, reveals other patterns.

In the area of democratic development, Canada's support evolved considerably from its focus on the elections in 2005–2006. CIDA is supporting new initiatives in this domain:[9]

- A CA$15 million project (managed by the OAS) to modernize the Haitian National Identification Office's civil registry. The civil registry is a key instrument for voter registration. It is also the starting point for broader citizenship, for example to access social services, jobs and property titles. This is critical in a country where large numbers of persons have been unregistered and disenfranchised for generations.
- A CA$5 million project managed by the Canadian Parliamentary Centre, to strengthen the Haitian Parliament's capacity to provide oversight through its committees, make the Parliament more accessible to citizens and provide better administrative support for the work of parliamentarians.

- A CA\$4.4 million programme managed by Rights and Democracy, to strengthen the advocacy work of Haitian human rights organizations on key issues such as the right to food, the role of political parties in democratic development and women's rights.

Earlier initiatives like the Election Observer Mission, the Democracy and Peace Fund for Haitian CSOs were gradually completed. Ongoing and new projects during this period demonstrate that CIDA's portfolio promoted both the strengthening of procedural democracy and the broadening of democratic participation. However they also suggest that CIDA continued to channel most of its funds through international and Canadian institutions. While these projects usually aimed to strengthen Haitian state and civil society partners, few if any of the large programmes and projects were managed by Haitian institutions themselves.

By mid-2008, CIDA could already report initial results from some of these projects. These included the registration of a further 560,000 adults on the voters' list, bringing the level of its national coverage to 92 per cent. They also included the broadcasting of parliamentary sessions to make them more accessible to the public, and continued increases in CSOs' capacity for human rights advocacy (CIDA, 2008b). These promising initial results suggest that more transparent, systematic monitoring and evaluation would be useful to track outcomes over time. Nonetheless, Shamsie's analysis reminds us that few of these projects supported the self-organization of large and historically marginalized constituencies such as the rural poor, whose pressures from below would seem crucial to deeper changes in economic and social policy.

Women are one such constituency, yet they were sidelined by Canada during this period. For a decade CIDA supported networks of Haitian women's organizations that were at the forefront of proposing and often gaining major legislative and programmatic changes from the state.[10] Leaders of the women's movement were brought into the Préval government as ministers and senior officials. On the basis of these antecedents and new developments, CIDA officials formulated a CA\$17 million programme with two tracks. The first would have expanded Canadian support for the Ministry for the Rights of Women (MCFDF) and its efforts to mainstream gender in government. The second track would have expanded CIDA's support for the service provision and policy advocacy activities of women's CSOs. Despite the impressive record of CIDA gender programming in Haiti, and despite the conclusions by a global review of 10 years of CIDA gender programming that a two–track approach was essential, in 2008 the Conservative minister of international development decided not to approve this programme. Minister Oda's rationale was that equality between men and women should become a "cross-cutting priority" in all of CIDA's programming in Haiti. Nonetheless, CIDA officials and their Haitian counterparts quietly found other ways of maintaining some support for the women's organizations that they viewed as being critical for human development.[11]

Security is an area in which Canada became even more programmatically engaged under the Préval government, chiefly due to the establishment of the Stabilization and Reconstruction Taskforce in DFAIT, and its growing security sector programming in Haiti. Highlights of START's Haiti programming during this period include the allocation of:[12]

- CA$5.5 million to CANADEM to fund the deployment of Canadian police and correctional experts to MINUSTAH. This is in addition to the approximately CA$30 million allocated to the RCMP over these two years, for the deployment of active duty officers to Haiti via the Canadian Police Arrangement (CPA).
- CA$3.3 million via the International Organization for Migration (IOM) for the refurbishment of the National Police School, and of CA$3.5 million via the United Nations Development Programme (UNDP) to renovate several HNP stations in the South Departments. Also the allocation of CA$5 million via UNDP to renovate the infrastructure and equip the HNP Inspectorate General.
- CA$4.7 million via UNDP for a major disarmament and community security programme, and CA$0.4 million to the Brazilian NGO Viva Rio for a community security project in the Bel Air area of Port-au-Prince.
- About CA$6 million for several programmes and projects via the IOM and other international institutions to renovate the infrastructure and strengthen the capacity of border guards to control illicit activities such as arms smuggling and human trafficking.
- As part of its programming in this sector, START has played an active role in government–donor coordination mechanisms: for example, by chairing the Donor Table on Prisons and helping to establish the Border Management Working Group.

It is worth noting that despite the prominent roles played by DFAIT/START and the RCMP in the area of security, CIDA also made large grants in this area. It allocated CA$18.1 million to build and equip the new National Police Academy in Ganthier, outside Port-au-Prince. It allocated CA$16.5 million to train and otherwise enhance the administrative capacities of HNP managers. CIDA also allocated about CA$5 million to support the continuation of Viva Rio's community security programming in Bel Air.

A 2009 evaluation of START programming in Haiti, commissioned by DFAIT and the Canadian Office of the Inspector General, provides insights into the outcomes of Canadian engagement in this sector. It pointedly suggested that START's programming "reflects some OECD best practices for fragile state engagement and several of the principles on aid effectiveness" (DFAIT, 2009b: 15). Specifically, the evaluation observed that START programming is aligned with Haitian governmental priorities codified in the DSNCRP, and in more specialized documents such as the 2006 National Police Reform Plan. It noted that most START-supported projects aim to strengthen the infrastructure and human resources of key Haitian institutions such as the HNP, prisons and the institutions involved in border management. It suggested that most of these projects were appreciated by Haitian counterparts for their relevance and timeliness.

Yet the evaluation also noted some overarching challenges, in addition to numerous things that could be improved at the operational level. Though START deserved credit for convincing CIDA and other donors to make longer-term investments in key areas such as HNP reform, much remained to be done to ensure the sustainability of these investments. Critical challenges in this regard included deepening coordination with Haitian institutions and channelling more funds through the Haitian state. While recognizing the historic corruption and inefficiencies of Haitian institutions, the report recommended that START shift from its almost total reliance on international and Canadian implementing agencies, and increase the portion of funds channelled directly through the HNP and other Haitian government institutions (ibid.: 67, recommendation 9).

The report noted that sustainability also depends on the will and effectiveness of national actors in this sector. Indeed since 2004 the HNP, the judiciary and other state actors have slowed down or blocked internationally sanctioned reforms that they have viewed as too risky. Yet the international community's somewhat technocratic and state-centric approach to reform has also left it hostage to the whims of political and bureaucratic leaders. The lack of international follow-up to a HNP Reform Plan provision to hold public consultations on "what kind of police Haiti needs" has been a major problem in this area. In 2007 senior Haitian officials claimed that they wished to go ahead with these consultations. Yet key international actors, including MINUSTAH and Canada, withheld support for public consultations because they feared that this could further polarize public opinion on security matters. That may have been the case in 2007, but paucity or absence of parliamentary or citizen engagement in public security policy debates now makes it difficult for the international community to find allies in its quest to press the HNP on delicate matters such as the decertification of officers allegedly guilty of serious crimes (Fortin and Pierre, 2008), and debrief with senior Canadian police officers who served with MINUSTAH in 2008).

In the economic and social realm, during the 2006–2009 period CIDA's programming was based on its 2006 Interim Strategy, informed by the

Haitian DSNCRP, and affected by the destruction caused by the hurricanes in 2008. Highlights of CIDA's programming during those years reflect these diverse influences:

- A CA$13.8 million project to increase the capacity of several government of Haiti institutions to implement the DSNCRP.
- A CA$18.5 million project via the Canadian Border Services Agency to increase public revenues through improved Haitian border and customs controls.
- A CA$15.5 million project via the Ministry of the Economy and Finances, largely to reduce its short-term debt to the Inter-American Development Bank (IDB), and to strengthen public finances management.
- A CA$75 million project via the IDB to build a new road connecting the towns of Jérémie and Les Cayes in the south-western region, and another CA$19.8 million project via the IDB for the rehabilitation of other roads and basic infrastructure.
- A CA$20 million project via Canadian NGOs like Centre for International Studies and Cooperation (CECI), to promote local development and a CA$15 million project via Développement international Desjardins to support Haitian savings cooperatives.
- CA$5.3 million for the Pro Huerta project with the Inter-American Institute for Cooperation on Agriculture (IICA) and Argentine partners to foster community-based agriculture for food security for some of the poorest areas of the country.
- A CA$17.5 million project via the Pan-American Health Organization (PAHO) and Brazilian partners to support the Ministry of Health's Expanded National Vaccination Programme. Another CA$17.5 million project via the Université de Montréal to help the Ministry of Health strengthen its policies, planning, human resource management and stakeholder engagement processes. A CA$18.75 million project via the Canadian Embassy to help the Ministry of Health strengthen its regulatory role in the health sector.
- A portfolio of small grants, such as CA$750,000 granted to the World Food Programme for relief to hurricane victims in 2008.

In mid-2008, CIDA reported results from some of these projects. These included the reduction of Haiti's debt to the IDB; continued access to credit in 56 savings and credit cooperatives; the immunization of over 620,000 children and young people against polio, measles and rubella; "doubling, and in some cases even tripling, of agricultural production for people benefiting from local development projects" (CIDA, 2008b). These all seem to be significant outcomes.

Thorough studies would be required to assess results, yet several observations are possible. First, although most of CIDA's largest investments were still channelled via international and Canadian institutions, there were important projects being implemented by the Haitian state. These included a large project to strengthen the state's capacity to lead the implementation of the DSNCRP, a central development mission over the coming years. Other projects could strengthen the revenue generation or financial management capacities of key state institutions that may make them more investment-worthy and even self-sufficient in the future. Indeed, CIDA's support helped key ministries prepare the DSNCRP priority investment plan presented at the donors' conference in April 2009. That plan and measures to strengthen the accountability of public finances and increase customs revenues were crucial to regaining donors' confidence and obtaining a further cancellation of Haiti's external debt that year.[13]

Second, although most other projects addressed other important development needs – from debt relief and the construction of roads to the provision of basic services such as immunization and primary schooling – few except for Pro Huerta directly stimulate agriculture for local consumption. This is worrisome because food insecurity remained a major gap in Haiti's stabilization-to-development strategy, and other large donors did not seem to be offering help in this area (Droits et Démocratie et GRAMIR, 2008; Baranyi et al., 2009). The establishment of the National Commission for Food Security, the initiation of promising initiatives under its guidance and the involvement of innovative partners from Argentina may help attract more investment from traditional donors like Canada.

Third, given the scale of Canadian investments in the economic and social sectors, there was little investment in democratic debate on policy alternatives. The focus on strengthening state capacity and delivering essential services seems to have crowded out support for the organization of constituencies that could press for critical policy changes. Nonetheless, CIDA's support for the Rights and Democracy's programme to help rural producers lobby for increased investment in national agriculture, and its programme to help women lobby against gender-based violence, were steps forward in the direction of more participatory development.

## Conclusions

If nurturing national ownership of development processes was a challenge in Haiti after the intervention in 2004, it has become an enormous challenge after the earthquake in January 2010. The authority, capacity and legitimacy of an already fragile state have been greatly weakened, while the scope of international engagement has grown dramatically in quantitative and qualitative terms (Fatton, 2010). How has Canada acted in this even more difficult context?

Like many others moved by the dimension of the tragedy that befell Haiti on 12 January 2010, Canadians responded quickly and generously to the humanitarian crisis. Within a week Ottawa had deployed a thousand troops and disbursed funds to support several UN and NGO humanitarian assistance initiatives. On January 25 Canada hosted the first Ministerial Preparatory Conference, where core cooperation principles like national ownership, coordination and sustainability (which seemed threatened by certain large powers' militarized initial responses) were reaffirmed. Over the following weeks Canadian citizens donated a record $220 million to Haiti, while the government increased its financial commitments to keep up with the Canadian public and with other donors. At the International Donors' Conference on 31 March, Canada pledged an additional $400 million of assistance over two years.[14] On that basis it was given a seat on the Interim Commission for the Reconstruction of Haiti (CIRH).

Although it is too early to assess these commitments, one can piece together a sense of where Canada is focusing its contributions:

- Humanitarian aid: a large part of the funds allocated for 2010–2012 are earmarked for short-term relief and reconstruction activities.[15]
- Reconstruction and development: especially in CIDA's priority areas, namely economic reactivation, food security, as well as children and youth.
- Justice and security: support to rebuild the National Police and the broader rule of law system will remain a priority for DFAIT/START.
- Democratic governance: Canada disbursed modest sums to support the organization of the elections in November 2010.[16]

What do these initial post-earthquake actions and the longer record of Canadian engagement from 2004 to 2009 suggest about Canada's abilities to "walk the talk" of partnership in Haiti? What do the trends suggest about the debates noted in the introduction?

The historical record over the past five years supports Canadian officials' self-perception of Canada as a diplomatically active partner which tends to exceed its substantial aid pledges. It confirms their claims that Canadians coordinate their efforts fairly well through whole-of-government, bilateral and multilateral mechanisms. The record also demonstrates that Canada has been active in several important sectors – from democratization and public security to economic and social development, as well as humanitarian assistance – and that before the earthquake some Canadian-supported initiatives were yielding developmental results.

The record shows that building the capacity of Haitian state institutions has been a priority of Canadian development assistance since 2004, and that Ottawa has increased the funding it channels directly through state agencies since the elections in 2006. Indeed, Canada seems unique among traditional donors in having targeted some of its assistance to strengthen the capacity of key state institutions to plan and implement overarching development processes such as the DSNCRP. It has also targeted funds to help border and customs agencies increase public revenue, help the Ministry of Finance manage public finances more effectively and help both the National Police and the Ministry of Health manage their human resources more professionally. All of these initiatives are critical to the goals of strengthening the Haitian state and its ability to own and orientate development processes in the country.

This tendency helps qualify suggestions made by Jean-Max Bellerive when he was minister of planning: namely, that Canada and other traditional donors have not adapted their cooperation to reflect Haiti's advances and are not investing sufficient Official Development Assistance (ODA) funds through the Haitian state. While the data presented in this study confirm that Canada still channels the lion's share of its assistance through international and Canadian executing agencies, it also shows that Canada has strategically invested in projects to strengthen the Haitian state and its absorptive capacity. The big question is whether this approach will be sustained over the coming years given the unpromising convergence of dramatically weakened state capacity/legitimacy and equally dramatic increases in international engagement.

National ownership involves much more than state ownership. Canada's support for inclusive, free and fair elections, its support for Parliament and other aspects of procedural democracy, are important contributions to democratizing national ownership. In the past, CIDA has invested ODA funds to foster organization and constructive policy advocacy by constituencies such as women that have an interest in policy change. Yet these investments in the social basis of democracy have been minute compared to Canadian investments in state institutions and procedural democracy. Before the earthquake, Canada still invested little in supporting policy advocacy by small rural producers and consumers, two constituencies whose engagement is essential to reversing the critical problem of food insecurity in Haiti. Similarly, DFAIT/START's important investments in security sector reform (SSR) have also largely neglected the democratic dimension of SSR. Clearly, there is scope for improvement if Canada aspires to pursue the democratic approach to national ownership codified in the Paris Declaration and in the DAC Principles for Good Engagement in Fragile States.

One of the most complex dimensions of development cooperation in a context like Haiti is the interface between democratic ownership and policy choices. Donais, Shamsie and others have argued that Western donors and multilateral institutions have encouraged democratic ownership but only within the bounds of liberal orthodoxies like macroeconomic stability, fiscal restraint and social compensation typical of the post-Washington Consensus era. This model may have made sense immediately after the 2004 intervention, when stabilization was the main goal. But as Robert Fatton Jr. (2010) and others have argued cogently, at a time when key sectors of the Haitian economy like agriculture need to be revitalized, when the provision of basic social services is unlikely to become more socially inclusive without greater public-sector activism, it seems important to give Haitians space to explore policy mixes that might be more appropriate to their situation. That is also what Jean-Max Bellerive has been asking for since 2008.

That brings us back to the core of ownership, namely national agency. A former chief of a ministerial cabinet in the Alexis government has suggested that: "When the state asserts itself, certain donors follow."[17] This suggests that when national ownership emerges from the inside and when it is seen as legitimate by the international community, it can provide a focus for external engagement. Shamsie and Donais remind us that democratic support is another crucial ingredient of national ownership: state elites can assert themselves vis-à-vis external actors, but their capacity to sustain such efforts rests on their ability to marshal broad support for their positions. That, in turn, depends on being able to translate public policy into tangible benefits for broad constituencies – by stimulating and regulating the creation of more jobs with better incomes, affordable food, transportation and housing, public security, as well as better education and health care for the majority of citizens. It is these synergies between national ownership, democratic support and public policy effectiveness that require careful nurturing in Haiti.

If one believes that there is room for creative agency in history despite the weight of social structures or the devastating effect of natural disasters, then it may be possible for the next leaders of Haiti to move ahead with the institutional and policy reforms that the country needs, and build the multiparty and multiconstituency alliances required to sustain such reforms. It may also be possible for international actors like Canada to support such reforms and help Haitians nurture the social bases of change, even when some movements' discourses differ from liberal norms. That would require an imaginative leap beyond current practices of technical assistance for elections, institutional strengthening and the reconstruction of infrastructure. It would also require more investment in public agency (as opposed to just "agencies"), as well as in public accountability through parliamentary and other participatory mechanisms.

If Canada and its partners in Haiti rise to this historic challenge, they may find themselves "walking the talk" of national ownership and sustainable development in Haiti. Yet if the earthquake and its aftermath do not lead to this qualitative leap, many Haitians may ask themselves what their leaders and their partners are really up to. Some will ask whether, despite their stated intentions, Canada, the United Nations and other partners are actually perpetuating Haiti's condition of fragility and dependence.[18] And Canadians might well ask whether the considerable investments made since 2004 have really been worthwhile, as they are currently asking about Canada's precarious role in Afghanistan.

Before readers dismiss this scenario too quickly, they might reflect on words written by Lyonel Trouillot, one of Haiti's most prominent intellectuals, in April 2010:

> The "chiefs", the big men ... might speak of reconstruction led by Haitians, but it is not what is happening ... In the street, in the homes of honest citizens ... there is a sense of defeat ... An impression ... that what is being built is improvised, leaving much room for the private calculations of a few Haitian politicians and businessmen. The impression that a few international officials, "experts" ... and NGOs will play the sorcerer's apprentice to justify their nice salaries ... In the street, a wave of anger is rising that we would be wrong to under-estimate. (Trouillot, 2010, author's translation)

## Notes

1. Pledges made at the International Conference on Haiti on 31 March 2010, suggest that Venezuela has replaced Canada as the second bilateral donor and that it may have replaced the United States as the lead donor (PRH, 2010).
2. The original version of this speech was given at CIDA on 18 November 2008. Government of Haiti representatives in Canada continued to echo this view in mid-2009 (see Collins, 2009).
3. Several primary research methods were used for this study. We examined documents issued by the governments of Canada and Haiti, conducted over 20 off-the-record key informant interviews and participated in numerous policy forums from 2007 to 2010. The interviews have been kept confidential to protect informants' identities. The author thanks Michèle Meilleur Sarazin for her research assistance on this project. I am also grateful to Isabelle Fortin for her detailed comments on a draft as well as to the two anonymous reviewers of the book manuscript.
4. For a historical account of Canada–Haiti relations, see Keating (2001).
5. CIDA (2006) reports that it disbursed CA$23.85 million to Haiti in 2002–2003 and CA$27.5 million in 2003–2004. See Muggah (2007) for details on Canadian assistance from the mid-1990s to 2004. See Sanders (2007 and 2008) for a more critical view of Canadian assistance via civil society organizations between 2000 and 2004.

6. The last claim was confirmed in interviews with senior DFAIT officials in Ottawa and senior diplomats in Port-au-Prince in 2008 and 2009.
7. Muggah (2007) draws the same conclusion based on his analysis of Canadian governance programming in Haiti.
8. The preparation of the *Plan d'investissement prioritaires du DSNCRP (2008–2010)* and its presentation at the April 2009 donors' conference contributed greatly in this regard. See République d'Haïti (2009).
9. The project descriptions in this section (except those financed by DFAIT/START) are adapted from CIDA's on-line project browser, accessed between June and August 2009.
10. For a detailed analysis of Canada's gender equity programming in Haiti, see Salahub (2008).
11. Discussions with Canadian officials, Haitian officials and Haitian activists in Port-au-Prince in June 2009 as well as in Ottawa during the autumn of 2009.
12. These project descriptions are taken from the DFAIT/START website and from the February 2009 draft evaluation report.
13. See Collins (2009) for an analysis of Canada's role in the forgiveness of Haiti's debt.
14. Ottawa and Quebec also introduced measures to make it easier for certain Haitians to stay in or immigrate to Canada. Ottawa repatriated most of the 2,000 or so Canadian troops deployed in Haiti by March 2010, as MINUSTAH ramped up its new deployments. Data on these actions was obtained from Government of Canada press releases and other statements posted on DFAIT and CIDA websites during that period, particularly the periodic updates on the DFAIT website titled "Canada's response to the earthquake in Haiti".
15. A CIDA News Release on 9 July 2010 notes that CIDA has allocated over $150 million to humanitarian assistance in Haiti since the earthquake.
16. In addition to the CIDA news release noted above, this composite picture draws on DFAIT (2010) and as well as Montpetit (2010).
17. Interview on 7 June 2009.
18. The increase of social protests in Haiti since May 2010 suggests that this is not only an academic preoccupation. See RNDDH (2010) and Péan (2010) for analyses of the national government and the international community's actions six months after the earthquake, and their differing views on where current trends might lead Haiti.

## REFERENCES

Baranyi, Stephen (2007) "Le Canada, Haïti et les dilemmes de l'intervention dans les 'États fragiles'." Paper presented at the Congress of the Latin American Studies Association, Montréal, 7 September.

Baranyi, Stephen, Pierre Beaudet and Isabelle Fortin (2009) *De la stabilisation et la reconstruction au développement. Enjeux pour Haïti, le Brésil et la Canada.* Ottawa: EDIM.

Bellerive, Jean-Max (2008) "Présentation du ministre de la planification et de la coopération externe d'Haïti", Presentation at *De la stabilisation et la reconstruction au développement international. Enjeux pour Haïti, le Brésil et le Canada.* International Symposium, University of Ottawa, 11 December.

Brigagao, Clovis and Fernanda Fernandes (2007) "Política externa brasileira e o Haiti", *Pensamiento propio*, 12. Available at http://www.gloobal.net/iepala/gloobal/fichas/ficha.php?entidad=Textos&id=5113&opcion=documento

CIDA (2006a) *Statistical Report on Official Development Assistance. Fiscal Year 2004–2005*. Ottawa: CIDA.

CIDA (2006b) "Coopération Canada-Haiti. Synthèse des résultats dans le contexte du Cadre de Coopération Intérimaire (Avril 2004–Mars 2006)", Gatineau, QC, Unpublished paper.

CIDA (2008a) *Statistical Report on Official Development Assistance: Fiscal Year 2005–2006*. Ottawa: CIDA.

CIDA (2008b) "Haiti: CIDA Results (2007–2008)", August. Available at http://www.acdi-cida.gc.ca/inet/images.nsf/vLUImages/Haiti/$file/HaitiResults07-08-eng.pdf

CIDA (2009) *Statistical Report on International Assistance: Fiscal Year 2006–2007*. Ottawa: CIDA. Available at http://www.acdi-cida.gc.ca/acdi-cida/ACDI-CIDA.nsf/eng/FRA-7994831-J7V

Collins, Michelle (2009) "Debt Relief Brings Hope for Troubled Haiti's Future", *Embassy*, 8 July.

Donais, Timothy (2009) "Peacebuilding and the Dilemmas of Local Ownership: The Case of Haiti", *International Journal*, 44(3): 753–773.

DFAIT (2009a) "Canada's Contribution to Haiti: Four Years of Progress", Department of Foreign Affairs and International Trade, Canada, website. Available at http://www.international.gc.ca/start-gtsr/haiti-progress-progres-haiti.aspx?lang=eng

DFAIT (2009b) *Summative evaluation of START's Global Peace and Security Fund – Haiti*. Department of Foreign Affairs and International Trade Canada. Available at http://www.international.gc.ca/about-a_propos/oig-big/2009/evaluation/gpsf_fpsm_haiti09.aspx?lang=eng

DFAIT (2010) "Statement by Minister Cannon on Haiti: Reaffirming Canada's Commitment Six Months after the Haiti Earthquake", Ottawa, 12 July. Available at http://www.international.gc.ca/ministers-ministres/Cannon_audio_haiti_earthquake_seisme_2010-07-10.aspx

Droits et Démocratie et GRAMIR (2008) *Le Droit a l'Alimentation en Haïti. Rapport d'une Mission Internationale d'Observation*. Montréal: Droits et Démocratie.

Fatton Jr., Robert (2010) "Towards a New Haitian State", *The Root*, 9 February. Available at http://www.theroot.com

Fortin, Isabelle and Yves-François Pierre (2008) "La réforme de la Police Nationale d'Haïti". Working paper, December, North-South Institute, Ottawa.

Government of Canada (2007) *Government Response to the Fourth Report of the Standing Committee on Foreign Affairs and International Development. Canada's International Policy Put to a Test on Haiti*. Ottawa: House of Commons.

Hallward, Peter (2007) *Damning the Flood: Haiti, Aristide, and the Politics of Containment*. New York: Verso Books.

House of Commons (2006) *Canada's International Policy Put to the Test in Haiti. Report of the Standing Committee on Foreign Affairs and International Development*. Ottawa: House of Commons, Parliament of Canada, December.

International Crisis Group (2008) *Reforming Haiti's Security Sector*. Latin America/Caribbean Report No. 28, 18 September.

Keating, Tom (2001) "Promoting Democracy in Haiti: Assessing the Practical and Ethical Implications" in R. Erwin (ed.) *Ethics and Security in Canadian Foreign Policy*. Vancouver: UBC Press, pp. 208–226.

Montpetit, Jonathan (2010) "Canada Calls for Haitian Vote by Year's End", *Globe and Mail*, 22 May.

Muggah, Robert (2007) "The Perils of Changing Donor Priorities in Fragile States: The Case of Haiti" in Jennifer Welsh and Ngaire Woods (eds) *Exporting Good Governance: Temptations and Challenges in Canada's Aid Program*. Waterloo: CIGI and Wilfrid Laurier University Press, pp. 190–223.

OECD (2005) *The Paris Declaration on Aid Effectiveness*. Paris: OECD-DAC.

OECD (2006) *Piloting the Principles for Good International Engagement in Fragile States and linkages to the Paris Declaration: Haiti report to the DAC Fragile States Group*. Paris: OECD.

OECD (2007) *Principles for Good International Engagement in Fragile States and Situations*. Paris: OECD-DAC.

OECD (2009) *Aid Effectiveness: A Progress Report on Implementing the Paris Declaration*. Paris: OECD-DAC.

Péan, Leslie (2010) "Haïti-Élections: Avec la publication du calendrier électoral, les dés sont jetés", *AlterPresse*, 19 July.

PRH (Plateforme pour la Refondation d'Haïti) (2010) "Pledge List: Financial Contributions". Available at http://www.refondation.ht/index.jsp?sid=1&id=191&pid=126

République d'Haïti (2009) *Plan d'investissements prioritaires du DSNCRP (2008–2010). Pour réussir le saut qualitatif*. Port-au-Prince: Government of Haiti.

RNDDH (Réseau National des Droits Humains d'Haïti) (2010) "RNDDH: Situation du pays 6 mois après le séisme", Radio Kiskeya, 18 July.

Salahub, Jennifer Erin (2008) "Canada, Haiti, and Gender in a 'Fragile State'" in The North-South Institute, *Fragile States or Failing Development? Canadian Development Report 2008*. Ottawa: North-South Institute, pp. 49–68. Available at http://www.nsi-ins.ca/english/pdf/CDR_2008.pdf

Sanders, Richard (2007) "A Very Canadian Coup D'état in Haiti: The Top 10 Ways that Canada's Government Helped the 2004 Coup and its Reign of Terror", *Press for Conversion*, 60: 44–45.

Sanders, Richard (2008) "Putting the Aid in Aiding and Abetting: CIDA's Agents of Regime Change in Haiti's 2004 Coup", *Press for Conversion*, 62: 3–5.

Shamsie, Yasmine (2006) "It's Not Just Afghanistan or Darfur: Canada's Peacebuilding Efforts in Haiti" in Andrew Cooper and Dane Rowlands (eds) *Canada Among Nations*. Ottawa: Carleton University Press, pp. 209–230.

Trouillot, Lyonel (2010) "Appel aux citoyens du monde: La reconstruction d'Haïti prise en otage", Radio Kiskeya, 23 April.

# 13

## US policy towards Haiti under the administrations of George W. Bush and Barack Obama

*Robert Maguire*

The advent of the Obama administration has brought opportunities for a fresh approach in US policy towards Haiti. This chapter provides a summary of US interests in Haiti and an overview and assessment of US Haiti policy during the administration of George W. Bush. It then explores how the Obama administration has begun to pursue policies – both before and after the catastrophic earthquake that struck Port-au-Prince and environs on 12 January 2010 – that will serve US interests while fostering improved bilateral and multilateral relationships to strengthen prospects for stability, development, improved governance, greater equality and economic growth in the impoverished Caribbean nation.

### Interests and interest groups

With an area the size of Maryland and a population of 9.7 million, Haiti is a small country that would not normally be viewed as having critical importance in US foreign policy. Yet, over the past 24 years, since the demise of the 29-year Duvalier family dictatorship (1957–1986), Haiti has loomed disproportionately large on the US policy radar screen. Its blip was particularly big on two occasions of extreme political crisis: from 1990 to 1994, when the presidential election of Jean-Bertrand Aristide was followed by Aristide's violent ouster in a military coup d'état, three years of rapacious de facto military rule and his restoration to office

*Fixing Haiti: MINUSTAH and beyond, Heine and Thompson (eds),*
*United Nations University Press, 2011, ISBN 978-92-808-1197-1*

following a UN-sanctioned and US-led armed intervention; and from 2003 to 2006, when political violence resulted not only in a re-elected Aristide's second ouster but in a second UN-sanctioned and US-led armed intervention. This time, however, Aristide was not restored to office. Rather, Haiti was governed for two years by an appointed interim regime, while conflict and instability continued despite the presence of a UN Stabilization Mission in Haiti (MINUSTAH).

Relative calm returned following the February 2006 election and May inauguration of a government headed by President René Préval. During 2008 and again in 2010 calamities beyond Préval's control cast a cloud over the relative political calm and the progress that accompanied it. In 2008, progress was jeopardized first by escalating food and fuel prices that led to widespread unrest and the Haitian Parliament's removal of the country's prime minister followed by months of political instability, and subsequently by massive economic and social devastation caused by four powerful storms that hit the country in quick succession, leaving massive destruction, hundreds dead, tens of thousands homeless and a third of the population at risk for moderate or severe malnutrition. In 2010, Haiti suffered a severe set-back when the 7.0 magnitude earthquake that struck on 12 January killed at least 230,000 of the 3 million residents of the Port-au-Prince metropolitan area, left another 300,000 injured and 1.3 million homeless, and left behind damage estimated at $7.9 billion, or 120 per cent of Haiti's 2009 GDP. As the Haitian government and people struggled with these setbacks, MINUSTAH's mandate has been extended twice, most recently in October 2010 for yet another year.

In between major crises, Haiti has kept the attention of the US foreign policy community because of constant concern over illegal migration, a worry that is heightened by the periodic outflow towards south Florida of large numbers of desperate boatpeople. Every American president from Jimmy Carter to George W. Bush has had to confront the immigration "hot rail" of US policy towards Haiti and toward Haitians (Maguire, 2003).

The usual American response to Haitian refugees seeking entry to the United States has been Coast Guard interdiction on the high seas, with a pro forma shipboard asylum interview and a rapid return to Haiti or, if the refugee reaches US soil, incarceration, a pro forma asylum interview and deportation to Haiti.[1]

On-going interest also centres on Haiti's role in narco-trafficking. The weak state is located in the crosshairs of a drug-trafficking network that originates in Colombia, ends in North America, fuels corruption and violence in Haiti and funnels approximately 8 per cent of the cocaine consumed annually in the United States (Perito and Maley, 2007). Additionally, US interests relate to issues of humanitarianism (especially in the aftermath of natural disaster), development assistance (Haiti is by far the largest recipient in the Caribbean of US foreign aid) and democratization (the United States typically engages in the promotion, funding and monitoring of elections in Haiti).

Contributing to the policy focus on Haiti are several constituencies in the United States with ongoing interests in the Caribbean country. One group is Haitian-Americans, aka "the diaspora". While its exact number is not known, estimates of this group range up to two million. Although Haitian immigrants are present in all 50 states, the largest populations are concentrated in Florida, New York, Massachusetts, New Jersey and Connecticut. Combined, these states make up some 90 per cent of the total of foreign-born Haitians in the United States (Newland, 2004).

Another constituency with strong interests in Haiti is African-Americans. High-profile manifestations of this group's interest have emanated from such leaders as Andrew Young and Jesse Jackson and from within the US Congress by the members of the Congressional Black Caucus (CBC). The CBC's focus on Haiti goes back to the 1970s, under the leadership of Representatives Shirley Chisholm, William Grey and Walter Fauntroy. It continued thereafter with engagement by such members as Charles Rangel, John Conyers, Donald Payne, Maxine Waters and Barbara Lee and, more recently, by Kendrick Meek, Alcee Hastings, Gregory Meeks, Donna Edwards and Yvette Clarke. In mid-September of 2008, the latter two congresswomen joined Meek on a post-hurricane fact-finding visit to the country not too far from his south Florida congressional district. At a hearing on Haiti shortly thereafter, the Miami-based congressman and other CBC members urged the Bush administration to provide Temporary Protected Status (TPS) in the post-storm period to Haitians already in the United States. TPS designation allows certain foreign nationals to remain temporarily in the United States when extraordinary conditions, including environmental disaster, pose a threat to personal safety or prevent them from returning home. As TPS advocacy illustrates, African-American interests focus not only on policy towards Haiti but also on the treatment of Haitians in the United States. CBC members have been in the forefront of US political engagement with Haiti after the earthquake.

Haiti's location 90 minutes by air from Miami broadens political interest. Elected officials from throughout the state of Florida – in national, state and local offices, and of both political parties – keep an eye on Haiti, and on Haitian-American voters in their districts. Growing numbers of Florida's estimated 400,000 Haitian-Americans are registered to vote. Three Republican members of south Florida's congressional delegation – Ileana Ros-Lehtinen, Lincoln Diaz-Balart and Mario Diaz-Balart – are actively involved in legislative issues linked to Haiti. In September 2008 all three joined the CBC to urge TPS designation for Haitians, a position not embraced by President Bush. Other members of Congress who are neither members of the CBC nor located in Florida also follow Haiti carefully. This group includes Representatives William Delahunt (D-Mass), whose district contains many Haitian-Americans; James Oberstar (D-Minn), who was involved in a training mission in Haiti several decades ago; and Senator Christopher Dodd (D-Conn), who served as a Peace Corps Volunteer in the neighbouring Dominican Republic.[2]

Finally, two other US groups – humanitarians and businessmen – help to maintain US interest. Among the former are tens of thousands of congregants of diverse religious denominations whose churches sponsor visits to Haiti and mobilize resources to support humanitarian work there. A North American parish twinning scheme of the Catholic Church, for example, lists over 345 parishes in its programme (*Catholic News*, 2008). Doctors and nurses engaged in Haiti medical missions along with a plethora of US-based non-governmental organizations supporting social and economic development there round off this broad and diverse humanitarian constituency which has played a critical role in post-quake relief and recovery operations. Businessmen involved in Haiti are a somewhat small but influential group mostly involved with import–export operations or Haitian-based assembly plants. The passage of Congressional legislation providing trade advantages for products assembled in Haiti (the HOPE and HOPE II Acts) was boosted by the engagement of this constituency (Hornbeck, 2008), which is actively seeking an expanded role in rubble removal, reconstruction and job creation after the earthquake.

## US–Haiti policy during the administration of George W. Bush

Under the Bush administration, US policy toward Haiti rested on four pillars: "foster and strengthen democracy; help alleviate poverty, illiteracy, and malnutrition; promote respect for human rights; and counter illegal migration and drug trafficking" (USAID, 2007). Not all of these components, however, were accorded equal and consistent attention during the Bush years. Efforts to counter and contain illegal migration were the most consistent feature of the Bush Haiti policy. The administration supported robust US Coast Guard interdiction of Haitians on the high seas and their return to Haiti, and provided assistance to the Haitian Coast Guard to improve its capacity to deter migration even when, from 2001 to 2003, virtually all other US bilateral assistance was suspended. Deportations of Haitians illegally in the United States, and of Haitian resident aliens found guilty of a criminal transgression, were consistently conducted (Bracken, 2007). In late September 2008, responding to congressional pressure following Haiti's storm-related devastation, the administration temporarily suspended Haitian deportations but resumed them by mid-December, enraging Haiti advocates in Congress (Hastings, 2008).

Efforts to counter drug trafficking, while another steadfast element of the administration's focus, did not match the magnitude or success of actions related to the interdiction or deportation of people. Although support of Haitian government bodies mandated to curb trafficking was provided, and pressure on Haitian officials to arrest and hand over drug traffickers resulted in occasional success, the aforementioned fact that significant quantities of cocaine continue to flow through the country indicates the insufficiency of these efforts. Some of this inadequacy is linked to the location of US interdiction assets. Coast Guard cutters ply the waters between Haiti and Florida, where they have been more effective in controlling the northward flow of people than of cocaine. While people originate in Haiti, narcotics stemming from Colombia or Venezuela often move from Haiti into the Dominican Republic before entering North America. As a rule, American interdiction assets were not deployed between South America and Haiti by the Bush administration. When two Drug Enforcement Administration (DEA) helicopters operated along Haiti's southern coast for six weeks in 2007 to assist drug interdiction efforts, however, the flow of cocaine into the Caribbean country was virtually halted. But when "Operation Rum Punch" ended, narco-trafficking into southern Haiti increased beyond previous levels (US Department of State, 2008; *Miami Herald*, 2007).

Other key elements of the Bush Haiti policy – democracy strengthening, poverty alleviation and human rights promotion – were pursued less consistently or vigorously over what were two somewhat distinct policy periods during that administration: 2001–2004 and 2005–2008. During the former period, when terrorism and war pushed Latin America and the Caribbean to the back burner, US Haiti policy reflected the persona of the two assistant secretaries in the State Department's Bureau of Western Hemisphere Affairs responsible for its oversight: Otto Reich (1/02–11/02) and Roger Noriega (7/03–10/05). They exerted a mostly aggressive and negative stance towards Haiti's government, especially its leader, President Jean-Bertrand Aristide.[3] Throughout this period, the administration seemed willing either to call upon, or to turn a blind eye to, external actors working with Haitian forces opposing Aristide, notably the International Republican Institute for International Affairs (IRI) (Bogdanich and Nordberg, 2006).

Throughout 2001–2003, the approach towards Haiti was to exert heavy pressure on Aristide to acquiesce to US demands, while suspending or removing desperately needed economic assistance, fostering international isolation and sending signals to opposition forces that their efforts to ultimately unseat the elected government merited support. The Haitian government did little to help its own cause vis-à-vis relations with the United States. In spite of sporadic efforts to meet US demands, its less-than-democratic practices, including election tampering, matched by an inability or lack of interest to defuse politically linked violence, fuelled the already negative stance of the Bush administration.

To sum up, during this first period, Bush administration policy towards Haiti was largely one of estrangement, with most bilateral assistance suspended, humanitarian aid redirected through non-governmental organizations and pressure exerted on multilateral donors to replicate this approach (Maguire, 2003). As a result, suspended aid and loan disbursements to the impoverished country and its government totalled more than $500 million by the beginning of 2003. By the end of that year, with US estrangement matching politically infused violence running rampant in Haiti, the policy boiled down to one resembling support of regime change. On 29 February 2004, Aristide was deposed and those who opposed him acquired power. Bush policy immediately shifted from estrangement to vigorous engagement.

Of the 2,700 strong UN Multinational Force that occupied Haiti the day Aristide departed, 1,740 of these were US soldiers (United States Southern Command, 2004). In July 2004, at an international donors' conference where $1.085 billion was pledged in support of the installed interim government, the US offered $230 million (Taft-Morales, 2005). Within two years, US disbursements to Haiti reached $390 million. The administration pushed for and eagerly supported MINUSTAH, organized in April 2004, through the allocation of financial resources (not troops) for the South American-led operation. Regime change in Haiti, however, quickly deteriorated into two years of uncontrolled violence, criminality and politically charged confrontation. Administration support of MINUSTAH, including its 50-member US civilian police unit, continued, along with support for the interim government.

As Bush policy moved into its second phase following Aristide's ouster, it gradually evolved from one driven by emotion to one construed through rationality. This trend was enhanced when Roger Noriega was removed as assistant secretary of state in late 2005 and career diplomat Thomas Shannon was appointed to the post (Council on Hemispheric Affairs, 2007). Under Shannon, a more rational policy included an intensified push for national elections as a means for bringing greater stability and prospects for development to the country. Those elections were held in February 2006.

The aftermath of that successful ballot witnessed heightened demonstrations of rationality in US Haiti policy. René Préval had the good fortune of being elected president around the time Shannon proclaimed the Bush administration's "Year of Engagement" in the Western Hemisphere (Crawley, 2007). President Bush offered Préval congratulations on his electoral victory and welcomed him to Washington, and the administration dialogued with him and his government regularly after that. Also, it tolerated Préval's pragmatic approach to foreign policy and development assistance, which includes participation in Cuba's programme of educational exchanges and the provision of some 575 doctors in Haiti; Haiti's membership in Venezuela's Petro-Caribe initiative and its observer status in ALBA, a Venezuelan-sponsored regional grouping; and the latter's provision of humanitarian, education and health assistance, and an oil refinery and three electricity plants.

Engagement also translated into significant and steadfast resource allocations. In addition to supporting MINUSTAH and the active engagement of such multilateral organizations as the World Bank and the Inter-American Development Bank, the administration maintained a consistent direct flow of aid to its Caribbean neighbour. In July 2006 high-ranking officials participated in another international donors' meeting, pledging $210 million of the $750 million mobilized to support Haiti's recovery over two years. In fiscal year (FY) 06 and in FY 07 the administration granted $226 million and $215 million in bilateral aid, respectively. In FY 08, $201 million was accorded to Haiti, representing 61 per cent of the entire US aid package for the Caribbean (Veillette et al., 2007). Subsequently, aid allocations for FY 08 rose to $279 million, including the addition of at least $27.3 million in post-storm relief operations, some of which were undertaken by the Miami-based US Southern Command (Bureau for Democracy, Conflict and Humanitarian Assistance, 2008).[4] Despite high-profile relief operations, the lion's share of FY 08's bilateral aid went towards more routine activities such as HIV/AIDS funding, economic support and food aid; 15 per cent was allocated to development assistance. As has been the case over most of the past two decades, even in the aftermath of elections aid to Haiti continued to be channelled principally through US-linked NGOs, bypassing the country's government. The parliamentary sacking of the prime minister in April 2008, leaving a caretaker government in place for five months, reinforced the tendency to work through NGOs.

In Washington, the Bush administration's more rational engagement with Haiti translated into greater bipartisanship, in spite of its aggressive containment and interdiction policy and refusal to provide TPS designation, two issues that angered human rights and Haiti advocates in Congress. Bipartisanship was demonstrated during the passage of the aforementioned HOPE and HOPE II Acts to promote investment and job creation in Haiti's assembly plant sector, as well as by congressional approval of the administration's budget requests.[5] Of critical importance, Washington's new-found bipartisanship took the wind from the sails of those who periodically re-emerge seeking support for an agenda of destabilization and regime change in Haiti.[6] Hovering over rational engagement and bipartisan gains during the latter Bush years was Jean-Bertrand Aristide. The former president, ensconced in South Africa since the middle of 2004, was – and remains – a highly polarizing figure both in Haiti and in Washington (Charles, 2008). In that regard, statements or actions that even appear to clear the way for his return to Haiti run the risk of creating chaos in Haiti and undermining bipartisanship towards Haiti in Washington.

## A new US approach towards Haiti

A new US approach towards Haiti under the Obama administration includes opportunities for improving relations and strengthening prospects for stability, democratization and more effective support for economic growth, poverty alleviation and the country's reconstruction particularly in the aftermath of the earthquake. Equally important opportunities for the Obama administration include seeking rational and constructive engagement with Haiti and its elected government, eschewing any prospect of mixed messages that can destabilize an already fragile political environment. During his campaign, candidate Obama singled out the suffering of Haitian people "under governments that cared more about their own power than their people's progress and prosperity," adding that it is "time to press Haiti's leaders to bridge the divides between them" (Obama, 2008a). This statement is on target. It is important for the new administration to rely on it in its approach toward Haiti.

Application of this approach has translated thus far into strong and consistent engagement with Haiti's elected government, led by Préval and Prime Minister Michele Pierre-Louis, succeeded by Jean-Max Bellerive. To the Haitian president's credit, following his 2006 inauguration Préval endeavoured to bridge divides among Haitians by supporting coalition government, seeking moderation, reinstilling respect for the dignity inherent in all Haitians and fostering the opportunity for all Haitians to have greater inclusion in developing their country. To the credit of his political opponents, most accepted this opportunity – at least tentatively, as have Haitians from a wide array of social and economic sectors. This tentative embrace was reinforced by the aforementioned bipartisanship in Washington.

A variety of political pressure points, however, including the lengthy delay of senate elections scheduled for late 2007, a tendency in 2008 among some parliamentarians to place self above country in the midst of national crisis, and post-quake efforts by some political adversaries to undermine Préval have all pushed against Haiti's fragile political détente. In 2011, it faced multiple crises. Not only was Haiti still reeling from the shocks of 2008 and the devastation wrought by the earthquake, it was also coping with a national cholera epidemic that began in mid-2010 and had killed over 4,000 by year's end. Further, its fragile political détente was on the verge of unravelling following hotly contested, badly organized and fraud-stained parliamentary and presidential elections in late November 2010 that yielded not a successor to Préval but protracted confrontation over which two candidates would face one another in a presidential run-off. The unexpected return to the country in mid-January of former dictator Jean-Claude Duvalier following 25 years of exile further threatened the country's nascent political stability. With the future of Haiti's movement towards the politics of moderation and inclusion suddenly uncertain, it has become even more important for the Obama administration to press all Haitian sides strongly, clearly and consistently to respect human dignity and the rules of the democratic game as a means of helping the country maintain recent political gains and move forward.

In the aftermath of Haiti's 2008 storm-wrought devastation, candidate Obama urged the United States to work "in partnership with President Rene Préval and ... [then] Prime Minister Michele Pierre-Louis, and with key international actors: the United Nations Mission in Haiti [MINUSTAH], the Inter-American Development Bank, the World Bank, the Organization of America States, and crucial bilateral donors" in helping it recover (Obama, 2008b). Since taking office, Obama has maintained the position that his administration should work in partnership with these key actors not just for immediate relief and recovery but to achieve stability, improved governance, social inclusion and economic growth, and the reconstruction of Haiti over the longer term, particularly in the post-quake period.

Continued support by Obama of MINUSTAH as a UN Chapter VII undertaking is critically important in view of its role both as a security umbrella that limits instability fuelled by criminal gangs, former soldiers and opportunistic politicians and as a front-line responder to disasters, natural and man-made. At such a time when MINUSTAH's security umbrella can be lowered, support for transition to a Chapter VI development operation, facilitating, in the words of Préval, "more tractors and fewer tanks", would become appropriate. In the meantime, efforts by MINUSTAH, multilateral or bilateral funders and their Haitian partners to improve public safety through police, judicial and penal reform and strengthened rule of law should receive strong Obama support. Improved public safety and rule of law are essential elements for stability, institution-strengthening and growth. Tolerance of corruption and patterns and practices of impunity from the law continue to plague Haiti's evolution toward a free, fair and developed democratic society.

Within the framework of partnership, the Obama administration has connected with Haiti's other neighbours, including the Caribbean Community (CARICOM) and its individual member states, the Dominican Republic and even Cuba, to facilitate relief and recovery operations following the earthquake. Taking these connections one step further, an Obama-inspired US – Caribbean consortium could serve as a focal point for regional engagement with Haiti on such shared concerns as sound democratic governance, natural disaster mitigation and response, drug trafficking, poverty alleviation and the detrimental impact of ineffective, externally applied, "top-down" development models. Leadership from the Obama administration in recognizing – and acting upon – issues of climate change, particularly as they relate to the vulnerabilities of coastal areas in island states, will be embraced by all Caribbean nations, including Haiti. US leadership that takes a holistic approach to the island of Hispaniola and assists Haiti and the Dominican Republic to resolve cross-border issues, including migration and shared resource management, will not only be beneficial to each country but will also represent a refreshing approach to US–Caribbean relations.

Actions to cool down the migration "hot rail" are urgently overdue. More effective approaches to improve conditions that fuel emigration through the rehabilitation of the natural environment and the productive infrastructure, and the expansion of employment opportunities and economic growth, are explored below. There is no doubt that the United States must take measures to control the flow of people across its land and maritime borders, and follow legislative mandates related to that flow. Policies and practices that respect the dignity of desperate, impoverished and frightened people fleeing their homeland in search of safety and opportunity, however, must replace those that result in perfunctory or coercive practices that do not accord individuals a fair chance to gain protection under the umbrella of US and accepted international law. Broader immigration reform efforts undertaken by the Obama administration should have provisions that ensure universal fair treatment of Haitians, including the possibility of guest worker arrangements and the suspension of perfunctory shipboard asylum interviews. Haitians interdicted by the US Coast Guard on the high seas should be afforded a

US-supervised land-based interview in a secure and non-intimidating environment. Collaboration with Haitian authorities, including its Coast Guard, to deter potential migrants and reintegrate those who are deemed ineligible for entry to the United States, should be a stated principle and practice of Obama's policy.[7]

In spite of early expectations that President Obama would accord to Haitians in the United States Temporary Protected Status, it was not granted during the administration's first year in office.[8] In the immediate aftermath of Haiti's devastating earthquake, however, Obama accorded TPS to cover the estimated 200,000 Haitians illegally in the United States at the time of the disaster. A sore point in US–Haiti relations for more than a decade has been the deportation of Haitian aliens convicted of a criminal transgression. In the quake's aftermath, deportations have been suspended. Before they are eventually reinstituted, the Obama administration should work with Haitian authorities to ensure that facilities and resources to secure criminal deportees are in place, and that facilities and programmes enabling the reintegration of non-violent criminal deportees receive adequate US government support.[9]

Since his inauguration in May 2006, President Préval has spoken repeatedly about the obstacles placed in Haiti's path by narco-trafficking, requesting heightened assistance from the United States in combating what he sees as essentially a US problem brought upon Haiti as an accident of geography. As described earlier, the temporary deployment of US drug interdiction assets to the southern coast of Haiti was effective. MINUSTAH, as part of its mandate to increase border protection, deployed 16 Uruguayan-purchased Boston Whalers in late 2008 to enact maritime border patrols with the Haitian Coast Guard. This welcome initiative should be strengthened by greater, sustained deployment of US assets, particularly to Haiti's southern areas, including helicopters and other surveillance equipment, to assist drug interdiction efforts. Additionally, as part of the aforementioned US support of Haitian–Dominican collaboration, the administration should support more robust monitoring and seizure of narcotics moving across the Haiti–Dominican border and from the Dominican Republic towards Puerto Rico and the US mainland.

During the campaign, candidate Obama spoke of the need for a "southbound strategy [that] will target the trafficking of guns, money, and stolen vehicles that go virtually unchecked from the US south into Mexico and beyond" (Obama, 2008a). President Préval has repeatedly complained to Washington about the negative impact in Haiti of unchecked, illicit trade emanating in the United States from the Miami River and other points. In this regard, the application of the proposed southbound strategy should be extended to Haiti, where it will be welcomed.

US leadership on Haiti was largely absent, detrimental or outsourced during most of the administration of George W. Bush. President Obama has begun to act on the opportunity to change this by solidifying partnerships and providing direction throughout his presidency. This has been evident during both the international donors' conference on Haiti held in Washington in April 2009 and another conference at the United Nations in New York City in March 2010. In both instances, US sponsorship and leadership were key to the successful outcome of these gatherings where donors discussed and responded to the Haitian government's poverty alleviation and economic growth strategy in 2009 and post-quake recovery plan in 2010. Beyond doubt, the Obama administration, under the tutelage of Secretary of State Hillary Clinton, participated robustly in these pivotal events, assuming leadership not only in decisions made among donors but in how they are to be enacted, thus establishing its lead role in forging a consistent and constructive international engagement with Haiti (Maguire, 2009 and Maguire and Copeland, 2010).[10]

In the past, international donors have tended to prescribe solutions for Haiti either without including its government as a full partner or by-passing the Haitian government altogether. At times, this has occurred for good reason in that past Haitian governments – labelled predatory by many scholars – cared little about the well-being of their citizens (see, for example, Fatton Jr., 2002). International concern about the weakness of state institutions and the questionable ability for sound fiscal management has also been justified. What has not been justified, however, is an approach towards reconstruction – and now, post-quake recovery – that focuses heavily on tamping down problems without addressing root causes or seeking sustainable solutions. While stability must be attained so that other social, economic and political initiatives have an improved chance for success, the international tendency to emphasize quick impact projects whose aim is strictly to achieve stability in the short run, without effective strategies and programmes for expanding opportunities for Haiti's people and meeting longer-term development goals, has done little over the long haul to stabilize or reconstruct Haiti.

As evidenced by several development and recovery strategies created by the Haitian government between 2007 and 2010 that have been endorsed by the International Monetary Fund (IMF), the World Bank and leading multilateral and bilateral donors, the current government of Haiti wishes not to prey upon its citizens but rather to engage them constructively, providing the social and economic services a government should render over the long term to its people as well as seeking solutions to causes of their country's poverty (Government of Haiti, 2007; 2009; 2010). As an outcome of a US government-wide review of US assistance policy towards Haiti initiated in May 2009, the Obama administration has espoused an approach that will refrain from diagnosing problems and pre-scribing solutions without the requisite participation of Haitian officials (US Department of State, 2009; 2010). The administration should seize its review of how the US delivers assistance to Haiti as an opportunity to build a new consensus towards international engagement that vigorously includes "bottom-up" approaches as fully legitimate means of assisting governments to serve their people. The emphasis on prescribed, top-down approaches as opposed to home-grown, bottom-up initiatives has resulted not only in Haiti becoming a country of failed or unsustainable projects but also in the failure to address the legitimate aspirations of Haiti's poor – namely, that meaningful opportunity that enables them to provide for themselves be expanded. Support for development of Haiti's rural areas, where more than half of its people live, is particularly urgent given its past neglect and current importance and, in the aftermath of the earth-quake, the flow of some 700,000 displaced people to rural communities. US support of a collaborative, bottom-up approach would send a mes-sage to future governments in Haiti – and elsewhere – that it is in their best interest to emulate a collaborative model of governance that en-gages all the nation's citizens in the national development process (see Maguire, 2008).

As the Obama administration has forged a new path for US relations with Haiti and of leadership in global international relations, it has recog-nized the necessity of resolving the dilemma of weak and neglected Hai-tian public institutions wishing to take their responsibility but unable to do so. This condition, exacerbated by the destruction of government fa-cilities and the death of some 17 per cent of Haiti's civic servants during the earthquake, has been reinforced by international tendencies to by-pass state institutions and allocate development resources largely to non-governmental organizations. Especially as Haiti endeavours to build back from earthquake devastation, greater balance must be sought in allocat-ing resources to non-governmental partners and providing resources for the strengthening of state institutions and their ability to render services to their citizens. Such resource allocation must be accompanied by close monitoring of all development actors and incentives that will support continued improvement and the achievement of stated goals.

Contributing to the weakness of Haiti's public institutions has been the debt burden inherited from past governments. At the end of 2008, Haiti's external debt stood at $1.7 billion, serviced to the amount of some $1 million a month (Perito, 2008). Much of that debt, however, was cancelled by mid-2009 after Haiti fulfilled the World Bank's Heavily Indebted Poor Countries (HIPC) completion point requirements. Haiti's debt was fur-ther reduced following the earthquake. As a candidate, Barack Obama called for wiping out debt incurred by poor countries. As president, his administration has taken leadership in supporting the cancelation of practically all of Haiti's external debt, conditional on parallel efforts that help to assure not just sound, prompt and effective resource management, use and accountability but that also address the need to strengthen Haitian executive branch institutions.

With as many as 1.5 million of its 9.7 million people displaced in the aftermath of January's earthquake and a much higher number of the 78 per cent of Haiti's entire population who must get by on earnings of less than $2 a day facing the prospect of unceasing poverty accompanied by hunger, disease and malnutrition, a compelling urgency confronts Haiti today. Without doubt, humanitarian relief programmes that provide food to displaced and impoverished people is a top priority. A competing priority, however, is to focus on medium- and long-term development needs that include support of efforts that will enable Haitians to grow their own food. The aforementioned government development strategies dwell on the dilemma of Haiti's extreme vulnerability to global increases in the cost of imported food and fuel that exacerbate widespread citizen suffering (Government of Haiti, 2010).

Important ideas emanating from among Haitian authorities suggest that poverty alleviation and economic growth must go beyond initiatives that provide only short-term, stop-gap opportunities or that offer poor Haitians only the prospect of jobs in "make-work" projects or assembly plants. Those ideas focus on the dire need not just to rebuild the earthquake-ravaged areas but also to rehabilitate the country's severely damaged environment and productive infrastructure, to invest in food crop production and in the creation of jobs in rural areas and to expand opportunities for Haiti's increasingly alienated youth (60 per cent of its population is under 25) (Maguire, 2008; Government of Haiti, 2010).

Even before the earthquake, Haiti's National Council for Food Security (CNSA) identified seven immediate and longer-term post-storm recovery and rebuilding priorities, including the rehabilitation of damaged physical infrastructure, recapitalization of farming operations (including livestock) and the protection of watersheds.[11] Post-quake studies, including a post-disaster needs assessment conducted prior to the March 2010 donors' conference reiterated these priorities. Before the quake, Haitian officials, including Prime Minister Pierre-Louis, had begun to consider the idea of creating a National Service Corps similar to the US Depression-era Civilian Conservation Corps (CCC) as a means of addressing long-term infrastructure rehabilitation, production and job-creation needs (Maguire, 2009). Such an institution, they thought, would play a key role not only in rehabilitating Haiti and creating meaningful jobs but also in creating opportunities for its youth to gain a stake in their country's future through involvement in rebuilding it. Additionally, such a service corps would provide "green" jobs in reforestation and land reclamation, and would contribute towards building institutional capacity for disaster mitigation and relief. Discussion and consideration of these ideas continues in the post-quake period. In responding to and supporting Haitian initiatives, it is incumbent upon the Obama administration to recognize these priorities, listen to Haitian ideas and lead others in working in partnership with the Haitian government to draw upon them as possible "game changers" that will assist the Caribbean country to overcome the grave challenges in the post-quake period.

In conclusion, as the Obama administration pursues its approach towards Haiti after the massive earthquake, the basic components of US policy – fostering and strengthening democracy; alleviating poverty through expanded opportunities for economic growth coupled with improved education and healthcare; promoting respect for human rights; countering illegal migration and drug trafficking – do not have to change. What should change is the way they are conceived and implemented. In that regard, the most important change is for the United States to work in greater partnership with Haiti's government and its people. In so doing, it must listen to them, urge them to work together and respect each other, and treat them with the dignity and respect they deserve as a people striving to rebuild a country that has been brought to tatters by decades of bad governance, lack of inclusion, incomplete or flawed partnerships and inappropriate or badly applied solutions prescribed to a country and people who deserve better.

## Notes

1. In 1981, the US practice of interdicting Haitians on the high seas and returning them to Haiti, begun following a prior agreement between the Duvalier and Reagan governments, was codified in the Omnibus Immigration Control Act (see Wasem, 2005).
2. This array of elected officials engaged with Haiti has changed since the November 2010 congressional elections in the United States. Delahunt and Dodd have retired, and Meek and Oberstar are no longer members of the US Congress. Meek gave up his House seat and ran unsuccessfully for the US senate and Oberstar was defeated in the general election.
3. In early 2001, prior to his July 2003 confirmation as assistant secretary, Noriega was appointed US Ambassador to the Organization of American States, where he was also actively engaged with Haiti.
4. By mid-December, the figure spent in post-storm relief operations had risen to $33.7 million, which includes unspecified allocations from the FY 09 budget.
5. HOPE I legislation was passed in December 2006; HOPE II was passed in September 2008 and extended following the earthquake.
6. US Ambassador to Haiti Brian Dean Curran famously labelled those in Washington advocating that US engagement should foster instability in Haiti "the *Chimeres* of Washington", using a Haitian expression for gang members or political spoilers (cited in Maguire, 2009).
7. Many of these recommendations were made in 2002 in Bach and Maguire (2002).

8. For example, TPS was accorded to citizens of Central American countries devastated by Hurricane Mitch in 1998 (see Schneider, 2008).

9. On 20 January 2011, the Obama administration resumed criminal deportations when 27 Haitians were sent back to Haiti by the US Department of Homeland Security (DHS). Upon arrival, the deportees were detained by Haitian authorities.

10. See Maguire (2009), and Maguire and Copeland (2010) for an assessment of the 2009 and 2010 Haiti donors' conferences.

11. The other priorities are: increase agricultural production including cereal crops serving as a substitute for imported food; promote investments in key productive economic sectors to reduce unemployment; expand activities that mitigate chronic malnutrition, including investments in health, nutrition, water and sanitation; reinforce institutional capacities to coordinate, monitor and evaluate development programmes and crisis response operations (see *Haiti en Marche*, 2008).

## REFERENCES

Bach, Robert L. and Robert Maguire (2002) "Next Steps for US Policy Toward Haiti", 6 November. Available at http://www.pcgroup.biz/IRSP/archive015.htm

Bogdanich, Walt and Jenny Nordberg (2006) "Democracy Undone: Mixed US Signals Helped Tilt Haiti toward Chaos", *New York Times*, 29 January.

Bracken, Amy (2007) "Influx of Deportees Stirs Anger in Haiti", *Boston Globe*, 11 March.

Bureau for Democracy, Conflict, and Humanitarian Assistance (2008) "Haiti-Storms", *Fact Sheet #6, FY 2008*, Office of US Foreign Disaster Assistance, US-AID, 18 December.

*Catholic News* (2008) "North American Volunteers Say Efforts in Haiti Empower its Citizens", 24 July. Available at http://www.americancatholic.org/features/dailynews/todays.asp?date=7/24/2008

Charles, Jacqueline (2008) "Aristide's Backers Demand Return to Haiti", *Miami Herald*, 1 March.

Council on Hemispheric Affairs (2007) "Tom Shannon Inherits the Wreckage of the Bureau of Western Hemisphere Affairs", 2 January. Available at http://www.coha.org/2007/01/tom-shannon-inherits-the-wreckage-of-the-bureau-of-western-hemisphere-affairs/

Crawley, Vince (2007) "State's Shannon Offers Details on 2007 Goals for Latin America, United States", US Information Agency, 31 January. Available at http://news.findlaw.com/wash/s/20070131/20070131105431.html

Fatton Jr., Robert (2002) *Haiti's Predatory Republic: The Unending Transition to Democracy*. Boulder: Lynne Rienner Publishers.

Government of Haiti (2007) *Pour Réussir le Saut Qualitatif: Document de Stratégie Nationale pour la Croissance et la Réduction de la Pauvreté*. November.

Government of Haiti (2009) *Toward a New Paradigm of Cooperation*. 14 April.

Government of Haiti (2010) *Action Plan for National Recovery and Development of Haiti*. March. Available at http://www.haiticonference.org/Haiti_Action_Plan_ENG.pdf

*Haiti en Marche* (2008) "L'insecurite alimentaire nous guette, selon la CNSA", 1 October.

Hastings, Alcee L. (2008) "Inhumane to Deport Haitians", *Miami Herald*, 29 December.

Hornbeck, J.F. (2008) "The Haitian Economy and the HOPE Act", Congressional Research Service, *CRS Report for Congress*, October.

Maguire, Robert (2003) "US Policy Toward Haiti: Engagement or Estrangement?" Trinity College Haiti Project, *Haiti Papers* No. 6, November. Available at http://www.trinitydc.edu/academics/depts/Interdisc/International/PDF%20files/hbp8.pdf

Maguire, Robert (2008) "Towards the End of Poverty in Haiti", United States Institute of Peace, *USIPeace Briefing*, 24 December. Available at http://www.usip.org/pubs/usipeace_briefings/2008/1224_haiti_poverty.html

Maguire, Robert (2009) *Haiti After the Donors' Conference*. Special Report 232, October. Washington, DC: United States Institute of Peace. Available at http://www.usip.org/publications/haiti-after-the-donors-conference

Maguire, Robert and Casie Copeland (2010) "The International Donors' Conference and Support for Haiti's Future", United States Institute of Peace, *Peace Brief*, 26, 6 May. Available at http://www.usip.org/publications/the-international-donors-conference-and-support-haiti-s-future

*Miami Herald* (2007) "Rum Punch Spikes Caribbean Drugs", 1 July.

Newland, Kathleen (2004) "Spotlight on Haitians in the United States", Migration Policy Institute, April. Available at http://www.migrationinformation.org/usfocus/display.cfm?id=214

Obama, Barack (2008a) "Renewing US Leadership in the Americas", Speech, Miami, Florida, 23 May. Available at http://www.barackobama.com/2008/05/23/remarks_of_senator_barack_obam_68.php

Obama, Barack (2008b) "Barack Obama Statement on the Need for Humanitarian Assistance to Haiti Following Devastating Hurricane and Storms", Press Release, 7 September. Available at http://my.barackobama.com/page/community/post/kristenpsaki/gG5p9p

Perito, Robert (2008) "After the Storms: Weather and Conflict", United States Institute of Peace, *USIPeace Briefing*, November. Available at http://www.humansecuritygateway.com/documents/USIP_Haiti_AfterTheStorms.pdf

Perito, Robert and Greg Maly (2007) "Haiti's Drug Problems", United States Institute of Peace, *Peace Brief*, June.

Schneider, Mark (2008) "In the Aftermath of Hurricanes, Haiti Situation is Critical", *World Politics Review*, 20 October.

Taft-Morales, Maureen (2005) "Haiti: International Assistance Strategy for the Interim Government and Congressional Concerns", Congressional Research Service, *CRS Report for Congress*, November.

USAID (2007) "Haiti Overview" in USAID, *Latin America and the Caribbean*. USAID online. Available at http://www.usaid.gov/locations/latin_america_caribbean/country/haiti/

US Department of State (2008) "2008 International Narcotics Control Strategy Report", 28 February. Available at http://www.haiti-info.com/spip.php?page=imprimer&id_article=4552

US Department of State (2009) "Haiti Policy and Foreign Assistance Review", September, Unpublished document.

US Department of State (2010) "From Natural Disaster to Economic Opportunity", April, Unpublished document.

United States Southern Command (2004) "Situation Report for Media: Multinational Interim Force-Haiti", Press Release, 14 March. Available at http://www.globalsecurity.org/military/library/news/2004/03/mil-040314-southcom01.pdf

Veillette, Connie, Clare Ribando and Mark Sullivan (2007) "US Foreign Assistance to Latin America and the Caribbean: FY2006–FY2008", Congressional Research Service, *CRS Report for Congress*, 28 December.

Wasem, Ruth (2005) "US Immigration Policy on Haitian Migrants", Congressional Research Service, *CRS Report for Congress*, November.

# Conclusion: Fixing Haiti— MINUSTAH and beyond

*Jorge Heine and Andrew S. Thompson*

Crises are watershed moments that mark a profound break from the past. It is not yet clear whether the earthquake of January 2010 will constitute such a tipping point, although it is easy to conceive of at least two opposing scenarios that could emerge from the disaster. The first is that Haiti never recovers, that the earthquake has the effect of exacerbating insecurity and instability to the point that Haiti, to borrow a term from Jared Diamond, "collapses" under the weight of its own fragility (Diamond, 2005). In such a circumstance, it is not impossible to imagine widespread political violence and mass human rights violations that far exceed those of previous periods of turmoil such as the popular revolution of 1986 that brought an end to Duvalierism, the difficult transition from authoritarianism to democracy from 1987 to 1990 or the respective anti-Aristide coups of 1991 to 1994, and 2004. Nor is it impossible to imagine a further and drastic decline in food security, as well as social, health and economic development, which were already among the lowest in the world. Under such a scenario, the common perception of Haiti as the "basket case of the new world" would not only be reinforced but the Caribbean country would come to constitute an even greater threat to regional peace and security than it has in the past.

The second scenario is more hopeful, although, sadly, less plausible. While the earthquake caused a systemic breakdown, the magnitude of which few countries have ever had to endure, the possibility remains that the events of January 2010 presented Haiti with an opportunity to effectively start over, a chance to forge a stable and cohesive society with a

*Fixing Haiti: MINUSTAH and beyond, Heine and Thompson (eds),*
*United Nations University Press, 2011, ISBN 978-92-808-1197-1*

functional and effective state. In this scenario, infrastructure would be rebuilt and extended throughout the country, Haitian agriculture would move beyond subsistence levels, human development indicators would rise, poverty would be reduced and the political system would become inclusive to all.

Granted, at the time of writing, such an outcome seemed far removed from present-day realities. The challenges arising from the earthquake alone were tremendous and should not be underestimated – more than one million people displaced and living in temporary shelters, the destruction of what limited infrastructure had existed in the Port-au-Prince area, serious food and water shortages. In the months following the earthquake the international response was both generous and expeditious; as a result, thousands of lives were saved, and a basic level of security, which had always been tenuous, was maintained. Nonetheless, while the relief effort will likely be hailed as proof of the international community's collective ability to rally together in times of humanitarian crisis, Haiti's reconstruction will ultimately be judged by the profundity and efficacy of domestic and international actors' collective resolve to mid- and long-term rebuilding.

There are no guarantees that either are up to the challenge. Prior to the earthquake, Haiti saw political discord and upheaval, systemic human rights violations and wide-spread poverty, gang and criminal activities, and further environmental degradation. State institutions remained weak and incapable of either delivering services or responding in any meaningful way during moments of crisis. Haiti also suffered from a battered infrastructure and a lack of concrete civil society mechanisms for engagement in the political process. Moreover, the United Nations Stabilization Mission in Haiti (MINUSTAH) has been both a success and a work in progress. In many ways, it has helped to bring a semblance of order to the country and stabilize the situation enough that a general election could occur. On the other hand the situation in Haiti was – and remains – far from stable. Indeed, the historic and tragic circumstances in Haiti have been well chronicled. It has a history of failed governments and only a fraction of its presidents have finished their terms (Shamsie and Thompson, 2006). As indicated above, it has for some time been mired in a perilous and insecure situation, its fragility encompassing the most fundamental aspects of society – economics, food security and the environment, weak police and judicial structures (International Crisis Group, 2009). Currently, Haitians are dependent on the international community for assistance. Still, despite these ailments, there were signs of hope prior to the earthquake for a country that has the potential to capitalize on its scenic beauty, proximity to the major centres of the Western Hemisphere and a cultural legacy. For the better part of two decades, Haiti had been in the process of shedding its bleak past, while contending with its contemporary problems – and making the transition towards a democratic and stable society.

*Fixing Haiti: MINUSTAH and Beyond* examines both the governance challenges facing the country and the international commitment to helping Haiti stabilize during the period from the country's insurrection of February 2004 to the earthquake of January 2010. It would be an understatement to say that this six-year period was a difficult one for Haiti. And yet, the resilience of the Haitian people was met – and still is being met – with a commitment from the United Nations as well as Haiti's international neighbours to seek a way out of perpetual problems. The successes and failures of this process showcase a society where weakness and insecurity are being addressed at the same time that civil society and state institutions have begun to mature. In this sense, the book has not just been about Haiti and the struggles it has been enduring. Rather it is about the changes that have taken place internationally since the UN interventions of the mid- to late 1990s, specifically those relating to new trends in peacebuilding, most notably the adoption of human rights and human security into Chapter VII mandates, and the emergence of new actors from the region who have, for one reason or another, chosen to play an active role in securing Haiti's future. It is these dual developments that provide a measure of hope that Haiti's fate, despite its recent struggles, does not have to resemble the first scenario outlined above.

## The need for civic-mindedness

A common conclusion among many of the contributors is that one of the impediments to peacebuilding is the absence of a sense of civic-mindedness or citizenship in Haiti. Amélie Gauthier and Madalena Moita, Mirlande Manigat, Robert Fatton Jr. and Patrick Sylvain each lament in their own way that there is neither a social contract between the state and its citizens nor a sense of constitutionalism that binds Haitians to the rule of law or to each other but rather a sentiment of "clientelism" that inhibits governance for the collective good. The reasons for this are detailed throughout the volume; however, the result has been a collective inability to cope with the challenges that have arisen as a result of systemic and chronic underdevelopment, which has been exacerbated by the neo-liberal economic system, and extreme weather and natural disaster. Haiti's social malaise and poor governance is both a product of and a contributor to the deep political and economic inequities that exist in Haiti, inequities which can only be overcome through dialogue and reconciliation between the masses and the elites. Whether Haitians are prepared to develop this sense of cohesiveness remains to be seen. However, without it, governance reforms – including reform of the 1987 constitution, should that ever occur – are not likely to amount to any real substantive change.

## MINUSTAH: Regaining stability and moving forward

There remains a strong role for the international community in assisting Haitians in this process of transformation, should it ever occur, particularly in the realm of security. MINUSTAH differs in significant respects from other previous UN missions, including the intervention of the 1990s. Rather than having a single-minded approach to restoring good governance and stabilizing the country, MINUSTAH has operated with a much broader emphasis. It has attempted to address many of the systemic issues that plague the country while also protecting the dignity of the Haitian people and promoting human rights. Learning from previous experiences, there has been a greater commitment to facilitating long-term security through the elimination of collective threats to the Haitian people.

The wide scope of MINUSTAH's involvement has not been helped by the mission's weak mandate. The logistical problems that have arisen between MINUSTAH forces and the Haitian National Police (HNP) have made operations more complicated. However, maintaining the operating capacity of the HNP is essential for Haiti, as the country needs to develop the institutions necessary for moving forward, as examined in Timothy Donais's chapter. Better and more efficient cooperation between MINUSTAH and Haitian actors is still a work in progress.

MINUSTAH began its mission in Haiti at a pivotal time for the country. It had been only a few months since President Jean-Bertrand Aristide had been forcefully removed from office (for more, see Farmer, 2004). The transitional government that took his place was ill-equipped to deal with the country's turmoil. Many in the international community saw the 2005 national elections – which would be postponed four times and held in February 2006 – as a potential turning point (International Crisis Group, 2004). A government that was democratically chosen by the Haitian people was regarded as one of the first steps towards progress. Haitian society was plagued by gang warfare, often centring around the drug trade, and the lack of economic and social infrastructure, leaving the Haitian people vulnerable (James, 2004). It was important – indeed essential – for MINUSTAH to engage the public in helping to build a more secure environment.

Having been extended for another term, until October 2011, it is clear that much remains to be done by MINUSTAH. Yet, the mission to date has helped to improve the situation considerably. The number of kidnappings, which once ravaged the population was, at the time of writing, down, and the capacity of the Haitian state and public had begun to improve prior to the earthquake (Deibert, 2009). This progress was always tentative, however. UN Secretary-General Ban Ki-moon remained cautious in his appraisals: "the progress that has been made remains extremely fragile, and is susceptible to setbacks or reversals" (Lederer, 2006).

MINUSTAH remains responsible for much of this progress. As Gerard Le Chevallier's chapter reveals, the mission provided the security necessary for the 2006 elections – elections that provided Haiti with a semblance of normalcy and a democratically elected government – at a time of weak government and an insecure future. René Préval's election victory marked a significant turning point for the country. The Préval administration has offered a sense of hope for the beleaguered population. This election represented "a major victory for what would be called the popular sector and a major defeat for those Haitian elite- and foreign-backed forces" (Dupuy, 2006). Since then, there has been a reluctant acknowledgment among many Haitians that if MINUSTAH were to leave then the fragile stability that has been achieved would quickly deteriorate.

## From the north Atlantic to the hemisphere

A host of external actors from the Americas have assisted Haiti. The United States and Canada remain key actors in Haiti's future. Still, as Robert Maguire's and Stephen Baranyi's respective chapters demonstrate, Washington and Ottawa have, at times, played less-than-constructive roles in Haiti, particularly around the events of the 2004 insurrection. Haiti's viability hinges in large part on enlightened North American leadership. If Haiti is to be integrated into the world economy, it will be because it can tap into the North American consumer market. If Haiti is to have political stability, it will be because the United States and Canada make commitments to support future democratically elected governments, including providing a deterrent against domestic insurrections or coups. If Haitians are to achieve sustainable economic growth, it will be because the international financial institutions, which are dominated by the countries of the North, extend just and equitable lending policies to them, including those that do not simply rely on neo-liberal or market-oriented growth strategies.

Whereas in the nineteenth and twentieth centuries Haiti fell under the hegemony of the north Atlantic region, in the twenty-first century the orbit in which it finds itself is hemispheric. Following the end of previous UN missions in the country, the Big Three have seen their roles in Haiti decline. In their places have stepped the ABCs: Argentina, Brazil and Chile. Playing a large role in the MINUSTAH mission – whose force commander is Major-General Floriano Peixoto Vieira Neto, a Brazilian – the ABC countries have demonstrated Latin America's commitment to making Haiti work. Whereas the Big Three are in Haiti because of long-standing ties and domestic diasporic communities, the ABCs – who have also been joined by a host of other Latin American and Caribbean countries, such as Bolivia, Ecuador, Guatemala, Peru and Uruguay – have assumed a regional responsibility for assisting a geographic neighbour. As José Raúl Perales explains in his chapter, intra-regional cooperation and participation in international institutions has emerged as one of the defining new developments within the Americas. With arguably more to lose than their northern counterparts – due to their proximity to Haiti and threats to regional security that would develop if this centrally located country slipped back into instability – the countries of Latin America and the Caribbean have engaged in an international reconstruction mission in unprecedented ways.

The participation of the ABC countries and the remaining MINUS-TAH contingents illustrate the region's rising international role (Cooper and Heine, 2009). As Brazil rises to the upper tier of the international system – as shown in its vocal role as a member of the burgeoning G20 group, its increasing presence in diplomatic affairs (opening 32 embassies between 2003 and 2008) and in its ongoing quest for a permanent seat on the United Nations Security Council – a number of regional middle powers have become more assertive. Chile, with its ambitious trade agenda, is perhaps the prototypical example of the increasingly globalized nature of the region. As well, the country has sustainably managed the economic impact of the 2007–2008 commodity shock, initiating sound social stability mechanisms as well as saving a share of the foreign-exchange earnings derived from high copper prices, which helped the country weather the global financial crisis of 2008–2009 in a better position than other developing countries (Moffett, 2009).

Prior to the MINUSTAH mission, the countries of the region had been reluctant partners in international peacekeeping missions. As shown in Johanna Mendelson Forman's chapter, in Haiti there has been a dramatic turn of events, the dawning of a "new age of regional security" that, at least in the case of the 2 × 9 process, does not include Washington. Since 2004, these countries "have perceived the MINUSTAH as an opportunity to deepen inter-state diplomatic and military coordination" (Hirst, 2007).

Brazil's leading role in MINUSTAH, as discussed in this volume by Marcel Biato, can help to address criticism against it as a regional leader. For many in the Latin American community there is a perception that Brazil speaks the rhetoric of regional leader but does not follow this up with concrete actions (for more, see Turcotte, 2009). The country's sustained and leading role with MINUSTAH belies this vision. As Brazil moves into the upper-echelon of global governance it must meet its economic and demographic strengths with international clout (Cooper and Antkiewicz, 2008). The peacekeeping and security sector reforms that Brazil is involved with as part of MINUSTAH are one way of doing so.

Latin America and the Caribbean (LAC) soldiers now comprise a majority of the mission's troops, which has given MINUSTAH a decidedly Latin American flair. For a region that is becomingly increasingly prominent in the global sphere, such activities provide international prestige and credibility (Cooper and Heine, 2009). At the same time, they help to strengthen a regional neighbour and the region in general. General Juan Emilio Cheyre provides unique insight into this process and what it means for the region and international relations. While none of these countries has been operating in Haiti for purely altruistic reasons, their presence, commitment and approach to peacebuilding have helped to bridge some of the cultural differences that existed between the Big Three and the people of Haiti. As regional neighbours, the LAC countries share a similar culture and historical lineage with the people of Haiti – perhaps, most explicitly, the historical legacy of colonization.

Indeed, at the heart of the Latin American involvement is a quiet confidence. Although their connections to Haiti are relatively nascent, it is the common bonds and shared experiences that inform their contributions to the reconstruction effort. At one point or another, the Latin American actors in Haiti have all had to grapple with political instability and civil conflict, issues of transitional justice and reconciliation, interference in their domestic affairs, as well as economic insecurity and poverty. While they may lack the material resources of the United States, France and Canada, General Eduardo Aldunate's chapter suggests that their comparative advantages lie in their empathy for their Haitian brethren, and the knowledge that countries and even regions can emerge stronger from times of uncertainty and turmoil.

## Moving forward: An emphasis on the Haitian way

While international actors have and will continue to play an important role in stabilizing Haiti, it is the people, institutions and government of Haiti that will have to shoulder the main burden of moving the country forward. The election of President René Préval in February 2006 generated much hope. From the outside, Préval was viewed with both optimism, that he could help Haiti on a progressive path, and concern – that he was or would be too close to the deposed former president Jean-Bertrand Aristide and Haiti would be stuck in an untenable situation. Domestically though Préval had the majority of the support of the Haitian electorate – which, after voting irregularities were dealt with, gave him 51 per cent of the votes and avoided a potentially divisive run-off election. One of MINUSTAH's crowning achievements has been that it stabilized the country so that these elections could be successfully held.

While safer, Haiti remains poor. Currently, approximately 80 per cent of the Haitian population lives on fewer than US$2 per day and the country remains heavily indebted to foreign creditors (Rabuffetti, 2009). It is the poorest country in the Western Hemisphere, where upwards of two-thirds of the population does not have a formal job, is ripe with illiteracy and suffers from riot-causing food shortages (Payton, 2009). For the lives of the Haitian people to improve, this economic situation must be reversed. This will take the commitment of the Haitian government, its citizens as well as the international community. In 2009, Bill Clinton, the former US president and the United Nation's new special envoy to Haiti, called on international donors to fulfil their pledges as the country had only received US$21 million of some US$760 million in pledges (Reuters, 2009). With Haiti's improving government and state structure, Clinton had called on these donors to do more.

Together, international donors and the Haitian government can move forward on issues of inequality and poverty. Financial aid could help to develop a functioning economy in Haiti, a country where manufacturing and tourism opportunities are substantial. Historically a textile manufacturing hub, this is one area where increased investment could benefit greatly. As Carlo Dade, the executive director of the Canadian Foundation for the America's (FOCAL) points out, the country's proximity to North America would help to offset the transportation costs and travel times, which are "a fraction of what [they are] from China. You can get perishable goods out quickly" (quoted in Payton, 2009). Rebuilding the Haitian manufacturing sector will give much needed jobs to the Haitian people, providing them with an alternative to a life of illicit activity. For this to be possible there must be coordinated action to improve the infrastructure of the country.

This development could also facilitate the creation of a vibrant tourism sector. General Aldunate's stories about his, and the MINUSTAH troops', much deserved excursions to Haitian beaches demonstrate the capacity for a small yet vibrant industry on the island. That Haiti's island neighbour, the Dominican Republic, already benefits from this lends further credence to this possibility. Becoming part of the region's tourist industry offers ample opportunities for job creation and foreign investment. The regional composition of the MINUSTAH mission has already brought closer ties between the country and its Latin American neighbours.

As much as the international community can do to help stabilize Haiti, it remains paramount that the local population has an active role in the reconstruction process. Haitians must lead the way in terms of rebuilding their country and, as argued by Eduardo Aldunate in this volume, it is important for external actors to appreciate Haitian society.

For Haiti to succeed, the country cannot remain solely dependent upon foreign actors. It is imperative for the Haitian people to take ownership of the situation and move forward.

## Conclusion: Shared sovereignty

The challenge for Haitians and the international community is how to rebuild in the wake of the January 2010 earthquake. Several of the contributors to this volume have stressed the need for integrative solutions to Haiti's problems that make explicit the link between economic and physical security. In order to address both simultaneously, Haiti will need a stronger and more functional state that is able to deliver services and provide protection to its citizenry. At present, the government of Haiti lacks the ability to govern effectively on its own.

Some, such as former media mogul Conrad Black (2010) and the *Economist* (2010) magazine have called for the establishment of a UN- and OAS-sanctioned trusteeship under the guidance of the United States, Canada, Brazil, and the EU in the case of *The Economist*. Given Haiti's governance challenges, this sentiment is understandable, but it is ultimately misplaced. It is worth stressing that Haitians did not forfeit their sovereignty with the earthquake, nor should they be expected to. An international protectorate would likely have no more legitimacy in the eyes of Haitians than would the re-emergence of an authoritarian regime. Although state capacity, which was already severely limited prior to the earthquake, has been further reduced, the solution is not for the international community to assume control of its governance, even if only in the immediacy of the crisis. What is required is more and better democracy, the terms of which the international community can support but not dictate. Nonetheless, as Fatton Jr. points out, Haiti is today a de facto trusteeship; for the foreseeable future, Haitians and the international community will have to accept "shared sovereignty" in which Haitian choice and autonomy are respected while allowing the burden of administration to rest with international stakeholders. Finding this delicate balance between the two will not be easy, and will undoubtedly be a constant work in progress, but it is necessary. For if Haiti is to move forward, both domestic and international actors will need to remain committed to ensuring that in the rebuilding effort Haiti remains not only a democratic project but a hemispheric project. As Kofi Annan (2004) has stated: "the stakes are high – above all for Haitians, but also for us. Getting it right this time means doing things differently. Above all, it means keeping international attention and resources engaged for the long haul."

## REFERENCES

Annan, Kofi A. (2004) "In Haiti for the Long Haul", *Wall Street Journal*, 16 March.

Black, Conrad (2010) "A Plan for Haiti", *National Post*, 6 February.

Cooper, Andrew F. and Agata Antkiewicz (eds) (2008) *Emerging Powers in Global Governance: Lessons from the Heiligendamm Process*. Waterloo: Wilfrid Laurier University Press.

Cooper, Andrew F. and Jorge Heine (eds) (2009) *Which Way Latin America? Hemispheric Politics Meets Globalization*. Tokyo: United Nations University Press.

Deibert, Michael (2009) "Tentative Calm Brings Optimism to a 'Failed' Haiti; Preval, U.N. credited", *Washington Times*, 19 July.

Diamond, Jared (2005) *Collapse: How Societies Choose to Fail or Succeed*. New York: Viking.

Dupuy, Alex (2006) "Haiti Election 2006: A Pyrrhic Victory for Rene Preval?", *Latin American Perspectives*, 33(3): 132–141.

Economist (2010) "After the earthquake: A plan for Haiti", 23 January.

Farmer, Paul (2004) "Who Removed Aristide?" *London Review of Books*, 15 April. Available at http://www.lrb.co.uk/v26/n08/farm01_.html

Hirst, Mônica (2007) "South American Intervention in Haiti", *FRIDE Comment*, April.

International Crisis Group (2004) "A New Chance for Haiti?", *ICG Latin America/Caribbean Report No. 10*, 18 November. Available at http://www.crisisgroup.org/home/index.cfm?id=3109&l=1

International Crisis Group (2009) "Haiti 2009: Stability at Risk", *ICG Latin America/Caribbean Briefing No. 19*, 3 March. Available at http://www.crisisgroup.org/home/index.cfm?id=5952&l=1

James, Erica Caple (2004) "The Political Economy of 'Trauma' in Haiti in the Democratic Era of Insecurity", *Culture, Medicine and Psychiatry*, 28(1): 127–149.

Lederer, Edith M. (2009) "U.N. Chief says Haiti has 'historic opportunity' to progress but says achievements are fragile", *Canadian Press*, 3 September.

Moffett, Matt (2009) "Prudent Chile Thrives Amid Downturn", *Wall Street Journal*, 27 May. Available at http://online.wsj.com/article/SB124337806443856111.html

Payton, Laura (2009) "Cautious Optimism", *Ottawa Citizen*, 12 September.

Rabuffetti, Mauricio (2009) "Five Years into U.N. Mission, Haiti Safer but Still Poor", *Agence France Presse*, 3 July.

Reuters (2009) "U.N. Envoy Bill Clinton Chides Donors over Haiti Aid", *Reuters News*, 9 September.

Shamsie, Yasmine and Andrew S. Thompson (2006) *Haiti Hope for a Fragile State.* Waterloo: Wilfrid Laurier University Press.

Turcotte, Joe (2009) *Inter-American Cooperation at a Crossroads*, CIGI Conference Report, 30 June. Available at http://www.cigionline.org/publications/2009/6/inter-american-cooperation-crossroads

# Index